Study Guide

for

Cole and Smith's

The American System of Criminal Justice

Eleventh Edition

Christina DeJong
Michigan State University

THOMSON
———
WADSWORTH

Australia • Brazil • Canada • Mexico
Singapore • Spain • United Kingdom • United States

Printed in the United States of America
1 2 3 4 5 6 7 09 08 07 06 05

Printer: Thomson West

ISBN 0-495-12940-2
Credit image: © PictureQuest

Thomson Higher Education
10 Davis Drive
Belmont, CA 94002-3098
USA

For more information about our products, contact us at:
Thomson Learning Academic Resource Center
1-800-423-0563

For permission to use material from this text or product, submit a request online at
http://www.thomsonrights.com.
Any additional questions about permissions can be submitted by email to **thomsonrights@thomson.com.**

Study Guide

for

Cole and Smith's

The American System of Criminal Justice

TABLE OF CONTENTS

CRIME AND JUSTICE IN AMERICA

OUTLINE

- The Main Themes of this Book
- Crime and Justice as Public Policy Issues
- Defining Crime
- Types of Crime
- The Crime Problem Today

CHAPTER 1
CRIME AND JUSTICE IN AMERICA

LEARNING OBJECTIVES

After covering the material in this chapter, students should understand:

1.   public policy concerning crime is determined in political arenas

2.   crime control in a democracy involves balancing the value of safety and security with protection of individuals' rights

3.   the comparison and reality of Packer's Crime Control Model and Due Process Model

4.   categorization of crime, including *mala in se*, *mala prohibita*, occupational, organized, visible, victimless, political, and cybercrime

5.   the extent of crime, crime trends, and related demographic influences

6.   the sources for measuring crime and the weaknesses of those sources (especially UCR and NCVS).

CHAPTER SUMMARY

This chapter explores the problems of dealing with crime and justice in a democracy. The public policy issues of crime and justice must strike a balance between law enforcement and protection of freedoms, which can be challenging. Herbert Packer's two models of the criminal justice process provide an ideal version, the due process model, with its emphasis upon freedom and justice, and the reality-based version, the crime control model, with its emphasis on efficiency and order.

Defining crime can be a difficult task for the researcher interested in studying criminal behavior. While some acts are easily defined as criminal (such as murder), others are not so easily defined (such as assisted suicide or drug use). Crimes that are *mala in se* are acts that are wrong in and of themselves. For *mala in se* offenses, the public generally agrees that the offenses should be illegal. However, crimes that are *mala prohibita* are defined by the government as criminal, while the American public might not agree that they should be crimes. Examples of *mala prohibita* crimes include smoking marijuana or public drunkenness. Many scholars argue that the government uses the law to impose values upon the public.

There are many different types of crime, such as occupational, organized, visible, political, crimes without victims, hate crimes, and cybercrime. Law enforcement authorities focus largely upon visible crime, which involves street crimes such as burglary or homicide, because people fear this type of crime more than any other. However, occupational crime and political crimes can impose great financial costs upon society.

The crime problem today is a difficult issue for researchers because data on crime are not reliable. The Uniform Crime Reports provides data reported to police but does not track the dark figure of crime, which is crime not reported to the police. The National Crime Victimization Survey interviews residents of the United States about their victimization experience, but respondents may not report accurately due to embarrassment, memory problems, or other issues.

CHAPTER OUTLINE

I.   THE MAIN THEMES OF THIS BOOK

Throughout the textbook, you will see the following themes discussed: 1) crime and justice are public policy issues; 2) criminal justice can best be seen as a social system; and 3) the criminal justice system embodies society's effort to fulfill American values, such as liberty, privacy, and individual rights.

II.   CRIME AND JUSTICE AS PUBLIC POLICY ISSUES

Reiman argues that our system is designed not to reduce crime but to project a visible image of the threat of crime. In a democracy, political leaders are greatly influenced by public opinion. However, legislators also know that they can cater to the American public's anxiety about crime and community safety. As a result, policies often appear to be enacted that are popular with the general public but that are thought by researchers to have little potential impact on the crime problem.

A.   The Role of Public Opinion
Crime and justice issues are usually decided by public opinion, but opinion frequently contradicts findings from crime data.

B.   Contemporary Policies
Conservatives and liberals have different opinions of the main focus of crime and justice policy (crime control versus protection of rights, respectively).

C.   Crime and Justice in a Democracy
It is difficult to achieve the goal of enforcing laws and protecting rights of individuals. Unlike in an authoritarian state, rights must be respected in a democracy. In a democracy, we assume all individuals are presumed innocent until proven guilty.

D.   Crime Control versus Due Process

Herbert Packer's two competing models describe two methods of how justice is dispensed. Packer recognizes that the administration of criminal justice operates within the contemporary American society and is therefore influenced by cultural forces that, in turn, determine the models' usefulness.

1.   **Crime Control Model: Order as a Value**
The goal of crime control is the repression of criminal conduct. This model stresses efficiency, and the process can be described as administrative and filtering. The main decision point is completed by on police and prosecutors, and they use discretion as the basis for decision-making. The best analogy for this model is the "assembly line".

2.   **Due Process Model: Law as a Value**
The goal of the due process model is to preserve individual liberties. This model stresses reliability (i.e., accurate decisions about guilt and innocence), and the process can best be described as adversarial. The main decision point is in the courtroom (i.e., trial), and they use law as the basis for decision-making. The best analogy for this model is the "obstacle course".

E.   The Politics of Crime and Justice
Criminal justice policies are developed in national, state, and local political arenas. There are risks that politicians will enact laws that they believe the people want, even though the resulting policies may have little or no impact on crime. The clearest link between politics and criminal justice can be seen in the competing statements and promises of Republicans and Democrats who run against each other for office.

Politics and politicians also control the budgets for criminal justice agencies. Large amounts are allocated for the war on drugs but limits are placed on spending for defense attorneys for indigent suspects. Local prosecutors and judges are elected to office through political campaigns. This may affect their priorities (for example, public safety versus re-election).

III. DEFINING CRIME

We can categorize crimes as either *mala in se* or *mala prohibita*. *Mala in se* crimes are wrongs in themselves (murder, rape, assault), based on shared values or consensus. *Mala prohibita* crimes are not wrongs in themselves but are punished because they are prohibited by the government. There is often a lack of consensus about whether such actions should be illegal (e.g., use of marijuana, gambling, and prostitution). Crime seriousness: How people rate seriousness of crimes depends on their race, sex, class, and victimization experience.

IV. TYPES OF CRIME

In addition to categorizing crime as *mala in se* or *mala prohibita*, we may also categorize them as felonies or misdemeanors. Crime can be described using other categories, based on level of risk and profitability, degree of public disapproval, or cultural characteristics of offenders.

A. Visible Crime
   Consists of street crime or "ordinary crime" primarily by lower classes and run the gamut from shoplifting to homicide (i.e., violent crimes, property crimes public order crimes). Visible crimes make up the FBI's Uniform Crime Reports.

   1. **Violent Crime**
      Crimes against individuals, in which either physical injury or death occurs. These offenses are usually considered the most serious.

   2. **Property Crime**
      Crimes involving theft, damage, or destruction of property. Some professional criminals earn their livelihood through the use of property crime.

   3. **Public Order Crimes**
      Crimes that threaten public "peace", such as disorderly conduct, vagrancy, and vandalism. These crimes increase citizen fear of crime, and some view them as contributing to a larger feeling of disorder and thus more serious crime.

B. Occupational Crime
   These are defined as violation of law committed through opportunities created in the course of a legal business or profession. Occupational crimes are sometimes referred to as "white collar crimes" although that does not encompass all categories of occupational crime. Despite sizable financial harm to corporations and individuals, occupational crimes often do not receive stiff punishments.

   1. **Crimes for the benefit of the employing organization**: price fixing or theft of trade secrets.

   2. **Crimes through the exercise of state-based authority**: politicians taking bribes or police officers stealing from the evidence room.

   3. **Crime by professionals in their capacity as professionals**: lawyers stealing from clients, stockbrokers engaged in insider trading, or doctors sexually exploiting patients.

   4. **Crimes committed by individuals as individuals where opportunities are not based on governmental power or professional position**: employee theft from the organization or filing false expense claims. Total losses due to employee theft are greater than all business losses from shoplifting, burglary, or robbery. Most such crimes do not come to public attention. Many businesses and professional organizations "police" themselves by firing employees who commit offenses.

C. Organized Crime
Social framework for the perpetration of criminal acts rather than specific acts themselves. Organized criminals provide goods and services to people, and will engage in any illegal activity as long as it is low risk and high profit (e.g., pornography, money laundering, illegal disposal of toxic waste).

Organized crime has been associated with many different ethnic and immigrant groups as they struggled to gain access to legitimate economic opportunities when they became more accepted in American society. There is an increasing problem with transnational criminal groups.

D. Crimes Without Victims
These are mainly offenses that are *mala prohibita*. Some argue there is no true "victimless" crime, as society is harmed by their commission. The "war on drugs" is one example of enforcement of victimless crime.

E. Political Crime
Crimes carried out that are ideological in nature. They can be committed against the government or by the government.

F. Cybercrime
Crime committed using technology, usually computers and the Internet. Possible victims include individuals, corporations/organizations, or the government.

V. THE CRIME PROBLEM TODAY

Americans generally believe that crime is increasing, but the overall crime rate has actually been decreasing since the 1990s.

A. The Worst of Times?
The crime rate has been much worse, and much better, in different times. The United States is currently not experiencing "the worst" in criminal behavior. Types of crimes change over time. At times, violent crime is a bigger problem than property crime; at other times, property crime is a more important issue.

B. The Most Crime-Ridden Nation?
It is difficult to make direct comparisons between countries. We should compare the United States to other similarly situated countries in the world. Compared to other industrialized countries, the United States has a significantly higher homicide rate. This could be due to the prevalence of handguns in the United States. Rates of property crime are lower in the United States than in other industrialized countries.

C. Keeping Track of Crime
The dark figure of crime is crime that is not reported to the police. Many people do not report criminal victimizations due to fear, embarrassment, retaliation or other reasons.

1. **Uniform Crime Reports**: uses official crime data from police departments. The National Incident-Based Reporting System (NIBRS): uses incident-based crime data that identifies individual offenses and offenders.

2. **National Crime Victimization Surveys**: surveys victims regarding their household and individual victimization

D. Trends in Crime
Analysis of crime trends indicates that crime is not on the increase. Both the UCR and NCVS reflect decreases in crime since the early 1980's. Several factors affect crime rates:

1. **Age**
Larger groups of people in the 16-24 age group can greatly affect the crime rate, so changes in this distribution over time must be analyzed.

2. **Crack Cocaine**
   The increased use of this illegal drug had significant effects on the crime rate in the 1990s

3. **Crime Trends: What Do We Really Know?**
   The causes of crime are extremely complex, and there are rarely simple answers for analyzing the crime rate.

REVIEW OF KEY TERMS

Fill in the appropriate term for each statement:

crime
public policy
crime control model
due process model
mala in se
mala prohibita
felony
misdemeanor
visible crime
occupational crime
organized crime
money laundering
crimes without victims
political crime
cybercrime
identity theft
dark figure of crime
Uniform Crime Reports (UCR)
National Incident-Based Reporting System (NIBRS)
National Crime Victimization Survey (NCVS)

1. _dark crime figure_ is the term used for the amount of crime that goes unreported to the police.

2. _Uniform Crime Reports_ is generated from a compilation of reports from law enforcement agencies throughout the country.

3. _visible crime_ is also known as "street crime" or "ordinary crime".

4. _Crimes without victims_ involve the willing and private exchange of illegal goods and services.

5. _mala in se_ are offenses that are wrong by their very nature.

6. _National Crime Victimization Survey_ measures the amount of crime from the perspective of victims.

7. _National Incident Base Reporting System_ measures crime by police officers recording and reporting each offense in a crime incident instead of merely describing the most serious crime in the incident.

8. _Occupational crime_ is conduct committed through opportunities created through professional or employment activities.

9. _political crimes_ are acts, such as treason and sedition, that constitute threats against the state.

10. ___mala prohibita___ are offenses that are banned by statute but are not inherently wrong.

11. ___organized crimes___ is a social framework for the perpetration of criminal acts, often on a basis that crosses state and national boundaries.

12. ___crime___ is a specific act of commission or omission in violation of the law, for which a punishment is prescribed

13. ___due process model___ depicts the criminal justice system as emphasizing reliable decisions that protect individuals' liberty through an adversarial process based on law.

14. ___crime control model___ depicts the criminal justice system as one that emphasizes efficient repression of crime through the exercise of discretion in administrative processing of cases.

15. Crime and Justice are ___public policy___ issues.

16. Offense committed through the use of computers are called ___cybercrime___.

17. The process of legitimizing illegally obtained funds is called ___money laundering___.

18. ___Identitity thefts___ is a crime in which an offender uses the personal information of another citizen to purchase goods and services.

19. Sentences of incarceration for longer than one year are handed down to people convicted of a ___felony___.

20. Sentences of incarceration for less than one year are handed down to people convicted of a ___misdemeanor___.

REVIEW OF KEY PEOPLE

Edwin Sutherland
Herbert Packer
John Gotti
James Kopp
Jeffrey Reiman

1. ___Herbert Packer___ developed the crime control and due process models as the means to provide new insights into the nature of the criminal justice system.

2. ___Edwin Sutherland___ developed the concept of "white collar crime" and led criminal justice scholars away from an exclusive focus on criminal behavior by lower class people. This individual also developed differential association theory.

3. ___Jeffrey Reiman___ argues that our system is designed to keep Americans in fear of crime, rather than reduce crime or achieve justice.

4. ___John Gotti___, who died in June 2002, was the boss of New York's Gambino crime "family" and the most important gangster since Al Capone.

5. ___James Kopp___ is an example of someone who committed a political crime. He was arrested for the murder of Dr. Barnett Slepian near Buffalo, New York because he performed abortions.

FILL-IN-THE-BLANK PRACTICE QUESTIONS

Although it does not accurately characterize the processing of most cases in the criminal justice system, the 1. _due process model_
was developed by 2. _Herbert Packer_ to illustrate how the system's primary goal in some cases could be to
preserve individual liberty through careful, reliable determinations of guilt or innocence.

Acts that are wrong by nature are called 3. _mala in se_ while acts prohibited by law but not wrong by
themselves are called 4. _mala prohibita_.

Two sources of data on crime are a reporting system where police describe each offense called the
5. _National Incident Base Reporting System_ and interviews of samples of the U. S. population called
6. _National Crime Vicimization Sur_. The 7. _Uniform Crime Report_ cannot adequately measure
8. _dark figure crimes report_ because reports from police departments are limited to crimes that are reported to or
discovered by law enforcement officials.

SELF-TEST SECTION

MULTIPLE CHOICE QUESTIONS

1.1 Which of the following is stressed by the crime control model?
   a) freedom
   b) order
   c) law
   d) socialism
   e) all of these

1.2 Which of the following is stressed by the due process model?
   a) democracy
   b) order
   c) law
   d) efficiency
   e) all of these

1.3 Which of the following refers to acts that are wrong by nature?
   a) *mala in se*
   b) dark figure of crime
   c) victimology
   d) *mala prohibita*
   e) *mala nocturnus*

1.4 Which of the following refers to acts prohibited by government?
   a) *mala in se*
   b) dark figure of crime
   c) victimology
   d) *mala prohibita*
   e) *mala nocturnus*

1.5 What law requires sex offenders to register with the authorities?
   a) Crime Control Bill of 1994
   b) Omnibus Crime Control Act
   c) Sex and Justice Act of 1999
   d) Uniform Crime Reports Act
   e) Megan's Law

1.6   Which of the following refers to an organized crime syndicate usually associated with "families"?
    a)   occupational crime
    b)   victimless crime
    c)   visible crime
    d)   organized crime
    e)   Cybercrime

1.7   Which of the following refers to crime committed using one or more computers?
    a)   online crime
    b)   high-tech crime
    c)   visible crime
    d)   cybercrime
    e)   intelcrime

1.8   The "war on drugs" is associated with what type of crime?
    a)   occupational crime
    b)   crimes without victims
    c)   visible crime
    d)   organized crime
    e)   cybercrime

1.9   If a doctor is murdered because he or she performs abortions, how might we best classify that crime?
    a)   occupational crime
    b)   victimless crime
    c)   visible crime
    d)   organized crime
    e)   political crime

1.10   What type of crime is homicide?
    a)   occupational crime
    b)   victimless crime
    c)   visible crime
    d)   organized crime
    e)   political crime

1.11   What type of crime is using "insider" stock trading information for personal gain?
    a)   occupational crime
    b)   victimless crime
    c)   visible crime
    d)   organized crime
    e)   political crime

1.12.   If current trends continue, what would you expect the murder rate to be in the year 2005? Use the chart below (which shows changes in the murder rate over the past century) for your answer.

    a)   5.5
    b)   6.7
    c)   10.2
    d)   2.2
    e)   8.9

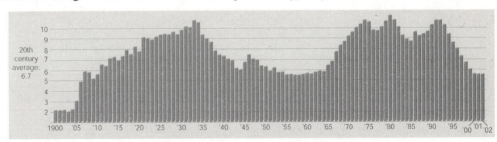

1.13. What is the name for crime not reported to the police?
   a) subtle crime
   b) victimless crime
   c) invisible crime
   d) silent crime
   e) dark figure of crime

1.14 What is the most accurate measure of crime in America?
   a) Uniform Crime Reports
   b) dark figure of crime
   c) National Incident-Based Reporting System
   d) National CrimeVictimization Survey
   e) there is no accurate measure

1.15 In which of the following places in the U. S. is gambling a legal business?
   a) Nevada
   b) New Jersey
   c) Michigan
   d) Indian reservations
   e) all of these

1.16 In which of the following places in the U. S. is prostitution a legal business?
   a) Nevada
   b) New Jersey
   c) Michigan
   d) Indian reservations
   e) all of these

1.17 Which measure of crime relies upon more detailed reports of crime by police agencies?
   a) FBI Statistics Data
   b) dark figure of crime
   c) National Incident-Based Reporting System
   d) National Crime Victimization Survey
   e) there is no such measure

1.18 What factor is the most likely to explain the difference in homicide rate between the United States and the United Kingdom?
   a) the death penalty
   b) native language
   c) climate
   d) availability of firearms
   e) government spending

1.19 Which of the following age groups commits the most crime?
   a) 15 and under
   b) 16-24
   c) 25-34
   d) 35-44
   e) 45 and over

1.20 Why was there an increase in violent crime in the late 1980s and early 1990s?
   a) spread of crack cocaine
   b) greater use of semi-automatic handguns
   c) fewer law enforcement personnel on the streets
   d) a and b
   f) none of these

1.21   The homicide rate in the U. S. is _____ as large as Canada.
   a)   twice
   b)   three times
   c)   four times
   d)   five times
   e)   ten times

1.22   According to your textbook, what factors might affect crime rates?
   a)   economic changes
   b)   law enforcement strategies
   c)   demographic changes
   d)   use of imprisonment
   e)   all of these

1.23   Which of the following is TRUE about Iceland?
   a)   Iceland has an extremely high crime rate
   b)   Iceland has a high crime rate
   c)   Iceland has an average rate of crime
   d)   Iceland has very little crime
   e)   Iceland has the same rate of crime as the U. S.

1.24   The rate of serious property crime in the U. S. is…
   a)   higher than most countries
   b)   about the same as most countries
   c)   lower than most countries
   d)   the U. S. does not measure property crime because it is a capitalist nation
   e)   the U. S. has the highest property crime rate of any country

1.25   The risk of lethal violence in the U. S. is…
   a)   higher than most countries
   b)   about the same as most countries
   c)   lower than most countries
   d)   the U. S. does not measure lethal crime
   f)   the U. S. has the lowest risk of lethal violence of any country

TRUE/FALSE QUESTIONS

1.   _F___   Most hate crimes are committed by groups representing hate-based organizations.
2.   _T___   Crime and justice are public policy issues because they are addressed by the government.
3.   _F___   Reiman urges criminalizing the acts of the poor and less affluent.
4.   _T___   There have been significant decreases in every type of violent crime in the U. S. in recent years.
5.   _F___   Political leaders are not influenced by public opinion in a democracy.
6.   _F___   Crime today is at an all-time high.
7.   _T___   The crime control model emphasizes order as a value.
8.   _T___   The due process model emphasizes law as a value.
9.   _F___   Megan's Law was designed to prosecute white-collar criminals.
10. _T___   Americans are not in agreement about which acts are criminal.
11. _T___   *Mala prohibita* crimes are acts prohibited by government.
12. _T___   *Mala in se* are acts wrong by nature.

13. _F_ The U. S. has only one source of data on crime, the Uniform Crime Reports.

14. _T_ Law enforcement officials focus largely upon visible crime.

15. _F_ Violent offenders are more likely to victimize strangers than offenders.

16. _T_ The Iran-Contra scandal is an example of a political crime.

17. _F_ Iceland has very high crime rates compared to the United States.

18. _F_ Persons usually provide accurate information when interview about their experiences with crime.

19. _T_ Organized crime is associated with many different ethnic and racial groups.

20. _F_ Cybercrime is not a problem yet because only middle and upper-income persons have computers and they usually do not commit crimes.

ANSWER KEY

Key Terms
1.   dark figure of crime
2.   Uniform Crime Reports
3.   visible
4.   crimes without victims
5.   *mala in se*
6.   National Crime Victimization Survey
7.   National Incident-Based Reporting System
8.   occupational crime
9.   political crime
10.   *mala prohibita*
11.   organized crime
12.   crime
13.   due process model
14.   crime control model
15.   public policy
16.   cybercrime
17.   money laundering
18.   identity theft
19.   felony
20.   misdemeanor

Key People
1.   Herbert Packer
2.   Edwin Sutherland
3.   Jeffrey Reiman
4.   John Gotti
5.   James Kopp

General Practice Questions
1.   due process model
2.   Herbert Packer
3.   mala in se
4.   mala prohibita
5.   National Incident-Based Reporting System
6.   National Crime Victimization Survey
7.   Uniform Crime Reports
8.   dark figure of crime

Multiple Choice
1.   B
2.   C
3.   A
4.   D
5.   E
6.   D
7.   D
8.   B
9.   E
10.   C
11.   A
12.   A
13.   E
14.   E

15. E
16. A
17. C
18. B
19. B
20. D
21. A
22. E
23. D
24. C
25. A

<u>True/False</u>
1. F
2. T
3. F
4. T
5. F
6. F
7. T
8. T
9. F
10. T
11. T
12. T
13. F
14. T
15. F
16. T
17. F
18. F
19. T
20. F

WORKSHEET 1.1: CONSENSUS OR NOT?

For each of the following activities, consider the following criminal acts and explain whether you believe the law defining each as criminal is based on a consensus in American society:

Prostitution_____

_____

_____

_____

_____

Smoking Marijuana_____

_____

_____

_____

_____

Income Tax Evasion_____

_____

_____

_____

_____

Copying Computer Software Without Permission_____

_____

_____

_____

VICTIMIZATION AND CRIMINAL BEHAVIOR

OUTLINE

- Crime Victimization
- Causes of Crime

CHAPTER 2
VICTIMIZATION AND CRIMINAL BEHAVIOR

LEARNING OBJECTIVES

After covering the material in this chapter, students should understand:

1. the factors affecting victimization

2. how individual and structural factors affect the risk of criminal victimization

3. the costs of criminal victimization and how they are calculated

4. the different theories of criminal behavior, including classical and positivist theories, biological, psychological, sociological, life course, and feminist theories of criminal behavior

5. the policy implications of the respective theories about the causes of crime

CHAPTER SUMMARY

Victimology surfaced in the 1950s as a field of criminology that studied the role of the victim in the criminal act. Young male residents of lower-income communities are the most likely to be victimized by crime. Because of the connection between race and social status in the United States, African Americans are more frequently victimized by crime than are whites. Most crime is intraracial. A significant percentage of crimes are committed by acquaintances and relatives of victims, especially crimes committed against women. Crime has a significant impact on all of society when one recognizes the financial and emotional costs it produces. Government agencies have begun to be more sensitive to the needs of crime victims. Thus, there are now programs in many places to provide services and compensation.

The classical school of criminology emphasized reform of the criminal law, procedures, and punishments. The rise of science led to the positivist school, which viewed behavior as stemming from social, biological, and psychological factors. Positivist criminology has dominated the study of criminal behavior in the twentieth century. The criminality of women has only recently been studied. It is argued by some that as women become more equal with men in society crimes committed by females will increase in number. Recent data indicate this theory may not hold true.

CHAPTER OUTLINE

I. CRIME VICTIMIZATION

    The field of victimology emerged in the 1950s and 1960s to focus attention on who is victimized, the impact of victimization, and role of victims in preventing and/or precipitating attacks.

    A. Who Is Victimized?

        1. **Men, Youths, Nonwhites**
            While African-Americans are more likely than whites to be victims, most violent crime is intraracial (i.e., the offender and the victim are same race). Young people are more likely than old to be victims, and men and low-income city dwellers are more likely to be victims than women and those living in more wealthy and rural areas.

2. **Low-Income City Dwellers**
   Lifestyle-exposure theory: Violent crime is primarily an urban phenomenon, in areas with high incidence of physical deterioration, economic insecurity, poor housing, family disintegration, and transience.

B. <u>Acquaintances and Strangers</u>
   People are more likely to be victimized by people they know, especially in the cases of sexual crimes. Women are more likely to experience violent victimization by an acquaintance or intimate.

C. <u>The Impact of Crime</u>
   Costs of crime range from tangible losses (such as from theft, destruction, or vandalism of property) to those losses that are intangible (pain, trauma, loss of quality of life). Fear of crime is also a cost on which a dollar value cannot be placed.

   1. **Costs of Crime**: Estimates of losses from crime include those that are tangible ($105 billion), intangible ($450 billion) and must also include the costs of operating the criminal justice system (over $167 billion per year).

   2. **Fear of Crime**: Ironically, those who are least likely to be victims (women and the elderly) sometimes experience the most fear of crime. Americans tend to fear crime more than their individual victimization risk would suggest. This may be due to the large amount of attention given to criminal victimization by the media.

D. <u>The Experience of Victims within the Criminal Justice System</u>
   Victims have been traditionally overlooked and forgotten; they have often felt interrogated and have been poorly treated by criminal justice officials in addition to their emotional, economic, and physical injuries. During the past two decades, justice agencies have taken new interest in the treatment and welfare of crime victims. While the proposed "Victim's Rights" constitutional amendment was not passed, the "Justice for All Act of 2004" has helped to place additional emphasis on victim's rights. There may be instances in which victims' and offenders' rights are contrary to one another, based on new legislation.

E. <u>The Role of Victims in Crime</u>
   Victims may increase their risk of victimization through negligence, precipitation, or provocation.

II. CAUSES OF CRIME

These theoretical explanations of crime can help to identify factors that increase individual propensity for crime. They may also help to create policy designed to reduce criminal behavior. Early explanations for crime focused on the "work of the devil" and explained that people were "lured" to commit crime by evil forces. The eighteenth century brought with it new perspectives on understanding criminal behavior.

A. <u>Classical and Positivist Theories</u>

   1. **The Classical School**. Classical theories of crime focus on the rational nature of crime (i.e., that criminals make decisions about whether to engage in criminal behavior), and that offenders weigh the cost and benefits of crime. In addition, theorists argued that punishment should fit the crime, and those who commit the same crime should receive similar punishments. Neoclassical criminology is the variety of classical criminology that has recently resurfaced.

   2. **Positivist criminology** views criminal behavior as caused by biological, social, and psychological factors rather than free will. These theorists argue that punishment should be tailored to individuals.

B. <u>Biological Explanations</u>

   These theories explain criminal behavior using individual biological differences between criminals and non-criminals. Biological theories fell out of favor after World War II in favor of sociological theories.

However, there has been a renewed interest in biological theories of crime since the mid-1980's. Some genetic factors may increase an individual's propensity (risk) for criminal behavior. These factors are known as criminogenic factors.

1. **Renewed Interest in Biological Explanations.** Environmental influences may work in conjunction with biological factors to explain criminal offending. Policy driven by biological explanations of crime would focus on identifying those with biological predispositions to crime and using methods such as selective incarceration, intensive supervision, or drug therapies to reduce their criminal behavior.

2. **Policy Implications of Biological Explanations.** Policies based on biological explanations focus on controlling people with biological predispositions to crime. Some options already used by the criminal justice system include selective incapacitation, intensive supervision, or drug-based therapies.

C. Psychological Explanations
    Psychological explanations for offending focus on crime as caused by mental illness or limited intellect. Psychiatrists have linked criminal behavior to such concepts as innate impulses, psychic conflict, and the repression of personality.

    1. **Psychopathology**: Related theories claimed that some people were "psychopaths," "sociopaths," or has anti-social personalities." Critics, however, have noted that it is difficult to identify and measure emotional factors in order to isolate people thought to be criminogenic.

    2. **Policy Implications of Psychological Explanations**. Policy created based on psychological explanations of crime focuses on treatment and counseling for offenders.

D. Sociological Explanations

    Sociological explanations of crime assume that the offender's actions are molded by contact with the social environment and such factors as race, age, gender, and income. University of Chicago researchers in the 1920s looked closely at the ecological factors that gave rise to crime: poverty, inadequate housing, broken families, and the problems of new immigrants.

    1. **Social Structure Theories** attribute criminal behavior to the stratified nature of Western societies, giving particular prominence to the fact that classes control very different amounts of wealth, status, and power. Thus deprivations and inequality lead the lower classes to crime. Structural factors can permit *anomie* to develop, in which rules or norms that regulate behavior weaken or disappear.

        a) Some theorists believe that strain from negative relationships can begin criminal behavior.

        b) Policy based on sociological explanations focuses on improving negative structural factors that increase criminal behavior. Policies that reduce poverty, expand job opportunities and improve health care are derived from this model.

    2. **Social Process Theories**: this group of theories assumes that criminality results from the interactions of people with the institutions, organizations, and processes of society. Thus everyone has the possibility of being a criminal, regardless of social status or education.

        a) There are three types of social process theories. Learning theories hypothesize that criminal activity is normal learned behavior, and this behavior is learned from family and peers who are involved in crime. Control theories assume that all members of society have the potential to commit crimes, but most people are restrained by their ties to such conventional institutions and individuals as family, church, school, and peer groups. Criminality results when these primary bonds are weakened and the person no longer follows the expected norms for behavior. Labeling theories state that certain individuals come to be labeled as deviant by society after committing a crime. The stigmatized individuals then come to believe that the label is true and they assume a criminal identity and career. By arguing, in effect, that the criminal justice system creates criminals by labeling individuals as such, this approach advocates the decriminalization of certain offenses to avoid needlessly placing labels on people.

b) Policy implications from social process theories focus on the strengthening of conventional bonds, developing positive role models, and avoiding labeling. Thus there should be policies to promote stable families and develop community agencies to assist those in need.

3. **Social conflict theory** argues that criminal law and criminal justice are mainly the means of controlling society's poor and have-nots. The rich commit crimes but are much less likely to be punished since they have more power (socially, politically, and economically) than the poor.

a) Critical, radical, or Marxist criminologists argue that the class structure of society results in certain powerless groups in society being labeled as deviant. When the status quo is threatened, criminal laws are altered to label and punish threatening groups and deviant criminals.

b) Policy implications from social conflict theories are focused on developing policies that reduce class-based conflict and injustice. They stress equal enforcement and punishment for crimes committed by upper-class offenders.

E. Life Course Explanations
These theories examine criminal offending across an individual's life course, and hypothesize that crime is caused by a number of factors discussed in biological, psychological, and sociological theories of crime. Some theorists discuss pathways to crime, in which young offenders begin with minor crimes and then move into more serious offenses.

Policy implications of these theories focus on the decreased use of incarceration for first-time offenders, and attempt to encourage and support key turning points that can keep offenders from criminal behavior.

F. Women and Crime
Most theories about the causes of crime are based almost entirely on observations of males. Except with respect to prostitution and shoplifting, little crime research focused on women prior to the 1970s. It was assumed that women did not commit serious crimes because of their nurturing, dependent nature. Women offenders were viewed as moral offenders: "fallen women."

Freda Adler's work stressed the role of the women's movement in changing women's roles and making their criminal behavior more similar in the 1970s and thereafter. Rita Simon emphasized greater freedom and opportunities in the job market as the source of changes in women's criminality. The number of women being arrested seems to be growing faster than the growth of men in crime. However, the number of women arrested is still relatively small. Some researchers believe that women will become more involved in economic and occupational crimes as more women pursue careers in business and industry. In general, like male offenders, women arrested for crimes tend to come from poor families in which physical and substance abuse are present.

G. Assessing Theories of Criminality
The body of existing criminological theories addresses distinct aspects of criminal behavior, and some focus on specific types of offenders. Criminological theory would be improved by the development of integrated theory, which merges these disparate theories into a single theory of criminal behavior.

REVIEW OF KEY TERMS

Fill in the appropriate term for each statement

victimology
classical criminology
positivist criminology
criminogenic
biological explanations
psychological explanations
sociological explanations
social process theories
social structure theories
anomie
learning theories
differential association
control theories
labeling theories
social conflict theories
life course theories

1. _Social process theories_ assert that crime is normal behavior which may be undertaken by anyone depending on the social forces and groups that influence their behavior.

2. _Classical criminology_ asserts that criminal behavior stems from free will, and therefore the system should demand accountability from offenders through deterrence-oriented punishments.

3. _labeling theories_ assert that certain individuals are treated as criminals by the system, and thus these individuals receive a message from the system that leads them to act as lawbreakers.

4. _Social conflict theories_ assert that criminal law and the criminal justice system are primarily means of controlling the poor.

5. _anomies_ is a state of normlessness caused by a breakdown in the rules of social behavior.

6. _learning theories_ assert that is crime learned behavior.

7. _biological explanations_ assert that criminal behavior is caused by physiological and neurological factors.

8. _Social structure theories_ assert that crime is the creation of a lower-class culture as poor people respond to poverty and deprivation.

9. _Control theories_ assert that criminal behavior results when the bonds that tie an individual to others in society are broken.

10. _Victimology_ includes the study of how victims cope with crime and the social costs of crime.

11. _Positivist criminology_ asserts that criminal behavior is not based on free will, but stems from social, biological, and psychological factors.

12. _Criminogenic_ factors are influences that are thought to bring about criminal behavior in an individual.

13. _Psychological explanations_ hypothesize that crime must be studied over time, and many factors must be examined that can affect criminal behavior at individual points in time.

14. _differential association_ assert that mental processes and associated behaviors are the cause of criminal behavior.

15. _Social_ assert that people become criminals when they identify with family members and individuals who regard criminal activity as normal and usual.

16. _____ assert that social conditions are the causes of crime.

REVIEW OF KEY PEOPLE

Edwin Sutherland
Cesare Lombroso
Cesare Beccaria
Sigmund Freud
Robert Merton
James Q. Wilson & Richard Hernnstein
Emile Durkheim
Robert Sampson & John Laub

1. _Cesare Lombroso_ associated with the theory that criminality is biologically determined.

2. _James Q. Wilson & Richard Hernnstein_ wrote books examining research on the links between biological factors and criminal behavior.

3. _Robert Merton_'s work focuses on life course criminology.

4. _Sigmund Freud_ associated with social structure theories of criminality and the idea that anomie within society influences criminal behavior.

5. _Edwin Sutherland_ stated that as society becomes more complex, traditional standards decline and crime becomes more prevalent.

6. _Cesare Beccaria_ developed theory that behavior can be caused by mental activity that takes place outside of our conscious awareness

7. _____ developed the concept of "white collar crime" and led criminal justice scholars away from an exclusive focus on criminal behavior by lower class people. Also developed differential association theory.

8. _____ regarded as the originator of classical criminology.

FILL-IN-THE-BLANK PRACTICE QUESTIONS

1. _Cesare Beccaria_ established the groundwork for 2. _classic criminology_ by arguing that people choose to commit crimes and that fear of punishment keeps people in check.

With the development of 3. _positivist criminology_, science-based theories emerged about the causes of criminal behavior, including 4. _psychological explanation_ drawing from 5. _Sigmund Freud_'s assertions about the influence of mental processes over behavior.

Among the 6. Social process ~~theories~~, 7. ~~differentation association theory~~ posits that criminals identify and emulate people who view crime as normal, acceptable activity and 8. control theory asserts that criminal behavior stems from the deterioration of ties between an individual and conventional institutions and people that support and reinforce society's rules and values.

SELF-TEST SECTION

MULTIPLE CHOICE QUESTIONS

2.1.   What does the routine activities theory explain?
    a)   Why people commit violent offenses
    b)   Why some people desist from crime
    c)   Why some people are more likely to be victimized that others
    d)   How to calculate the losses from crime
    e)   Why crime can be traumatic for victims

2.2.   Which of the following is TRUE about crime and race?
    a)   most violent crimes are interracial but property crimes are intraracial
    b)   most property crimes are interracial but violent crimes are intraracial
    c)   both property and violent crimes are most interracial
    d)   both property and violent crimes are mostly intraracial
    e)   race is not a factor in property or violent crimes

2.3.   How is income and location of residence related to crime?
    a)   Crime is most likely to occur in upper-class, urban locations
    b)   Crime is most likely to occur in lower-class, rural locations
    c)   Crime is most likely to occur in lower-class, urban locations
    d)   Crime is most likely to occur in upper-class, rural locations
    e)   Crime occurs equally across all income and locations

2.4.   Which of the following is a consequence of crime?
    a)   higher taxes
    b)   higher prices
    c)   increased levels of fear in society
    d)   all of the above
    e)   none of the above

2.5.   Which of the following is TRUE about victims?
    a)   victims are most often elderly women
    b)   the criminal justice system in the U. S. focuses more on the victim than the offender
    c)   victims are a key source of evidence in a criminal investigation
    d)   victims are protected by a Victims Bill of Rights in the U. S Constitution
    e)   all of the above are TRUE

2.6.   Women are most likely to be sexually victimized by:
    a)   someone they know
    b)   a stranger
    c)   a co-worker
    d)   a family member
    e)   none of the above

2.7. Which of the following factors is considered to be criminogenic?
   a)   being born into a middle- to upper-class household
   b)   experiencing hereditary traits such as alcoholism, epilepsy, or syphilis
   c)   attending college
   d)   being employed full-time
   e)   being raised in a two-parent household

2.8. Which twentieth century thinker proposed a psychoanalytic theory of criminal behavior?
   a)   Cesare Lombroso
   b)   Cesare Beccaria
   c)   Sigmund Freud
   d)   Henry Goddard
   e)   Ada Jukes

2.9. What is the main focus of social process theory?
   a)   Biological factors cause people to commit crime
   b)   Crime is totally due to social structural factors
   c)   Mental illness causes criminal behavior
   d)   The criminal justice process labels people as deviant
   e)   Anyone has the potential to be criminal, depending on circumstances

2.10. Which of the following is the best definition of anomie?
   a)   the breakdown of social norms that guide behavior
   b)   the increase of women involved in crime
   c)   increasing numbers of people in poverty committing crime
   d)   a severe decrease in genetic predispositions to crime
   e)   the effect of unemployment and poverty on crime

2.11. What is the main assumption of social conflict theories?
   a)   the poor are the only people who commit crimes
   b)   criminal laws are designed to control the poor
   c)   people commit crimes because of personality disorders
   d)   criminal behavior is normal and functional
   e)   society is most often interested in allowing crime to flourish

2.12. Which of the following is TRUE about women and crime?
   a)   there has been more research about women as opposed to men
   b)   women commit the same types of crime as men
   c)   the number of crimes committed by women has increased recently
   d)   women account for one-half of all arrests
   e)   all of the above are TRUE

2.13. Which two terms best describe life course criminology?
   a)   anomie/disfunction
   b)   epilepsy/syphilis
   c)   predisposition/precipitation
   d)   poverty/economic inequality
   e)   pathways/turning points

2.14. Which of the following is an example of the problems faced by victims?
   a)   emotional stress
   b)   missed work
   c)   defense attorneys may attempt to question their credibility
   d)   all of the above
   e)   none of the above

2.15. Which of the following is TRUE about crime?
- a) the fear of crime is low compared to the reality of crime
- b) the fear of crime is high compared to the reality of crime
- c) the fear of crime is about right when compared to the reality of crime
- d) there has been no research on the fear of crime in relation to the reality of crime
- e) the media plays an insignificant role in regard to the public's fear of crime

2.16. Which of the following is most likely to be victimized?
- a) elderly person watching television at home alone
- b) white female shopping during the day
- c) young black male at a nightclub
- d) young Hispanic child at school
- e) none of the above are likely to be victimized

2.17. Overall, criminological theories…
- a) explain all kinds of crime very well
- b) are focused too strongly on gender issues
- c) do not explain crime using social class or poverty
- d) need to be merged into more general theories
- e) have not been tested in the literature

2.18. Which of the following are psychological or emotional costs of crime?
- a) cost of medical care
- b) lost property
- c) lost quality of life
- d) all of the above
- e) none of the above

2.19. According to the chart below, which of the following groups is most likely to be victimized?

- a) White females, aged 16-19
- b) White males, aged 50-64
- c) African American females, aged 50-64
- d) White males, aged 25-34
- e) African American males, aged 25-34

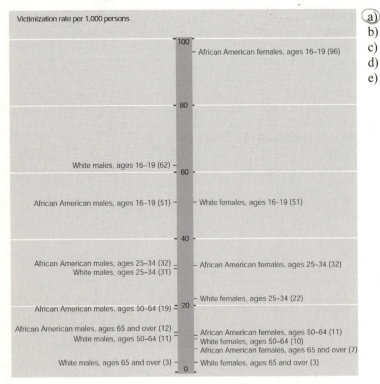

Victimization rate per 1,000 persons

African American females, ages 16–19 (96)

White males, ages 16–19 (62)

African American males, ages 16–19 (51)   White females, ages 16–19 (51)

African American males, ages 25–34 (32)   African American females, ages 25–34 (32)
White males, ages 25–34 (31)

White females, ages 25–34 (22)

African American males, ages 50–64 (19)

African American males, ages 65 and over (12)   African American females, ages 50–64 (11)
White males, ages 50–64 (11)   White females, ages 50–64 (10)
African American females, ages 65 and over (7)

White males, ages 65 and over (3)   White females, ages 65 and over (3)

2.20. Which of the following links criminal behavior to innate impulses, psychic conflict, and repressed personalities?
   a) biological theories
   b) psychological theories
   c) sociological theories
   d) legal theories
   e) conflict theories

2.21. Which of the following links criminal behavior to heredity?
   a) biological theories
   b) psychological theories
   c) sociological theories
   d) legal theories
   e) conflict theories

2.22. Which theoretical perspective would mandate counseling for criminal offenders?
   a) psychological theories
   b) conflict theories
   c) social structure theories
   d) sociological theories
   e) economic theories

2.23. How did Alder suggest the women's movement would affect crime?
   a) It would increase male crime but female crime would remain the same
   b) It would decrease female crime but male crime would remain the same
   c) Female crime would become more like male crime
   d) Male crime would become more like female crime
   e) Nothing would happen following the women's movement

2.24. What policy recommendation is most in line with social conflict theory?
   a) Programs should be developed that attempt to reduce poverty and aid people in need.
   b) Offenders should be sterilized to keep them from reproducing
   c) Trajectories should be identified to keep offenders from committing more crimes
   d) Counseling should be mandatory for criminal offenders
   e) Genetic testing should be required for recidivists

2.25. Which criminological theory would argue that sterilization should be used as a punishment to reduce criminal behavior?
   a) social process theory
   b) conflict theory
   c) biological theory
   d) strain theory
   e) labeling theory

TRUE/FALSE QUESTIONS

2.1. __T__ Women commit less crime than men.

2.2. __F__ There is general agreement within among criminologists that biological explanations of criminal behavior are the best.

2.3. __F__ A wealthy elderly women has a greater risk of becoming a victim of crime than the average citizen.

2.4. __F__ Crime does not impose any costs on the operation of the criminal justice system.

2.5. ___F___ Criminologists do not study characteristics of victims.

2.6. ___T___ Most people experience crime indirectly, such as through the media.

2.7. ___F___ The "Crime Victims' Bill of Rights" was ratified in April 2002 as the 28th Amendment to the U. S. Constitution .

2.8. ___T___ The criminal justice system focuses upon finding and prosecuting offenders.

2.9. ___F___ People cannot take precautions to protect themselves against criminals.

2.10. ___T___ Classical criminology portrays crime as a rational choice.

2.11. ___F___ Classical criminologists argue that laws and punishments should be hidden from the public.

2.12. ___F___ Learning theory is a biological explanation for criminal behavior.

2.13. ___T___ Sigmund Freud is most often associated with psychological explanations for criminal behavior.

2.14. ___F___ Residents in small towns and rural areas are more afraid to walk the streets than those residents in large cities.

2.15. ___T___ Positivist criminologists argue that criminals are different from noncriminals.

2.16. ___T___ According to a Seattle study, residential burglary is the most feared crime.

2.17. ___T___ Theories about the causes of crime can affect how crimes are punished.

2.18. ___T___ Theories about the causes of crime can affect how guilt or innocence is determined.

2.19. ___F___ The persons most likely to be victimized by crime are whites and people with high incomes.

2.20. ___T___ Demographic factors (such as age, gender and income) affect lifestyle, which in turn affects people's exposure to dangerous places.

ANSWER KEY

Key Terms
1. social process theories
2. classical criminology
3. labeling theories
4. social conflict theories
5. anomie
6. learning theories
7. biological explanations
8. social structure theories
9. control theories
10. victimology
11. positivist criminology
12. criminogenic factors
13. psychological explanations
14. differential association theories
15. sociological explanations

Key People
1. Cesare Lombroso
2. James Q. Wilson & Richard Hernnstein
3. Robert Merton
4. Sigmund Freud
5. Edwin Sutherland
6. Cesare Beccaria

General Practice Questions
1. Cesare Beccaria
2. classical criminology
3. positivist criminology
4. psychological explanations
5. Sigmund Freud
6. social process theories
7. differential association theory
8. control theory

Multiple Choice
2.1.   C
2.2.   D
2.3.   C
2.4.   D
2.5.   C
2.6.   A
2.7.   B
2.8.   C
2.9.   E
2.10. A
2.11. B
2.12. C
2.13. E
2.14. D
2.15. B
2.16. C
2.17. D
2.18. C

2.19. A
2.20. B
2.21. A
2.22. A
2.23. C
2.24. A
2.25. C

<u>True/False</u>
2.1.   T
2.2.   F
2.3.   F
2.4.   F
2.5.   F
2.6.   T
2.7.   F
2.8.   T
2.9.   F
2.10. T
2.11. F
2.12. F
2.13. T
2.14. F
2.15. T
2.16. T
2.17. T
2.18. T
2.19. F
2.20. T

WORKSHEET 2.1: THEORIES ABOUT THE CAUSES OF CRIME

On his way home from school, a fourteen-year-old boy from a poor family stops at a convenience store. When he thinks the clerk is not looking, he puts a bottle of orange juice under his coat and heads for the door. The clerk catches him and calls the police. How might one explain the boy's criminal action according to each of the following theories about causes of crime?

Biological Explanations_____

_____

_____

_____

_____

Psychological Explanations_____

_____

_____

_____

_____

Social Structure Theory_____

_____

_____

_____

_____

Social Process Theory_____

_____

_____

_____

THE CRIMINAL JUSTICE SYSTEM

OUTLINE

- The Goals of Criminal Justice
- Criminal Justice in a Federal System
- Criminal Justice as a System
- Operations of Criminal Justice Agencies
- The Flow of Decision Making in the Criminal Justice System
- Crime and Justice in a Multicultural Society

CHAPTER 3
THE CRIMINAL JUSTICE SYSTEM

LEARNING OBJECTIVES

After covering the material in this chapter, students should understand:

1.   the goals of criminal justice include doing justice, controlling crime, and preventing crime

2.   the existence, organization, and jurisdiction of national and state criminal justice systems, including the dual court system

3.   criminal justice as a "system," with specific characteristics: discretion, resource dependence, sequential tasks, and filtering

4.   the primary agencies of criminal justice and the prevalence of local agencies and institutions

5.   the flow of decision making in the criminal justice system, including the thirteen steps in the decision making process

6.   crime and justice in a multicultural society

CHAPTER SUMMARY

The three goals of criminal justice are doing justice, controlling crime, and preventing crime. The dual court system contains a national system and state systems of criminal justice that enforce laws, try cases, and punish offenders. Criminal justice is a system made up of a number of parts or subsystems--police, courts, and corrections. Exchange is a key concept for the analysis of criminal justice processes. The four major characteristics of the criminal justice system are discretion, resource dependence, sequential tasks, and filtering. The processing of cases in the criminal justice system involves a series of decisions by police officers, prosecutors, judges, probation officers, wardens, and parole board members. The criminal justice system consists of thirteen steps that cover the stages of law enforcement, adjudication, and corrections. The four-layered criminal justice wedding cake model indicates that not all cases are treated equally. The existence of unequal treatment of people within the criminal justice system would clash with the American values of equality, fairness, and due process. Racial disparities in criminal justice are explained in one of three ways: minorities commit more crimes; the criminal justice system is racist; the criminal justice system expresses the racism of society.

CHAPTER OUTLINE

I.   THE GOALS OF CRIMINAL JUSTICE

   A.   Doing Justice
        Without a system founded on justice there would be little difference between criminal justice in the United States and that in authoritarian countries. Elements of the goal include: offenders will be held fully accountable for their actions; the rights of persons who have contact with the system will be protected; like offenses will be treated alike; officials will take into account relevant differences among offenders and offenses.

B.   Controlling Crime
The criminal justice system is designed to control crime by apprehending, prosecuting, convicting, and punishing those members of the community who do not live according to the law. There is a constraint on that goal: efforts to control crime must be carried out within the framework of law.

C.   Preventing Crime
Crime prevention encompasses the deterrent effect of actions by the criminal justice system. Citizens can take an active role in crime prevention by simple actions. Unfortunately many people leave homes and cars unlocked, and take other actions that facilitate crime.

II.   CRIMINAL JUSTICE IN A FEDERAL SYSTEM

A.   Two Justice Systems
Federalism is a system in which power is divided between the federal government and the states. IN the United States. The federal and states systems of government are sometimes in conflict.

B.   Expansion of Federal Government
The United States government has expanded its role in law enforcement, especially after September 11th. With the development of the Department of Homeland Security, many more crimes are now defined as federal offenses.

III.   CRIMINAL JUSTICE AS A SYSTEM

A.   The System Perspective
The concept of system helps us to recognize that the agencies and processes of criminal justice are linked. One result is that the actions of the police, for example, have an impact on the other parts of the system prosecution, courts, and corrections.

One key concept is *exchange*, meaning the mutual transfer of resources among individual actors, each of whom has goals that he or she cannot accomplish alone. Plea bargaining is an obvious example of exchange. The prosecutor and defense attorney reach agreement on the plea and sentence. Each actor, including the defendant and the judge, gains a benefit as a result. The concept of exchange reminds us that decisions are the products of interactions among individuals in the system and that the subsystems of criminal justice are linked together by the actions of individual decision makers.

B.   Characteristics of the Criminal Justice System
1.   Discretion
At all levels of the justice process officials have significant ability to act according to their own judgment and conscience. Police officers, prosecutors, judges, and correctional officials may consider a wide variety of circumstances and exercise many options as they dispose of a case.   The need for discretionary power has been justified primarily on two counts: resources and justice.

2.   Resource Dependence: Criminal justice does not produce its own resources but is dependent on others for them. It must therefore develop special links with people responsible for the allocation of resources--that is, the political decision makers. Criminal justice actors must be responsive to the legislators, mayors, and city council members who hold the power of the purse. Justice officials seek to maintain a positive image in news reports and seek to keep voters happy.

3.   Sequential Tasks: Every part of the criminal justice system has distinct tasks that are carried out sequentially.
4.   Filtering: The criminal justice process may be viewed as a filtering process through which cases are screened: some are advanced to the next level of decision making, and others are either rejected or the conditions under which they are processed are changed.

IV. OPERATIONS OF CRIMINAL JUSTICE AGENCIES

    A. Police
        Complexity and fragmentation characterize the number and jurisdiction of the many public organizations in the United States engaged in law enforcement activities. Only fifty are federal law enforcement agencies; the rest are state and local.

        The responsibilities of police organizations include keeping the peace, apprehending law violators and fighting crime, engaging in crime prevention and providing social services.

    B. Courts
        The dual court system is used in the United States. There are separate judicial structures for each state in addition to a national structure. Interpretation of the law can vary from state to state. Judges have discretion to apply the law as they feel it should be applied until they are overruled by a higher court. Courts are responsible for adjudication, which involves determining whether defendants are guilty according to fair procedures.

    C. Corrections
        On any given day about 6 million Americans are under the supervision of the corrections system. Only about a third of convicted offenders are actually incarcerated; the remainder are under supervision in the community through probation, parole, community-based halfway houses, work release programs, and supervised activities. The federal government, all the states, most counties, and all but the smallest cities are engaged in the corrections enterprise. Increasingly, nonprofit private organizations such as the YMCA have contracted with governments to perform correctional services. For-profit businesses have undertaken the construction and administration of institutions through contracts with governments.

V. THE FLOW OF DECISION MAKING IN THE SYSTEM

    A. Steps in the Decision Making Process
        Remember that formal procedures outlined may not always depict reality. The system appears to be an assembly line as decisions are made about defendants. The process is shaped by the concepts of system, discretion, sequential tasks, filtering, and exchange.

        1.   **Investigation**: Police are normally dependent on a member of the community to report the offense.
        2.   **Arrest**: Taking a person into custody when police determine there is enough evidence indicating a particular person has committed a crime. Arrests are sometimes based on a warrant, but most times are not.
        3.   **Booking**: Procedure by which an administrative record is made of the arrest; a suspect may be fingerprinted, photographed, interrogated, and placed in a lineup for identification by the victim or witnesses. All suspects must be warned that they have the right to counsel, that they may remain silent, and that any statement they make may later be used against them.
        4.   **Charging**: Prosecuting attorneys determine whether there is reasonable cause to believe that an offense was committed and whether the suspect committed it.
        5.   **Initial Appearance**: Suspects must be brought before a judge to be given formal notice of the charge for which they are being held, to be advised of their rights, and to be given the opportunity to post bail. The judge determines if there is sufficient evidence to hold the suspect for further criminal processing.
        6.   **Preliminary Hearing/Grand Jury**: The preliminary hearing, used in about half the states, allows a judge to determine whether probable cause exists to believe that the accused committed a known crime within the jurisdiction of the court
        7.   **Indictment/Information**: The prosecutor prepares the formal charging document and enters it before the court.

8.   **Arraignment**: The accused person is next taken before a judge to hear the indictment or information read and is asked to enter a plea. The judge must determine if a guilty plea is made voluntarily and whether the person has full knowledge of the possible consequences of the plea.

9.   **Trial**: For the relatively small percentage of defendants who plead not guilty, the right to a. trial by an impartial jury is guaranteed by the Sixth Amendment for defendants facing charges which carry six months or more of imprisonment. Most trials are summary or bench trials conducted by a judge without a jury. It is estimated that only about 10-15% of cases go to trial and only about 5% are heard by juries.

10. **Sentencing**: The judge's intent is to make the sentence suitable to the particular offender within the requirements of the law and in accordance with the retribution (punishment) and rehabilitation goals of the system.

11. **Appeal**: Defendants found guilty may appeal their convictions to a higher court based on claims that the rules of procedure were not properly followed or that the law forbidding the behavior is unconstitutional. Defendants lose about 80 percent of appeals. A successful appeal typically leads to a new trial rather than release.

12. **Corrections**: Probation, intermediate sanctions, incarceration are the sanctions most generally impose and supervised by the corrections subsystem.

13. **Release**: Release may be accomplished through serving the full sentence imposed by the court or by returning to the community under supervision of a parole officer with restrictive conditions.

B. The Criminal Justice Wedding Cake
The key concept for differentiating cases according to the way in which criminal justice officials and the public react to it. Layer 1: Very few "celebrated" cases that are exceptional, get great public attention, result in a jury trial, and often have extended appeals. Layer 2: Felonies that are deemed to be serious by officials, e.g., crimes of violence committed by persons with long criminal records against victims unknown to them. Layer 3: Felonies by offenders who are seen as of lesser concern than those in Layer 2; many cases are filtered out of the system, and plea bargaining is encouraged. Layer 4: Misdemeanors encompassing 90% of all cases handled in the criminal justice system; processes are speedy and informal, and fines, probation, or short jail sentences result. Assembly-line justice reigns.

VI. CRIME AND JUSTICE IN A MULTI-CULTURAL SOCIETY

Disparity and Discrimination. African-Americans, Hispanics, and other minorities are drawn into the criminal justice system at much higher rates than the white majority.

A. Explanations for disparities
1.   **People of color commit more crimes**: There is no evidence of an ethnic link to criminal behavior. There is a link between crime and economic disadvantages which disproportionately affect these minority groups. Unemployment rates are higher and average family income is lower among these minority groups. Because most crime is intraracial rather than interracial, minority group members in poor neighborhoods also suffer from more significant victimization rates. African-Americans and Hispanics are arrested more often and for more serious crimes on average than whites. Analysts question whether crime control efforts should shift to an emphasis on reducing social problems that may contribute to crime.

2.   **The Criminal Justice System Is Racist**: Research indicates that people of color are arrested more often for drug offenses even though they do not engage in drug use more often than whites. Also, unfounded arrests of African-Americans occur at four times the rate of unfounded arrests of whites. The rate of incarceration for poor and minority citizens is greater than even their higher offense rates would justify. Disparities need not be the result of overt racism. For example, if police patrols concentrate on poor neighborhoods, more arrests will be made there than elsewhere. Poor people are less likely to make bail or hire their own attorneys, two factors that may contribute to a higher imprisonment rate.

3. **America Is A Racist Society**. There is some evidence of racism in the way that society asks the criminal justice system to operate. For example, federal sentencing guidelines punish users of crack cocaine about one hundred times more harshly than users of powder cocaine, even though the drugs are nearly identical. The only difference is that whites tend to use the powder form while people of color tend to use crack. Sentencing studies find a stronger link between unemployment and sentencing than between crime rates and sentencing. This suggests that prisons are being used to confine people who cannot find jobs. Drug law enforcement is aimed primarily at low-level dealers in minority neighborhoods. Numerous examples of African-American and Hispanic professionals who have been falsely arrested when police saw a person of color whom they believed was "out of place."

REVIEW OF KEY TERMS

Fill in the appropriate term for each statement:

federalism
system
exchange
plea bargain
discretion
filtering process
adjudication
dual court system
arrest
warrant
information
indictment
felonies
misdemeanors
disparity
discrimination

1. _____discretion_____ is the authority to make decisions by using one's own judgment and conscience which provides the basis for individualization and informality in the administration of justice.

2. _____Plea bargain_____ occur when the defense attorney and prosecuting attorney reach an agreement for the sentence of an accused.

3. _____arrest_____ is the physical taking of a person into custody.

4. _____information_____ is a document charging an individual with a specific crime prepared by a prosecuting attorney and presented to a court at a preliminary hearing.

5. A _dual court system_ has a separate state and national court system. Each case is tried in the jurisdiction in which the law was broken.

6. _____federalism_____ consists of separate judicial structures for states and for the national government.

7. _____disparity_____ is the unequal treatment of one group by the criminal justice system.

8. _____system_____ is a complex whole consisting of interdependent parts whose operations are directed toward goals and are influenced by the environment within which they function.

9. _____filtering process_____ is a characteristic of the criminal justice system that describes how one subsystem must complete its responsibilities before a case is passed to the authority of another subsystem.

10. _____warrant_____ is a court order authorizing law enforcement officials to take certain actions, for example, to arrest suspects or to search premises.

11. _____Discrimination_____ occurs when differential treatment of individuals occurs based on race, ethnicity, gender, sexual orientation or economic status rather than behavior or qualifications.

12. _____felonies_____ are serious crimes carrying penalties of one year or more imprisonment.

13. _____adjudication_____ is the process of determining whether or not a defendant is guilty.

14. _____exchange_____ is a mutual transfer of resources or information that underlies the motivations and decisions of actors within the criminal justice system.

15. _____Indictment_____ is a document returned by a grand jury as a "true bill" charging an individual with a specific crime.

16. _____misdemeanors_____ are less serious offenses carrying penalties of no more than one year of incarceration.

FILL-IN-THE-BLANK PRACTICE QUESTIONS

One example of the way in which 1. _political conversation_ affect the development of criminal justice policies is the power of elected officials serving in 2. _Congress_ to enact criminal laws and allocate budgetary resources for criminal justice agencies on behalf of the federal government.

Prosecutors exercise 3. _discretion_ in making decisions about which cases will leave the criminal justice system through the 4. _filtering process_ and which cases will be discussed with criminal defense attorneys in the 5. _Plea bargaining_ process that obtains convictions without taking cases to trial.

In states that do not initiate formal charges by having a prosecutor file an 6. _information_ , a group of citizens, known as the 7. _grand jury_ , decides whether or not there is sufficient evidence to pursue a case. If they find the existence of sufficient evidence, they issue an 8. _indictment_ .

Among the primary goals of criminal justice, 9. _preventing crime_ relies on the deterring effect of punishing offenders as well as the actions of private citizens.

Criminal justice agencies throughout the United States are characterized by 10. _decentralization_ and fragmentation. In the judicial branch, this is evident in the 11. _dual court system_ which is very different from the unified, national systems that exist in many other countries.

SELF-TEST SECTION

MULTIPLE CHOICE QUESTIONS

3.1.   Which of the following is a goal of the American criminal justice system?
   a)   consolidating power at the local level
   b)   preventing crime
   c)   consolidating power at the federal level
   d)   dramatizing crime
   e)   all of the above are goals of the criminal justice system

3.2.   Which of the following is TRUE about the American criminal justice system?
   a)   citizens have authority to enforce the law
   b)   most people take steps to protect themselves against crime
   c)   there is little difference between the U. S criminal system and authoritarian countries
   d)   criminal justice officials are limited by the constitutional rights of individuals
   e)   criminal justice officials never fall short of doing justice

3.3.   Which of the following is TRUE about discretion within the American system of criminal justice?
   a)   discretion not exist within the American system of criminal justice
   b)   discretion exists but for only a few participants
   c)   discretion exists for all participants but it does not limit the values of the American system
   d)   discretion exists and its use limits the values of the American system
   e)   discretion exists for only judges

3.4.   Which of the following is TRUE about the American system of criminal justice?
   a)   very few suspects who are arrested are then prosecuted, tried, and convicted
   b)   all suspects who are arrested are then prosecuted, tried, and convicted
   c)   no suspects who are arrested are then prosecuted, tried, and convicted
   d)   a large percentage of suspects who are arrested are then prosecuted, tried, and convicted
   e)   none of the above are TRUE

3.5.   Which of the following is an attribute of the American system of criminal justice?
   a)   mandatory actions
   b)   resource dependence
   c)   independence of actors
   d)   rigidity of institutions
   e)   independent subsystems

3.6.   How many state and local law enforcement agencies exist within the American system of criminal justice?
   a)   roughly 5,000
   b)   roughly 10,000
   c)   roughly 12,000
   d)   roughly 18,000
   e)   roughly 35,000

3.7.   In which layer of the "criminal justice wedding cake" (see below) does the O.J. Simpson murder case belong?

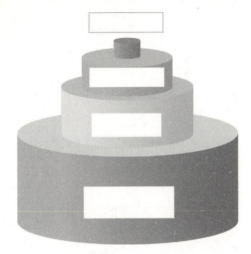

a) Layer 1
b) Layer 2
c) Layer 3
d) Layer 4
e) Layer 5

3.8.   Which state does NOT have a state law enforcement agency?
a) California
b) Ohio
c) New York
d) South Dakota
e) Hawaii

3.9.   Which of the following is likely to be a federal crime?
a) assault
b) larceny
c) arson
d) espionage
e) auto theft

3.10.   Which of the following are major duties of police agencies?
a) keeping the peace
b) apprehending criminals
c) providing social services
d) preventing crime
e) all of the above

3.11.   Which of the following duties is being performed if a police officer "directs traffic"?
a) solving crime
b) apprehending criminals
c) providing social services
d) preventing crime
e) all of the above

3.12.   Which of the following duties is being performed if a police officer "provides emergency aid"?
a) solving crime
b) apprehending criminals
c) providing social services
d) preventing crime
e) all of the above

3.13. Which of the following accounts for the smallest amount of an officer's time?
a) keeping the peace
b) apprehending criminals
c) providing social services
d) preventing crime
e) all of the above account for a great deal of an officer's time

3.14. Which of the following engage in corrections?
a) federal government
b) state government
c) most counties
d) most cities
e) all of the above

3.15. Which of the following has diminished the role of the Federal Bureau of Investigation in criminal investigation?
a) domestic violence
b) drug enforcement
c) homeland security
d) immigration
e) homicide

3.16. The right to a trial by an impartial jury is guaranteed by the...
a) First Amendment
b) Fifth Amendment
c) Sixth Amendment
d) Eighth Amendment
e) Tenth Amendment

3.17. The Department of Homeland Security oversees:
a) the Federal Bureau of Investigation
b) the Central Intelligence Agency
c) the Bureau of Alcohol, Tobacco, and Firearms
d) the Immigration and Naturalization Service
e) the Government Accounting Office

3.18. How many percent of criminal cases go before a jury?
a) five
b) ten to fifteen
c) twenty
d) thirty to forty
e) fifty

3.19. Where are accused offenders typically placed while awaiting arraignment?
a) a holding cell
b) a prison
c) a county jail
d) a community facility
e) a squad car

3.20. According to the chart below, which of the following groups is most likely to be stopped by the police?

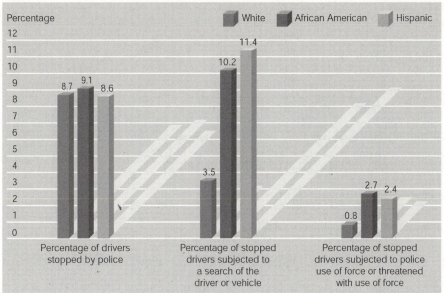

a) White
b) African American
c) Hispanic
d) Asian
e) All have an equal probability of being stopped

3.21. What layer of the criminal justice wedding cake contains ninety percent of all cases?
a) layer one (celebrated cases)
b) layer two (serious felony cases)
c) layer three (less important felony cases)
d) layer four (misdemeanor cases)
e) layer five (federal cases)

3.22. Which of the following is NOT a layer of the criminal justice wedding cake?
a) layer one (celebrated case)
b) layer two (serious felony case)
c) layer three (less important felony case)
d) layer four (misdemeanor case)
e) layer five (federal case)

3.23. Which group was on the minds of those who framed the Fourteenth Amendment's equal protection clause?
a) women
b) white men
c) African-Americans
d) handicapped persons
e) homosexuals

3.24. In what case did the U. S. Supreme Court declare that segregation (separate but equal) was unconstitutional?
a) *Marbury v. Madison* (1803)
b) *Plessy v. Ferguson* (1896)
c) *Shelley v. Kramer* (1948)
d) *Brown v. Board of Education* (1954)
e) *Roe v. Wade* (1973)

3.25. The link between crime and economic disadvantage is...
   a)   non-existent
   b)   slight
   c)   moderate
   (d)   significant
   e)   a universal law of causal and effect

TRUE/FALSE QUESTIONS

3.1. _F_   All laws are applied fairly in the United States

3.2. _F_   The easiest goal of the American system of criminal justice is to do justice.

3.3. _T_   The U. S. Constitution does not provide for a national police force.

3.4. _F_   There are no federal law enforcement agencies in the U. S.

3.5. _T_   Under the National Stolen Property Act, the FBI may investigate thefts of more than $5,000 in value.

3.6. _T_   Two-thirds of all criminal justice employees work for local government.

3.7. _F_   Discretion means that all actors in the criminal justice system enforce laws equally every time.

3.8. _T_   The subsystems of the American system of criminal justice are interdependent.

3.9. _F_   Eighty percent of American police are found at the federal level.

3.10. _F_   African-Americans are treated fairly within the American system of criminal justice.

3.11. _F_   All fifty states in the U. S. have state law enforcement agencies.

3.12. _F_   The U. S. criminal justice system processes most of its cases at the federal level.

3.13. _F_   State courts are required by the U. S. Supreme Court to decide all cases in a similar fashion.

3.14. _F_   Cases like Robert Blake's are typical of how the criminal justice system operates.

3.15. _F_   Citizens have the authority to arrest citizens.

3.16. _F_   Ninety percent of criminal cases involve serious felonies.

3.17. _F_   The drafters of the Fourteenth Amendment's equal protection clause were concerned solely with women's rights.

3.18. _T_   There is a large disparity between the sentences imposed upon those convicted for crack cocaine and those convicted for powder cocaine.

3.19. _T_   Some have argued that the "War on Drugs" was designed to disadvantage black youths.

3.20. _F_   The link between crime and economic disadvantage is not significant.

ANSWER KEY

Key Terms
1. discretion
2. plea bargains
3. arrest
4. information
1. dual court system
2. federalism
3. disparity
4. system
5. filtering process
6. warrant
7. discrimination
8. felonies
9. adjudication
10. exchange
11. indictment
12. misdemeanors

General Practice Questions
1. political considerations
2. Congress
3. discretion
4. filtering process
5. plea bargaining
6. information
7. grand jury
8. indictment
9. preventing crime
10. decentralization
11. dual court system

Multiple Choice
3.1.   B
3.2.   D
3.3.   D
3.4.   A
3.5.   B
3.6.   D
3.7.   D
3.8.   E
3.9.   D
3.10.   E
3.11.   C
3.12.   C
3.13.   B
3.14.   E
3.15.   C
3.16.   C
3.17.   D
3.18.   A
3.19.   A
3.20.   C
3.21.   D

3.22.   E
3.23.   C
3.24.   D
3.25.   D

<u>True/False</u>
3.1.   F
3.2.   F
3.3.   T
3.4.   F
3.5.   T
3.6.   T
3.7.   F
3.8.   T
3.9.   F
3.10.   F
3.11.   F
3.12.   F
3.13.   F
3.14.   F
3.15.   F
3.16.   F
3.17.   F
3.18.   T
3.19.   T
3.20.   F

WORKSHEET 3.1 SYSTEM ATTRIBUTES

Imagine that you are a county prosecutor. Briefly describe how the attributes of the criminal justice system (discretion, resource dependence, sequential tasks, and filtering) would affect your relationships, decisions, and actions with respect to each of the following.

Police_____

_____

_____

Defense Attorneys_____

_____

_____

_____

Trial Judges_____

_____

_____

_____

News Media_____

_____

_____

_____

County Commissioners_____

_____

_____

_____

CRIMINAL JUSTICE AND THE RULE OF LAW

OUTLINE

- Foundations of Criminal Law
- Substantive Criminal Law
- Procedural Criminal Law
- The Supreme Court Today

CHAPTER 4
CRIMINAL JUSTICE AND THE RULE OF LAW

LEARNING OBJECTIVES

After covering the material in this chapter, students should understand:

1.   the development of American criminal law from the English common law system

2.   the sources of criminal law

3.   the principles of substantive criminal law

4.   the accepted defenses and their justifications in substantive criminal law

5.   the importance of procedural due process

6.   the expansion of the meaning of the Bill of Rights and its protections for criminal defendants

CHAPTER SUMMARY

Criminal law focuses on prosecution and punishment of people who violate specific laws enacted by legislatures, while civil law concerns disputes between private citizens or businesses. Criminal law is divided into two parts: substantive law that defines offenses and penalties, and procedural law that defines individuals' rights and the processes that criminal justice officials must follow in handling cases. The common law tradition, which was inherited from England, involves judges' shaping law through their decisions. Criminal law is found in written constitutions, statutes, judicial decisions, and administrative regulations.

Substantive criminal law involves seven important elements that must exist and be demonstrated by the prosecution in order to obtain a conviction: legality, *actus reus,* causation, harm, concurrence, *mens rea,* punishment. The *mens rea* element, concerning intent or state of mind, can vary with different offenses, such as various degrees of murder or sexual assault. The element may also be disregarded for strict liability offenses that punish actions without considering intent. Criminal law provides opportunities to present several defenses based on lack of criminal intent: entrapment, self-defense, necessity, duress (coercion), immaturity, mistake, intoxication, and insanity. Standards for the insanity defense vary by jurisdiction with various state and federal courts using several different tests.

The provisions for the Bill of Rights were not made applicable to state and local officials by the U.S. Supreme Court until the mid-twentieth century, when the Court incorporated most of the Bill of Rights' specific provisions into the due process clause of the Fourteenth Amendment. The Fourth Amendment prohibition of unreasonable searches and seizures has produced many cases questioning the application of the exclusionary rule. Decisions by the Burger and Rehnquist Courts during the 1970s, 1980s, and 1990s have created several exceptions to the exclusionary rule and given greater flexibility to law enforcement officials. The Fifth Amendment provides protections against compelled self-incrimination and double jeopardy. As part of the right against compelled self-incrimination, the Supreme Court created *Miranda* warnings that must be given to suspects before they are questioned. The Sixth Amendment includes the right to counsel, the right to a speedy and public trial, and the right to an impartial jury.

The Eighth Amendment includes protections against excessive bail, excessive fines, and cruel and unusual punishments. Many of the Supreme Court's most well known Eighth Amendment cases concern the death penalty, which the Court has endorsed, provided that states employ careful decision-making procedures that consider aggravating and mitigating factors.

CHAPTER OUTLINE

I. FOUNDATIONS OF THE CRIMINAL LAW

A. Substantive Law and Procedural Law
Law must proscribe an act before it can be regarded as a crime and have accompanying punishment. Civil law concerns contracts, property, and personal injuries. Criminal law concerns conduct that is punished by the government.

Criminal law is divided into substantive and procedural law. Substantive law stipulates the types of conduct that are criminal and the punishments to be imposed. Procedural law sets forth the rules that govern the enforcement of the substantive law.

B. Sources of Criminal Law
Earliest known codes are the Sumerian (3100 B.C.) and the Code of Hammurabi (1750 B.C.). These written codes were divided into sections to cover different types of offenses.

1. **Common Law**: U.S. uses the Anglo-American common law system, which originated in England as primary source of its legal values and law. In the Anglo-American system of uncodified law, judges follow precedent set by earlier decisions when they decide new but similar cases. The common law system relies on doctrine of following earlier court rulings when making judicial decisions.

2. **Written Law**. The types of written law include constitutions, statutes, case law, and administrative regulations. Constitutions dictates the basic laws of a country or state; statutes are laws enacted by legislators; case law defines precedent from prior cases; administrative regulations focus on actions that may not be criminal but impact public health, environmental protection or workplace safety.

C. Felony and Misdemeanor
Felonies are punishable by more than one year of incarceration, while misdemeanors are punishable by one year or less. Felony offenders are often sent to state prison, but misdemeanants serve their sentence in local jails.

D. Criminal Law versus Civil Law
Criminal law defines an offense against society—the government punished violations of criminal law. Civil law defines relationships between individuals within society--civil wrongdoers pay compensation for the harms they cause. Criminal and civil law come together in civil forfeiture, which involves government seizure of property connected to criminal activity.

II. SUBSTANTIVE CRIMINAL LAW

A. Seven Principles of Criminal Law
1. **Legality**: existence of a law defining the crime. The U.S. Constitution prohibits *ex post facto* laws, or laws used to punish crimes that occurred before the law came into existence.

2. *Actus reus*: behavior of either commission or omission.

3. **Causation**: causal relationship between the act and the harm suffered.

4. **Harm**: damage inflicted on legally protected value (e.g., person, property, reputation). This also includes the potential for harm, as evidenced in inchoate offenses that are planned but not executed.

5. **Concurrence**: the simultaneous occurrence of the intention and the act.
6. *Mens rea* (a guilty state of mind): guilty mind requires intention to commit the act.

7. **Punishment**: the stipulation in the law of sanctions to be applied against persons found guilty of the forbidden behavior.

B.   <u>Elements of a Crime</u>
Three factors make up the elements of a crime. The act (*actus rea*), the attendant circumstances, and the intent to commit a crime (*mens rea*).

C.   <u>Statutory Definitions of Crimes</u>
1. **Murder and Nonnegligent Manslaughter**: murder requires "malice aforethought" or some other requirement of a higher level of intent.

2. **Rape** is a difficult crime to prosecute due to difficulties with finding corroborating evidence and with the public humiliation of the victim. In some jurisdictions, an absence of visible physical injury has been taken to mean that there was no force used and therefore there was consent.

D.   <u>Responsibility for Criminal Acts</u>
Mens rea is a key element for establishing perpetrator's responsibility. Guilt is decided based on whether a reasonable man in the defendant's situation and with his physical characteristics would have had a consciousness of guilt ("objective *mens rea*"). Accidents are not crimes because of the absence of *mens rea*, although acts of extreme negligence or recklessness may be criminal. Legislatures can criminalize acts without showing of intent, such as pure food and drug laws, housing laws, sanitation laws; such offenses usually do not lead to incarceration unless there is a refusal to comply after given notice of violation.

1. **Entrapment** is a defense claiming the absence of intent when the defendant lacks predisposition and government induced a law-abiding citizen to commit a crime.

2. **Self-defense** occurs when a person who feels in immediate danger of being harmed by another's unlawful use of force wards off the attack using physical means. Generally, individuals must use only the force level necessary to defend themselves.

3. **Necessity** can be used as a defense when a crime is committed for one's own preservation or to avoid a greater evil.

4. **Duress (or coercion)** occurs when a person has committed a crime by force.

5. **Immaturity**: traditionally Anglo-American law has excused criminal behavior by children under the age of seven on the ground that they are immature and not responsible for their actions.

6. **Mistake of fact** can be claimed when someone unwittingly commits a crime (although this does not cover ignorance of the law).

7. **Intoxication** is usually not defense to criminal behavior unless the crime required specific rather than general intent. For example, a person tricked into consuming an intoxicating substance can use intoxication as a defense.

8. **Insanity** is a controversial and relatively rare defense, successful in only about 1% of cases. The insanity defense is usually accompanied by civil commitment statute permitting insane acquittee to be hospitalized until condition improves.

III. PROCEDURAL CRIMINAL LAW

Procedural due process assures that accused offenders are accorded certain rights and protections in keeping with the Constitution of the United States. Procedures used may seek to advance truth seeking (e.g., trial by jury) or to prevent improper governmental actions (e.g., unreasonable searches and seizures).

A. Bill of Rights
These ten amendments added to the U.S. Constitution in 1789 include protections against self-incrimination and double jeopardy. The case of *Barron v. Baltimore* (1833) initially determined that Bill of Rights only provided protection for individuals against actions by the federal government, not actions by state governments. The constitutions of many states contained their own lists of protections for people within those states.

B. The Fourteenth Amendment and Due Process

During the twentieth century, the Supreme Court gradually made most of the provisions of the Bill of Rights applicable against the states (i.e., incorporation). The Court stated that individual rights had been incorporated into the 14th Amendment right to due process. The concept of "fundamental fairness" was used to determine which specific rights were applicable against the states as a component of the 14th Amendment right to due process.

C. The Due Process Revolution
The Warren Court (beginning in 1953) made decisions that mandated the states abide by due process protections set forth in the Fourteenth Amendment. This continued with the Burger Court (1969-1986) with the result that most criminal justice rights in the United States Constitution were applied to the states.

D. Fourth Amendment: Unreasonable Searches and Seizure
The Exclusionary Rule stated that illegally obtained evidence could be excluded from a criminal trial. Conservatives argue that exclusion is not effective against police misconduct and that it exacts a high price from society. Liberals argue that it is better for a few guilty people to go free than to permit police to engage in misconduct. Recent Supreme Court decisions give greater flexibility to police for conducting searches.

E. Fifth Amendment: Self-Incrimination & Double Jeopardy
The Constitution guarantees criminal defendants do not have to testify against themselves in court. This is the right against self-incrimination. In addition, criminal defendants are protected against double jeopardy—this means an individual cannot be tried twice for the same offense. Double jeopardy does not preclude the possibility of successive prosecutions in different (i.e., state or federal) jurisdictions.

F. Sixth Amendment: Right to Counsel and Fair Trial
1. **The Right to Counsel**: *Gideon v. Wainwright* (1963) required appointed counsel for indigent state court defendants facing six months or more of incarceration.

2. **The Right to a Speedy and Public Trial**: In some countries, people were incarcerated for years awaiting their trial, which was typically hidden from the public. In order to assure fairness, the Constitution requires a public trial.

3. **The Right to an Impartial Jury**: Citizens are guaranteed to be judged by a jury of their peers.

G. Eighth Amendment: Fines, Bail, and Punishment
1. **Release on bail**: Supreme Court decided that release is not required, but bail simply cannot be "excessive". Federal statutes permit holding defendants in jail after a finding that they may be dangerous to the community or that no conditions of release may prevent flight from the jurisdiction.

2. **Excessive fines** are prohibited by the United States Constitution, and these can include the value of property seized by law enforcement under civil forfeiture.

3. **Cruel and unusual punishment**. There has been significant debate about the use of the death penalty in the United States and whether it constitutes 'cruel and unusual punishment'. In 1972, the Court decided that the way in which the death penalty was being implemented amounted to cruel and unusual punishment (*Furman v. Georgia*). States changed their laws to create more extensive deliberative procedures, and the Supreme Court approved the use of the death penalty following those changes in 1976 (*Gregg v. Georgia*).

IV. THE SUPREME COURT TODAY

The current court has served with the same members for the past twelve years. Two new members will appear in 2005. With a Republican president currently serving his remaining term, the Court will likely become more conservative.

REVIEW OF KEY TERMS

Fill in the appropriate term for each statement

legal responsibility
civil law
substantive criminal law
procedural criminal law
common law
constitution
statutes
case law
administrative regulations
civil forfeiture
inchoate offense
mens rea
strict liability
entrapment
procedural due process
self-incrimination
double jeopardy
Barron v. Baltimore
Powell v. Alabama
fundamental fairness
incorporation
grand jury
Gideon v. Wainwright
indigent defendants

1. _Substantive criminal law_ defines the undesirable behaviors that the government will punish.

2. _indigent defendant_ do not earn enough money to afford a private attorney.

3. _civil law_ is the body of rules that regulate conduct between individuals in their private relationships.

4. _Procedural criminal law_ is a constitutional requirement that all people be treated fairly and equally by justice officials.

5. _legal responsibility_ is the accountability of an individual for a crime.

6. _incorporation_ is the extension of due process to make the Bill of Rights binding on state governments.

7. The basic laws of a country or state that define the structure of government is a ___Constitution___.

8. ___mens rea___ is the intent element of a crime.

9. ___Statues___ are laws passed by legislatures.

10. ___self-incrimination___ is the production of damaging testimony against one's self.

11. ___Procedural due process___ provides assurances that accused persons in criminal cases will be accorded certain rights and will be tried according to legally established procedures.

12. Court decisions that have the status of law and serve as precedents for later decisions are known as ___Case law___.

13. ___entrapment___ provides a defense when law enforcement officers are too aggressive in seeking to induce a particular individual to commit a crime.

14. ___administrative regulation___ are rules made by government agencies to implement specific public policies in areas such as public health, environmental protection and workplace safety.

15. ___Civil forfeiture___ is the seizure of property by the government.

16. ___Common law___ is the legal system that the United States inherited from Great Britain.

17. ___Strict liability___ can be used to charge someone with a crime without the required criminal intent.

18. ___double jeopardy___ occurs when one offender is tried twice for the same offense.

19. ___inchoate offense___ are crimes that include conspiracies and attempts.

20. In ___Barron v Baltimore___, the Supreme Court found that the Bill of Rights did not apply to the states.

21. ___fundamental fairness___ supports the idea that the Constitution has not been violated so long as a state's conduct maintains basic standards of fairness.

22. ___Gideon v Wainwright___ is the case that required states to provide attorneys for indigent defendants who faced serious criminal charges.

23. A body of citizens that determines whether a prosecuting attorney has enough evidence to bring charges against an accused is known as a ___Grand jury___

24. ___Powell v Alabama___ is the case that required offenders charged with capital offenses to receive benefit of counsel.

REVIEW OF KEY PEOPLE

Earl Warren
Warren Burger
Bill Clinton
King John of England
William Rehnquist

1. Many expected this Chief Justice of the U. S. Supreme Court to retire in 2005: ___William Rehnquist___

2. Chief Justice ___Earl Warren___ led a liberal revolution that included expanding the rights of criminal defendants.

3. ___King John of England___ issued the Magna Carta, promising that "no free man shall be arrested, or imprisoned, or disseized, or outlawed, or exiled, or in any way molested; nor will we proceed against him unless by the lawful judgment of his peers or by the law of the land."

4. ___Warren Burger___ was chief justice of the U. S. Supreme Court from 1969-1986.

5. President ___Bill Clinton___ appointed Justices Ruth Bader Ginsburg and Stephen Breyer to the U. S. Supreme Court.

GENERAL PRACTICE QUESTIONS

<u>Fill in the blanks with appropriate term, case, or person.</u>

When judges follow case precedents, they are adhering to the 1. common law system that the United States inherited from England.

When a defendant wishes to claim that he or she is not guilty by reason of 2. insanity , the rule applied by the court for determining capacity of criminal responsibility will vary from state to state.

When a defendant wishes to claim that he or she is not guilty by reason of 3. self defense ,the court will determine whether the level of force used was based on a reasonable fear and did not exceed the perceived threat.

Society has many rules for the behavior of its citizens. Under 4. substantive criminal law, the government defines rules that make violators subject to punishment by the government. By contrast, the rules known as 5. civil laws , govern disputes between individuals. Although there are formal rules that govern the processing of all cases, 6. Procedural criminal law rules are especially important for the protection of the rights of people who face criminal punishment.

Police behavior is controlled by a number of legal rules. For example, under the defense of 7. entrapment in substantive criminal law, a defendant may show that the police essentially initiated the commission of the crime. Procedural due process rules provide other controls by applying, for example, the 8. exclusionary rule when police obtain evidence without following proper procedures for respecting the Fourth or Fifth Amendment rights of suspects.

Under the leadership of Chief Justice Earl Warren, the Supreme Court decided a variety of cases, such as 9. Gideon v Wainwright , which provided a right to counsel for indigent defendants facing serious charges, through the process of 10. incorporation in which rights from the 11. Bill of Rights were recognized as applying to the states through the 12. Fourteenth Amendment. Under subsequent Chief Justices, such as Chief Justice William Rehnquist, who was appointed to be Chief Justice by President Reagan, the Supreme Court was less supportive of rights for criminal defendants.

SELF-TEST SECTION

MULTIPLE CHOICE QUESTIONS

4.1. What do most people fear about the powers of government in the wake of the September 11th terrorist attacks?
    a) government will not be powerful enough to protect our national security
    b) government will be too powerful and violate freedoms
    c) government will ignore the problem
    d) people are not in fear of the government
    e) none of the above

4.2. What type of law governs business deals, contracts, and real estate?
    a) civil law
    b) criminal law
    c) authoritarian law
    d) substantive law
    e) common law

4.3.   What type of law is based upon custom and tradition as interpreted by judges?
    a)   civil law
    b)   criminal law
    c)   authoritarian law
    d)   substantive law
    e)   common law

4.4.   What did the American Law Institute develop to make state laws more uniform?
    a)   Model Penal Code
    b)   The Bill of Rights
    c)   Victim's Bill of Rights
    d)   The Fourteenth Amendment
    e)   American Bar Association

4.5.   How are crimes classified within the American system of criminal justice?
    a)   by media attention
    b)   by seriousness
    c)   by victims
    d)   by federal or state
    e)   crimes are not classified

4.6.   A felony charge usually means that the offender may be given a prison sentence of more than...
    a)   one week
    b)   one month
    c)   one year
    d)   one decade
    e)   one life sentence

4.7.   Which of the following is NOT something that a person who committed a felony can be barred from doing in society?
    a)   serving on a jury
    b)   voting
    c)   practicing law
    d)   practicing medicine
    e)   getting married

4.8.   What is the burden of proof in a civil trial?
    a)   reasonable doubt
    b)   reasonable suspicion
    c)   probable cause
    d)   preponderance of the evidence
    e)   totality of the circumstances

4.9.   Which of the following permits law enforcement agencies to sell seized property and use the money for themselves?
    a)   search warrant
    b)   indictment
    c)   forfeiture law
    d)   arrest warrant
    e)   guilty verdict in a criminal trial

4.10.   The U. S. Supreme Court struck down a California law that made it a crime to be addicted to drugs in the case of...
    a)   *Cohen v. California* (1971)
    b)   *Rochin v California* (1954)
    c)   *Chimel v. California* (1969)
    d)   *Simpson v. California* (1995)
    e)   *Robinson v. California* (1962)

4.11.   Why are there alcohol restrictions in the state of Utah?
    a)   history of alcohol-related traffic accidents
    b)   high rate of underage drinking
    c)   high rate of liver disease
    d)   Mormon religion
    e)   high rate of domestic violence associated with alcohol

4.12.   Under Islamic law, what is the punishment for adultery?
    a)   probation
    b)   six months in jail
    c)   stoning to death
    d)   financial penalties up to $1000
    e)   there is no punishment

4.13.   Which of the following is NOT associated with Islamic criminal law?
    a)   the safety of the public from physical attack, insult, and humiliation
    b)   the stability of the family
    c)   the protection of property against theft, destruction, or unauthorized interference
    d)   the protection of the government and the Islamic faith against subversion
    e)   all of the above are associated with Islamic criminal law

4.14.   Which of the following is an example of a mitigating circumstance?
    a)   premeditation
    b)   waiving the right to remain silent
    c)   lying about the crime
    d)   a crime in the heat of passion
    e)   showing indifference to life

4.15.   The level of force used in self-defense cannot exceed the...
    a)   police's reasonable perception of the threat
    b)   person's (using self-defense) reasonable perception of the threat
    c)   judge's reasonable perception of the threat
    d)   average person's reasonable perception of the threat
    e)   threat as perceived by the person who is the attacker (not the person exercising self-defense)

4.16.   In the case of *The Queen v. Dudley and Stephens*, what was the defense's argument in the murder of a young sailor?
    a)   insanity
    b)   self-defense
    c)   necessity
    d)   entrapment
    e)   duress

4.17   Which Amendment covers the most points of contact in the criminal justice system?
   a)   Fourth
   b)   Fifth
   c)   Sixth
   d)   Seventh
   e)   Eighth

4.18.   Who issued the Magna Carta?
   a)   King Edward
   b)   King George
   c)   King John
   d)   Queen Victoria
   e)   Prince Alfred

4.19.   In what case did the U. S. Supreme Court rule that the Bill of Rights did not apply to the states?
   a)   *Marbury v. Madison* (1803)
   b)   *Barron v. Baltimore* (1833)
   c)   *Durham v United States* (1954)
   d)   *Mapp v. Ohio* (1961)
   e)   *Gibbons v. Ogden* (1824)

4.20.   What three amendments were added to the U. S. Constitution immediately after the Civil War?
   a)   First, Second, and Third
   b)   Fourth, Fifth, and Sixth
   c)   Tenth, Eleventh, and Twelfth
   d)   Thirteenth, Fourteenth, and Fifteenth
   e)   Twentieth, Twenty-First, and Twenty-Second

4.21.   Which of the following landmark U. S. Supreme Court cases stated that "cruel and unusual punishments" must be defined according to contemporary standards?
   a)   *Mapp v. Ohio* (1961)
   b)   *Weeks v. United States* (1914)
   c)   *Trop v. Dulles* (1958)
   d)   *Gideon v. Wainwright* (1963)
   e)   *Powell v. Alabama* (1932)

4.22.   Which of the following landmark U. S. Supreme Court cases stated that jury trials must be available in states to defendants facing serious charges?
   a)   *Duncan v. Louisiana* (1968)
   b)   *Weeks v. United States* (1914)
   c)   *Trop v. Dulles* (1958)
   d)   *Gideon v. Wainwright* (1963)
   e)   *Powell v. Alabama* (1932)

4.23.   Which of the following best explains Chief Justice Rehnquist's application of criminal defendants' rights?
   a)   Rehnquist has expanded the rights of criminal suspects
   b)   Rehnquist has eliminated the rights of criminal suspects
   c)   Rehnquist has narrowed the rights of criminal suspects
   d)   Rehnquist has created new rights for criminal suspects
   e)   Rehnquist has refused to hear cases dealing with the rights of criminal suspects

4.24. Which of the following rights has not been nationalized upon the states?
    a) right against double jeopardy
    b) right against unreasonable seizure
    c) right to an attorney
    (d) right to a grand jury trial
    e) all of the above have been nationalized

4.25. In what case did the U. S. Supreme Court declare that the death penalty was being used in an arbitrary and discriminatory way?
    a) *Furman v. Georgia* (1972)
    b) *Payne v. Tennessee* (1991)
    c) *McCleskey v. Kemp* (1985)
    d) *Atkins v. Virginia* (2002)
    e) *Gregg v. Georgia* (1976)

TRUE/FALSE QUESTIONS

4.1. _T_ In a criminal trial, guilt must be established beyond a reasonable doubt.

4.2. _F_ The U. S. criminal justice system operates according to common law.

4.3. _T_ A lawsuit involving slander or defamation is an example of civil law.

4.4. _F_ Precedent is the title given to the leader of the British system.

4.5. _F_ A misdemeanor is a very serious offense.

4.6. _T_ A felony is a very serious offense.

4.7. _T_ A person convicted of a felony may lose the right to vote.

4.8. _T_ A person cannot be arrested for simply being under the influence of drugs.

4.9. _F_ Islamic law has no penalty for adultery.

4.10. _F_ The Bill of Rights was nationalized through the Fifteenth Amendment.

4.11. _F_ Chief Justice Earl Warren narrowed the interpretation of criminal defendants' rights.

4.12. _T_ Self-defense is based on the defending person's perception of the threat.

4.13. _T_ The criminal defendants' rights are found in the Fourth, Fifth, Sixth, and Seventh Amendments.

4.14. _F_ Only a few of the Bill of Rights have been nationalized upon the states.

4.15. _F_ The Bill of Rights was ratified by the states at the same time as the U. S. Constitution.

4.16. _T_ The Fourth Amendment contains the right against unreasonable search and seizure.

4.17. _T_ The death penalty can be used by states against juveniles.

4.18. _F_ The death penalty can be used by states against the mentally retarded.

4.19. _T_ The Bill of Rights was influenced by the Magna Carta.

4.20. _F_ Chief Justice William Rehnquist's decisions have reflected a liberal viewpoint.

ANSWER KEY

Key Terms

1. substantive criminal law
2. indigent
3. civil law
4. procedural due process
5. legal responsibility
6. incorporation
7. constitution
8. *mens rea*
9. statutes
10. self-incrimination
11. procedural due process (?)
12. case law
13. entrapment
14. administrative regulations
15. civil forfeiture
16. common law
17. strict liability
18. double jeopardy
19. inchoate offenses
20. *Barron v. Baltimore*
21. fundamental fairness
22. *Gideon v. Wainwright*
23. grand jury
24. *Powell v. Alabama*

Key People

1. William Rehnquist
2. Earl Warren
3. King John of England
4. Warren Burger
5. Bill Clinton

General Practice Questions

1. common law
2. insanity
3. self-defense
4. substantive criminal law
5. civil law
6. procedural due process
7. entrapment
8. exclusionary rule
9. Gideon v. Wainwright
10. incorporation
11. Bill of Rights
12. Fourteenth Amendment

Multiple Choice

4.1.	B
4.2.	A
4.3.	E
4.4.	A
4.5.	B
4.6.	C
4.7.	E
4.8.	D
4.9.	C
4.10.	E
4.11.	D
4.12.	C
4.13.	E
4.14.	D
4.15.	B
4.16.	C
4.17.	A
4.18.	C
4.19.	B
4.20.	D
4.21.	C
4.22.	A
4.23.	C
4.24.	D
4.25.	A

True/False

4.1.	T
4.2.	F
4.3.	T
4.4.	F
4.5.	F
4.6.	T
4.7.	T
4.8.	T
4.9.	F
4.10.	F
4.11.	F
4.12.	T
4.13.	T
4.14.	F
4.15.	F
4.16.	T
4.17.	T
4.18.	F
4.19.	T
4.20.	F

WORKSHEET 4.1: PRINCIPLES OF CRIMINAL LAW

Acting in response to complaints about smokers gathering in the lobby of the library, the Board of Trustees of the Jonesville Public Library approves the following new rule on the evening of February 6th. The new rule states:

"It shall be unlawful for anyone to smoke at the public library. This rule shall take effect as soon as the Jonesville City Council meets to approve it."

The Jonesville City Council is scheduled to consider the new rule at its 7 p.m. meeting on February 15th. The Library's new smoking rule is the third item scheduled for discussion on the Council's agenda.
At 7:05 p.m. on February 15th, Sam Johnson leaves the public library. At the front door to the library he encounters his brother John. John is struggling while using both hands to carry ten overdue books. He has a lighted cigarette dangling from his mouth. "Hey, John," says Sam, "I don't think that you're supposed to smoke in the library anymore." "Really, I hadn't heard that," said John. "Say, while you're holding the door for me, Sam, can you take this cigarette and put it in that ashtray in the lobby? Thanks a million." As Sam took the cigarette from his brother's lips and walked toward the ashtray, a police officer coming out of the lobby arrested him for violating the library's anti-smoking rule.

You are asked to serve as Sam's attorney. Use four of the seven principles of criminal law to formulate arguments on Sam's behalf about why he should not be found guilty of violating the rule.

1._____

_____

_____

_____

2._____

_____

_____

_____

3._____

_____

_____

_____

4._____

_____

_____

WORKSHEET 4.2: INSANITY DEFENSE

Over the course of seven years, a mother has five babies and they all die during the first months of their lives. Doctors conclude that each child died from Sudden Infant Death Syndrome (SIDS) -- commonly known as "crib death" -- the unexplainable cause of death for 7,000 to 8,000 American babies each year. The woman's family doctor publishes an article about her family to show how SIDS tragically seems to run in families, perhaps for unknown genetic reasons. Years later a prosecutor notices the article and charges the woman with murdering all of her children. The woman initially confesses during police questioning but later claims that the police pressured her to confess. You are hired as her defense attorney. A psychiatrist friend of yours tells you that your client might suffer from a psychiatric condition known as "Munchausen syndrome by proxy." You hope to use this information to consider presenting an insanity defense.

1. Search the Internet for the term "Munchausen syndrome by proxy." What is the definition?

_____

_____

_____

2. Briefly explain whether or not your client's condition can fulfill the requirements of the various tests for the insanity defense.

M'Naghten:_____

_____

_____

Irresistible Impulse:_____

_____

_____

Durham:_____

_____

_____

Substantial Capacity:_____

_____

_____

Federal Comprehensive Crime Control Act:_____

_____

_____

WORKSHEET 4.3: FOURTH AMENDMENT AND EXCLUSIONARY RULE

A woman called the police to her home after her daughter was severely beaten earlier in the day by the daughter's boyfriend. The daughter agreed to use her key to let the officers into the apartment where the man was sleeping. The officers did not seek to obtain either an arrest warrant or a search warrant. After the daughter unlocked the apartment door, the officers entered and found a white substance, which later proved to be cocaine, sitting on a table. They arrested the sleeping man and charged him with narcotics offenses. The defendant sought to have the drugs excluded from evidence because the officers' warrantless search was based on permission from the girlfriend who had moved out of the apartment several weeks earlier and therefore had no authority to give the officers permission to enter and search.

As the prosecutor, think about possible exceptions to the exclusionary rule, such as those discussed for the Fourth and Fifth Amendments, to make arguments about why the evidence should not be excluded.

1._____

_____

_____

2._____

_____

_____

Now, imagine that you are the judge. Decide whether the evidence obtained in the warrantless search should be excluded. Provide reasons for your decision. Consider the words of the Fourth Amendment, the purposes of the Amendment, and the potential effects on society from the rule you formulate for this case.

_____

_____

_____

_____

_____

_____

_____

_____

_____

[Search the Internet for the case *Illinois v. Rodriguez*, 110 S.Ct. 2793 (1990). Compare your opinions with the actual findings of the court.].

WORKSHEET 4.4: FIFTH AND SIXTH AMENDMENTS

After arresting a suspect for burglary, police officers learned that the suspect's nickname was "Butch." A confidential informant had previously told them that someone named "Butch" was guilty of an unsolved murder in another city. The police in the other city were informed about this coincidence and they sent officers to question the suspect about the murder. Meanwhile, the suspect's sister secured the services of a lawyer to represent her brother on the burglary charge. Neither she nor the lawyer knew about the suspicions concerning the unsolved murder case. The lawyer telephoned the police station and said she would come to the station to be present if the police wished to question her client. The lawyer was told that the police would not question him until the following morning and she could come to the station at that time. Meanwhile, the police from the other city arrived and initiated the first of a series of evening questioning sessions with the suspect. The suspect was not informed that his sister had obtained the services of a lawyer to represent him. The suspect was not told that the lawyer had called the police and asked to be present during any questioning. During questioning, the suspect was informed of his *Miranda* rights, waived his right to be represented by counsel during questioning, and subsequently confessed to the murder.

1. If you were the defense attorney, what arguments would you make to have the confession excluded from evidence?

_____

_____

_____

_____

_____

_____

2. If you were the judge, would you permit the confession to be used in evidence? Provide reasons for your decision.

_____

_____

_____

_____

_____

_____

_____

[Search the Internet for the case *Moran v. Burbine*, 475 U.S. 412 (1985). Compare your opinions with the actual findings of the court.]

POLICE

OUTLINE

- The Development of Police in the United States
- Law Enforcement Agencies
- Police Functions
- Organization of the Police
- Police Policy
- Police Actions
- Police and the Community

CHAPTER 5
POLICE

LEARNING OBJECTIVES

After covering the material in this chapter, students should understand:

1.   the English origins from which American police eventually developed

2.   the history of American police, including the Political Era, the Professional Model era, and the Community Model era

3.   organization of the police in the American federal system, including federal, state, and local

4.   police functions and the extent of those functions, including order maintenance, law enforcement, and service

5.   the organization of the police, including the bureaucratic elements of police work

6.   police policy, and how it affects police action

7.   police actions and the use of discretion

8.   the relationship between the police and the community

CHAPTER SUMMARY

The police in the United States have their roots in the early nineteenth-century developments of policing in England. Similar to England, the American police have limited authority, are under local control, and are organizationally fragmented. The three eras of American policing include the political era (1840-1920), the professional era (1920-1970), and the community policing era (1970-present). In the U.S. federal system of government, police agencies are found at the national, state, county, and municipal levels. Improvements have been made during the past quarter-century in recruiting more officers who are women, racial and ethnic minorities, and well-educated applicants. The functions of the police are order maintenance, law enforcement, and service. Police agencies are organized in a hierarchical fashion, with division of labor and strict chain of command. Agencies are divided into organization units that handle specific kinds of cases, such as patrol, investigation, traffic, vice and juvenile. Police officers have an enormous amount of discretion, and make difficult decisions about whether to arrest citizens for breaking the law or handling some cases informally. Police-community relations are extremely important, since citizens can assist in maintaining order in communities. Officers must be aware of changes in our increasingly multicultural society and how that relates to criminal behavior.

CHAPTER OUTLINE

I.   THE DEVELOPMENT OF THE POLICE IN THE UNITED STATES

A.   The English Roots of the American Police
Three major traditions passed from England to the United States: limited authority, local control, and organizational fragmentation. In early England, the frankpledge system required that groups of ten families, called tithings, agree to uphold the law, maintain order, and commit to court those who had violated the law. Every male above the age of twelve was required to be part of the system. The tithing was fined if members did not perform their duties.

The parish constable system was established in England in 1285 under the Statute of Winchester. All citizens were required to pursue criminals under direction of constables—this traditional system of community law enforcement was maintained well into the eighteenth century.

The early English police mandate was to maintain order while keeping a low profile. Officers attempted to use nonviolent methods and minimize conflict between police and public. Leaders feared that if the police were too powerful or too visible, they might threaten civil liberties.

B. Policing in the United States

1. **The Colonial Era and the Early Republic**. Before the Revolution, Americans shared the English belief that community members had a basic responsibility to help maintain order. Over time, ethnic diversity, local political control, regional differences, the opening up of the West, and the violent traditions of American society were factors that brought about a different development of police in the United States compared with that in England.

2. **The Political Era: 1840-1920**. Growth of cities led to pressure for modernization of police forces. Social problems were focused on ethnic conflicts as a consequence of massive immigration, hostility toward non-slave African-Americans, and mob actions against banks and other institutions during economic declines. Styles of policing differed dramatically in different regions of the United States.

3. **The Professional Model Era: 1920-1970**. Based on a progressive reform movement pushed by upper-middle-class, educated Americans that sought to professionalize police and remove the connections between police and local politicians. The Progressives were primarily concerned with creating efficient government and using government services to improve services for the poor.

4. **The Community Model Era: 1970-Present**. James Q. Wilson and George Kelling argued in their "broken windows thesis" that a focus on controlling less serious crime problems (such as maintenance of order, provision of services, and strategies to reduce the fear of crime), would reduce community fear and improve quality of life by preventing neighborhood disorder and deterioration. This method was also theorized to improve public attitudes toward the police by moving to a problem-oriented approach.

5. **Homeland Security: The Next Era for Policing?** The terrorist attacks on September 11, 2001 increased the focus of policing on national security and antiterrorism. Increasing numbers of police departments are training their officers on these issues to provide an adequate response in the face of threats to security.

II. LAW ENFORCEMENT AGENCIES

Most law enforcement officers in the United States can be found working in local police agencies. Federal agencies make up the smallest percentage of officers in the United States, but the number of federal agents has been increasing since September 11th.

A. Federal Agencies
1. **FBI**. This agency has the power to investigate all federal crimes that are not already being investigated by other agencies. Their priorities have shifted to include threats from terrorism and foreign intelligence/espionage.

2. **Specialization in Federal Law Enforcement**. The remaining federal agencies are quite specialized and focus their enforcement activities on a smaller range of crimes. Agencies under the command of the Department of Justice include the Drug Enforcement Administration (DEA), the Bureau of Alcohol, Tobacco, and Firearms (ATF), and the U.S. Marshals Service. Several other federal law enforcement agencies are subsumed under the umbrella of the Department of Homeland Security, including Customs and Border Protection, the Secret Service, and the Transportation Security Administration (TSA). Many other agencies exist that help to enforce federal laws.

3. **Internationalization of U.S. Law Enforcement**:
The U.S. government has increasingly stationed officers overseas to address terrorism, drug trafficking, and other trans-border problems. U.S. officials have limited authority on foreign soil, yet agents have been successful in tracking down terror and drug suspects abroad.

B. State Agencies
Every state except Hawaii has a state police force. In many states they fill the void for enforcement in rural areas, and they might also administer the state crime lab available to all local law enforcement agencies.

C. County Agencies
Sheriffs are found in almost all of the 3,100 counties in the U.S. Traditionally, they have had responsibility for rural policing and maintain responsibility for the local jail. Sheriffs may be selected by election or by political appointment depending on the state.

D. Native American Tribal Police:
Native American tribes have significant autonomy. Tribal law enforcement agencies may enforce laws on Native American reservations.

E. Municipal Agencies:
Most police officers in the United States are employed by local law enforcement agencies. These local agencies enforce the laws of their jurisdictions, but also work with other agencies at the county, state, and national level to combat crime.

III. POLICE FUNCTIONS

Police provide other services besides law enforcement. They protect constitutional guarantees of free speech and assembly, facilitate movement of people and vehicles, resolve conflicts, identify problems, create and maintain feeling of security in community, and assist those who cannot care for themselves.

A. Order Maintenance
Police officers frequently work to prevent disturbances and threats to public peace. Order Maintenance requires the exercise of significant discretion when officers decide how to handle situations as they arise.

B. Law Enforcement
The law enforcement mandate of the police is frequently the most visible to the public. In these situations, the law has been violated and police work to determine the identity of the guilty parties. Enforcement of the law can be especially difficult when victims delay calling the police, thereby reducing the likelihood of apprehending the offender.

C. Service
Police officers frequently provide assistance to the community by administering first aid, rescuing animals, and extending social welfare services, especially to lower class citizens. Many of these functions may assist crime control, such as checking the doors of buildings, dealing with runaways and drunks, and settling family disputes.

D. Underline: Implementing the Mandate
    Police administrators have learned that they can gain greater support for their budgets by emphasizing the crime-fighting function. Some have argued the police do not prevent crime, however, because (a) there is no connection between number of officers and the crime rate, and (b) primary strategies adopted by the police have not been shown to affect crime.

IV. ORGANIZATION OF THE POLICE

Most law enforcement agencies are organized using a military hierarchy, but they are also bureaucracies concerned with efficiency and meeting objectives.

A. Bureaucratic Elements
    1. **Division of Labor**: Tasks are typically divided among units of the police department to increase efficiency. Units within each department can be very specialized (training and crime scene investigation, for example).

    2. **Chain and Utility of Command**: The militaristic character of police departments results in a chain-of-command, which makes clear the powers and duties of officers at each level.

    3. **Rules and Procedures**: More complex organizations required complex regulations and guidelines to maintain efficiency and order. While there cannot be a rule for every possible circumstance, agencies attempt to guide their officers' behavior through official rules.

B. Operational Units
    These specialized units focus on their respective assignments. Units typically take the form of patrol, investigation (detectives), traffic, vice, and juvenile. Larger police departments tend to have a larger number of specialized units (for example: robbery/homicide, domestic violence, and internal affairs).

C. The Police Bureaucracy and the Criminal Justice System
    The discretion used by police officers affect the entire criminal justice system—police officers have enormous control over who is arrested, and the crime with which they are charged. However, after offenders enter the system the police have little control over the process. Officers are also expected to follow commands but also use discretion, and these two tasks are sometimes at odds with one another.

V. POLICE POLICY

Police policies reflect specific styles of policing used by police agencies to meet their many goals. There are three main types of policing styles used in the United States: watchman, legalistic, and service. These styles are influenced by the characteristics of the jurisdiction and the city government.

The watchman style of policing emphasizes order maintenance. These types of departments are most likely to be found in cities that are declining industrial towns, racially heterogeneous, and/or blue-collar.

Legalistic styles of policing emphasize law enforcement. These departments tend to be found where the city government is focused on reform, and/or has a mixed socioeconomic composition.

The service style of policing emphasizes the balance between maintaining order and law enforcement. This model is typically found in middle-class suburban communities.

VI. POLICE ACTIONS

A. Encounters Between Police and Citizens
    The probability that a citizen will be arrested is related to the accessibility of the police to the citizen, the complainant's demeanor and characteristics, and the type of violation committed. Citizens exercise control over police work by the decisions about whether to call the police. Many people fail to call the police to report crimes because they believe that it is not worth the effort and cost of the citizens"time.

B. Police Discretion

Discretion is a characteristic of organizations: officials are given the authority to base decisions on their own judgment rather than on a formal set of rules. Formal rules cannot cover all situations; officers must have a shared outlook that provides a common definition of situations that they are likely to encounter.

Discretion increases as one moves *down* the organizational hierarchy: patrol officers have the greatest amount of discretion in maintaining order and enforcing ambiguous laws such as disorderly conduct, public drunkenness, or breach of the peace. Officers exercise discretion in a number of ways including noninvolvement (i.e., doing nothing), arrest, or informal handling of incidents.

C. Domestic Violence

Domestic violence perpetrated by men against women is consistent across racial and ethnic boundaries. African-American women, women aged 16-24, those living in urban areas, and those from lower income families are the most likely to be victims of violence by an intimate. It has been estimated that 30% of all female murder victims were killed by intimates.

Until mid-1970s, often not treated as serious criminal matter despite the fact that many women are victimized repeatedly. Concerns were expressed that police would make the situation worse for the victim by intervening into a "private family matter." Intervention in domestic disputes can also be dangerous to police officers. Domestic disturbances are volatile, emotional situations and citizens are typically hostile to the police.

Many police agencies use "mandatory arrest" policies for domestic violence, although there is some evidence this is not the correct response for each situation. In some cases, women injured in domestic assaults have filed suit against police departments, claiming that police ignored evidence of criminal assaults.

VII. POLICE AND THE COMMUNITY

A. Special Populations.
Urban police have the complex task of working with social service agencies in dealing with special populations such as the homeless, runaways, mentally ill, drugs addicts, and alcoholics.

B. Policing a Multicultural Society
Policing can be a difficult task, especially in urban areas where there is distrust of police and a lack of cooperation among some citizens. The increasing ethnic diversity of the United States has resulted in poor police-citizen relations, which may be the result of stereotypes, cultural differences, and language barriers.

Some research has indicated that police officers may have biased attitudes toward the poor and members of racial minority groups. In addition, the military organization of police and the "war on crime" mentality many encourage violence by police toward inner city residents.

C. Community Crime Prevention
Police officers cannot control of crime and disorder without the assistance of citizens. There are currently many mechanisms for community involvement in crime control, including neighborhood watch, "crime stopper" programs on television and radio and "Weed and Seed" programs.

REVIEW OF KEY TERMS

Fill in appropriate term for each statement

frankpledge
order maintenance
law enforcement
service

1. _law enforcement_ is the function that the public often believes is the primary focus of police resources.

2. _service_ is the function provided by the police that provides assistance to the public, usually in matters unrelated to crime.

3. _frankpledge_ provided the early English system of families committing themselves to protect each other and their communities.

4. _order maintenance_ emphasizes the prevention of behavior that either disturbs or threatens to disturb the public peace.

REVIEW OF KEY PEOPLE

Fill in the appropriate name

Henry Fielding
J. Edgar Hoover
August Vollmer
James Q. Wilson & George Kelling
Sir Robert Peel
O.W. Wilson

1. _J. Edgar Hoover_ was responsible for professionalizing the FBI.

2. _James Q Wilson & George Kelling_ developed the "broken windows thesis."

3. _Henry Fielding_ established the first unofficial police force in London.

4. _August Vollmer_ advocated professionalization of police and police intervention into the lives of citizens before they entered into crime.

5. _Sir Robert Peel_ oversaw the development of the official police force in England.

6. _O. W. Wilson_ was an ardent proponent of motorized patrols and rapid response as the means to facilitate effective crime fighting.

GENERAL PRACTICE QUESTIONS

Although many Americans believe the police devote their primary efforts to the
1. _law enforcement_ function, in part because the police created this image with the emphasis they developed
during the 2._Professional Model_ era, most scholars recognize that officers devote more time and tasks to the 3. _service_
function.

Among the 4. _federal agencies_ concerned with law enforcement responsibilities, the
5. _____ has the broadest responsibilities. However, they do not have responsibilities for as many
crimes as local officials, such as the county 6. _sheriff_ .

When police officers perform their 7. _order maintenance_ function, such as when they are called to
8. _domestic violence_ situations, they must use 9. _discretion_ to determine whether or not make arrest.

SELF-TEST SECTION

MULTIPLE CHOICE QUESTIONS

5.1.   How many families were in a tithing?
   a)   one
   b)   two
   c)   five
   d)   seven
   e)   ten

5.2.   Why did an organized police force develop in England during the eighteenth century?
   a)   growth of commerce and industry
   b)   decline of farming
   c)   social disorder in the large cities
   d)   all of the above
   e)   none of the above

5.3.   Federal law enforcement agencies are part of what branch of government?
   a)   judiciary
   b)   executive
   c)   legislative
   d)   local
   e)   state

5.4.   Where is the International Criminal Police Organization (Interpol) based in the world?
   a)   Stuttgart, Germany
   b)   New York, New York
   c)   Brussels, Belgium
   d)   Moscow, Russia
   e)   Lyons, France

5.5.   Which of the following best describes police organization in France?
   a)   decentralized
   b)   highly centralized
   c)   highly decentralized
   d)   somewhat centralized
   e)   there is no police organization in France

5.6.   For the most part, what role is emphasized by the police?
    a)   crime fighter
    b)   social service provider
    c)   crime preventer
    d)   crime investigator
    e)   social service investigator

5.7.   What community would you most likely find the legalistic style of policing?
    a)   reform-minded city
    b)   middle class suburban
    c)   mixed racial/ethnic composition
    d)   blue collar
    e)   all of the above

5.8.   What community would you most likely find the service style of policing?
    a)   reform-minded city
    b)   middle class suburban
    c)   mixed socio-economic
    d)   blue collar
    e)   all of the above

5.9.   What community would you most likely find the watchman style of policing?
    a)   blue collar
    b)   mixed racial/ethnic composition
    c)   declining industrial city
    d)   all of the above
    e)   none of the above

5.10.   What community would you most likely find the legalistic style of policing?
    a)   blue collar
    b)   middle class suburban
    c)   mixed socio-economic
    d)   blue collar
    e)   all of the above

5.11.   The beating of Rodney King is an example of an abuse resulting from the...
    a)   watchman style
    b)   service style
    c)   legalistic style
    d)   all of the above
    e)   none of the above

5.12.   Who developed the three styles of policing-watchman, legalistic, and service?
    a)   Robert Peel
    b)   James Q. Wilson
    c)   J. Edgar Hoover
    d)   Henry Fielding
    e)   August Vollmer

5.13.   Who was chief of police in Berkeley, California (1909-1932) and a leading advocate of professional policing?
    a)   Robert Peel
    b)   James Q. Wilson
    c)   J. Edgar Hoover
    d)   Henry Fielding
    e)   August Vollmer

5.14. Who wrote the book, Fixing Broken Windows, about strategies to restore order and reduce crime in the U. S.?
    a) Robert Peel and James Q. Wilson
    b) O. W Wilson and August Vollmer
    c) J. Edgar Hoover and Henry Fielding
    d) George Kelling and Catherine Coles
    e) Wyatt Earp and Mark Moore

5.15. What are the three historical periods of policing?
    a) political, professional, and community model
    b) pre-colonial, colonial, and post-colonial
    c) crime fighter, crime preventer, and service provider
    d) watchman, legalistic, and service
    e) crime control, crime and order, and order

5.16. As chief of police of Wichita, Kansas, who promoted the use of motorized patrols and rapid response?
    a) Robert Peel
    b) James Q. Wilson
    c) J. Edgar Hoover
    d) O. W. Wilson
    e) August Vollmer

5.17. Who wrote the article, "Broken Windows: The Police and Neighborhood Safety" about how police should work more on little problems?
    a) Robert Peel and Bat Masterson
    b) O. W Wilson and August Vollmer
    c) J. Edgar Hoover and Henry Fielding
    d) George Kelling and James Q. Wilson
    e) Wyatt Earp and Mark Moore

5.18. What year did the Fraternal Order of Police form?
    a) 1896
    b) 1902
    c) 1915
    d) 1924
    e) 1972

5.19. What year did the International Order of Chiefs of Police form?
    a) 1896
    b) 1902
    c) 1915
    d) 1924
    e) 1972

5.20. Where did the term "posse" originate?
    a) Latin term for " police"
    b) French term for "public"
    c) Old English term for "possessing the convict"
    d) Latin term for "power of the country"
    e) German term for "capture of prisoners"

5.21. During what policing era does fingerprinting develop?
    a) political
    b) professional
    c) community
    d) all of the above
    e) none of the above

5.22. During what policing era does close personal contact between officers and citizens occur?
    a) political
    b) professional
    (c) community
    d) all of the above
    e) none of the above

5.23. During what policing era does the use of motorcycle units occur?
    a) political
    (b) professional
    c) community
    d) all of the above
    e) none of the above

5.24. During what policing era do political machines dominate?
    (a) political
    b) professional
    c) community
    d) all of the above
    e) none of the above

TRUE/FALSE QUESTIONS

5.1. _T_ The roots of American policing derive largely from England.

5.2. _F_ The organization of police in France is decentralized.

5.3. _T_ British police did not have to deal with ethnic diversity.

5.4. _T_ The professional era of policing involved staying out of politics.

5.5. _F_ The urban riots of the 1960s did not affect the assumptions of the professional model.

5.6. _T_ Community policing involved more foot patrols.

5.7. _F_ Within the United States, Native Americans tribes have no sovereignty.

5.8. _T_ Providing first aid is an example of a service function.

5.9. _F_ The service style of policing is most likely found in a declining industrial city.

5.10. _F_ American policing did not develop differently in the South as opposed to the Northeast.

5.11. _T_ British police are called "bobbies" after Sir Robert Peel.

5.12. _F_ In the United States, police power resides with the federal government.

5.13. _T_ One aspect of American policing is limited authority.

5.14. _F_ Community policing began in the 1920s.

5.15. _F_ A tithing is a group of two families.

5.16. _T_ The political era of policing involved police corruption.

5.17. __F__ France has a stable history and, therefore, maintaining order is not a priority.

5.18. __T__ The service style of policing places a balance between law enforcement and order maintenance.

5.19. __F__ The watchman style of policing emphasizes law enforcement.

5.20. __T__ Public confidence is important for police if they are to do their job well.

ANSWER KEY

Key Terms
1. law enforcement
2. service
3. frankpledge
4. order maintenance

Key People
1. J. Edgar Hoover
2. James Q. Wilson & George Kelling
3. Henry Fielding
4. August Vollmer
5. Sir Robert Peel
6. O.W. Wilson

General Practice Questions
1. law enforcement
2. Professional Model
3. service
4. federal agencies
6. sheriff
7. order maintenance
8. domestic violence
9. discretion

Multiple Choice
5.1.   E
5.2.   D
5.3.   B
5.4   E
5.5.   B
5.6.   A
5.7.   A
5.8.   B
5.9.   D
5.10.   C
5.11.   A
5.12   B
5.13.   E
5.14.   D
5.15.   A
5.16.   D
5.17.   D
5.18.   C
5.19.   B
5.20.   D
5.21.   B
5.22.   C
5.23.   B
5.24.   A

<u>True/False</u>

5.1.	T
5.2.	F
5.3.	T
5.4.	T
5.5.	F
5.6.	T
5.7.	F
5.8.	T
5.9.	F
5.10.	F
5.11.	T
5.12.	F
5.13.	T
5.14.	F
5.15.	F
5.16.	T
5.17.	F
5.18.	T
5.19.	F
5.20.	T

WORKSHEET 5.1: ORGANIZATION OF THE POLICE

Imagine that you are a member of Congress. One of your staff assistants brings you a proposal to nationalize law enforcement throughout the United States. The proposal calls for abolishing state police agencies, county sheriffs, and local police departments. Instead, Congress would create a new U.S. Department of Law Enforcement. A Secretary of Law Enforcement would oversee a national police agency which would have units established in each state, county, city, and town. Your assistant argues that the new organization would save resources by coordinating the work of every law enforcement officer in the nation and creating a standard set of law enforcement policies and priorities. In addition, the plan would standardize training, salary, and benefits for police officers everywhere and thus raise the level of professionalism of police, especially in small towns and rural areas.

        Before you decide whether or not to present this proposal to Congress, respond to the following questions.

1. Are there any undesirable consequences that could develop from putting this plan into action?

_____

_____

_____

_____

_____

2. As a politician, you are concerned about how others will react to the plan. How do you think each group would react and why?

        a. Voters_____

_____

_____

        b. State and local politicians_____

_____

_____

        c. Police officers_____

_____

_____

3. Will you support the proposal? Why or why not?

_____

_____

WORKSHEET 5.2: POLICE POLICY

You are a retired police chief. A state government has hired you to provide advice on the appropriate police policy to implement in several jurisdictions. You advise them on whether to choose the watchman, legalistic, or service style. Explain why.

A. A city of 100,000 that contains a diverse mixture of Whites, African-Americans, Asian-Americans, and Hispanics. The unemployment rate is high. Few wealthy people live in the city. Most people are middle-class, but 25 percent of the citizens qualify for government assistance. The police department reflects the racial/ethnic mix of the city's population.

B. A small town of 2,000 residents. Most residents work in one lumber mill or in businesses that serve loggers and farmers who live in the area. The town's population is almost entirely white, except when large numbers of people from various minority groups arrive in the summer and fall to work on local farms.

C. A suburb with 15,000 residents. Twenty percent of the residents are members of minority groups. Nearly all of the town's residents are white-collar or professional workers with high incomes. Most people commute to a big city to work.

A._____

_____

_____

_____

_____

_____

B._____

_____

_____

_____

_____

_____

C._____

_____

_____

_____

_____

_____

POLICE OFFICERS AND LAW ENFORCEMENT OPERATIONS

OUTLINE

- Who Are the Police?
- The Police Subculture
- Police Response and Action
- Delivery of Police Services
- Issues in Patrolling

CHAPTER 6
POLICE OFFICERS AND
LAW ENFORCEMENT OPERATIONS

LEARNING OBJECTIVES

After covering the material in this chapter, students should understand

1.   the recruitment, training, and socialization of police officers

2.   the recruitment and integration of women and minority officers

3.   the police subculture, including the working personality and the elements of danger and authority

4.   the organization of police departments and their allocation of resources

5.   police action and decision making, including organizational response and productivity issues

6.   the role of detectives and the investigation function, including the apprehension process and forensic techniques

7.   the role of specialized operations in traffic, vice, and drug enforcement.

CHAPTER SUMMARY

The police must recruit and train individuals who will uphold the law and receive citizen support. Improvements have been made during the past quarter-century in recruiting more officers who are women, racial and ethnic minorities, and well-educated applicants. The police work in an environment greatly influenced by their subculture. The concept of the working personality helps us understand the influence of the police subculture on how individual officers see their world. The isolation of the police strengthens bonds among officers but may also add to job stress. Police operations are shaped by their formal organizational structures and also influenced by social and political processes both within and outside the department. The police are organized along military lines so that authority and responsibility can be located at appropriate levels. Police services are delivered through the work of the patrol, investigation, and specialized operations units. The patrol function has three components: answering calls for assistance, maintaining a police presence, and probing suspicious circumstances. The investigation function is the responsibility of detectives in close coordination with patrol officers. The felony apprehension process is a sequence of actions that includes crime detection, preliminary investigation, follow-up investigation, clearance, and arrest. Specialized units dealing with traffic, drug, and vice are found in large departments.

CHAPTER OUTLINE

I.   WHO ARE THE POLICE?

     A strong police force is vitally important to the protection and safety of society. Unfortunately, many police officers receive low pay for their work and experience high stress while on the job. Individuals interested in becoming police officers are attracted to many aspects of this job, including investigation, catching suspects, and serving the public.

A. Recruitment

Some departments pay officers quite well, but salaries are extremely varied. Departments are increasingly able to attract college educated recruits. Due to the expansion of undergraduate criminal justice programs, it has become much easier for police departments to find candidates with college degrees.

B. The Changing Profile of the Police

Historically, police departments contained mainly white, male officers. This changed following several police-community relations problems, urban riots in the 1960's that were caused by conflict between the police and minority communities, and equal opportunity laws.

1. **Minority Police Officers**: The percentage of minority police officers has increased dramatically in the past 30 years. This change reflects the changing demographics of the United States.

2. **Women on the Force**: Traditional beliefs about police being "men's work" have kept women off of the force. This has changed in recent years, with more women serving than ever before. Most women have easily met performance requirements, but it is at the social level that they have met their greatest resistance. Male officers sometimes doubt that women can physically back them up in crime situations or disturbances. Resistance may also be based on cultural expectations by male officers and the public about the women's role in policing. Women police officers may also be subjected to sexual harassment.

C. Training

Police academies may be run by large departments for their own officers, or by the state for rural and town recruits. Community colleges also offer police academies for prospective officers. Recruits are often told that real learning will take place on the job. This process of *socialization* includes learning informal practices as well as formal rules. In addition, officers work in an organizational framework in which rank carries privileges and responsibilities. Performance is usually measured by their contribution to the group's success.

II. THE POLICE SUBCULTURE

A subculture is a smaller part of a larger societal culture that has a shared system of beliefs, values and attitudes. The shared values of the police lead them to have shared expectations about human behavior. Subcultures can change over time, especially when the department changes with regard to ethnicity and gender composition.

A. The Working Personality

Police officers' working personalities shape the way they interpret events. There are two important elements that define the working personality: danger and authority.

1. Danger: Police are especially attentive to signs of potential violence because they work in dangerous situations. The socialization process teaches recruits to be cautious and suspicious. Their orientation toward watching and questioning citizens can contribute to tension and conflict in contacts with the public. Police officers are constantly on edge, watching for unexpected dangers whether on or off duty.

2. Authority: Police officers, a symbol of authority with low occupation status, must often be assertive in establishing authority with citizenry. This can lead to conflict, hostility, and perhaps overreaction and police brutality. Officers are expected to remain detached, neutral, and unemotional even when challenged and in situations of conflict.

B. Police Morality

There is a high sense of morality in the law enforcement subculture. Morality helps police overcome dilemmas that they frequently encounter on the street, and the fact that it is sometimes very difficult to determine the correct course of action to reduce crime.

C. Police Isolation

The public is generally supportive of the police, but police perceive the public to be hostile. Officers' contacts with the public are frequently during moments of conflict, crisis, and emotion—this creates isolation. In addition, officers tend to socialize primarily with other officers. Because police officers are so identified with their jobs, members of the public frequently treat them as police, even when they are off-duty.

D. Job Stress

The police working environment and subculture both affect physical and mental health in the form of marital problems, health problems, and drinking problems. In addition, suicide can be a problem among officers. They experience several kinds of stress (emotional, organization, personal and operational). Police departments had been slow to address issue of stress, but many have developed counseling, liberal disability rules and other mechanisms.

III. POLICE RESPONSE AND ACTION

Police in a democracy are organized mainly to be *reactive* (citizen-invoked calls for service) rather than *proactive* (police-invoked). Police arrive after the fact, thus reports by victims and observers define the boundaries of policing. The public has come to expect that police will respond to every call. This results in incident-driven policing. Police employ proactive strategies such as surveillance in some contexts. As more police personnel are allocated to proactive operations, the number of resulting arrests is likely to rise.

A. Organizational Response

Administrative environment and organization of department affect the way in which calls are processed as well as the nature of police response. Centralization of communications (i.e., 911 numbers and two-way radios) has altered past practices of individual officers observing and addressing crime problems in neighborhoods. Police departments use *differential response strategies* for calls. Dispatchers make decisions about whether or not a patrol car needs to rush to the scene of each call. A delayed response may be just as effective depending on the nature of the call. Advocates of community policing believe that advances in communication technology further isolate the officers from the community and prevent them from building rapport.

B. Productivity

Following the lead of New York City's Compstat program, several cities now emphasize accountability at the precinct level. Police have difficulty in measuring the quantity and quality of their work, and tend to focus on crime rates and clearance rates. The clearance rate varies by the nature of the offense. Police often use "activity" as a measure (i.e., tickets issued, arrests made, suspects stopped for questioning), although this does not necessarily reflect the complete range of order maintenance functions. It may actually be more beneficial for society when police spend their time calming conflicts, becoming acquainted with citizens, and providing services and information for people.

VI. DELIVERY OF POLICE SERVICES

Line functions directly involved field operations, and account for the majority of police personnel. Within this group of officers, the patrol bureau is generally the largest.

A. Patrol Functions

Patrol officers make up two-thirds of all sworn officers. In small communities, the patrol force constitutes the entire department. The patrol function has three components: answering calls for assistance, maintaining a police presence, and probing suspicious circumstances. When not responding to calls, officers engage in preventive patrol--making the police presence known to deter crime and to be available to respond to calls. Patrol officers' presence in a community can be major factor in reducing *fear* of crime. Patrol may also improve community relations and increase citizen cooperation with police.

B. Investigation

Most police departments have detective units, which are responsible for the investigation of criminal cases. Detectives are often organized by the type of crime they investigate (homicide, robbery, forgery, burglary, etc.). Detective work is largely reactive—detectives typically wait until a crime is reported before their work can begin. Even though detectives are responsible for investigating most crimes in a jurisdiction, other officers (such as patrol, traffic, vice and juveniles) also have some investigative functions.

1. **Apprehension**: Apprehension of suspects has three stages. First, the crime is detected (whether reported or discovered). Next, preliminary investigation is begun—usually by a patrol officer. Follow-up investigation is next, often done by detectives in larger cities. The final stages of apprehension are clearance and arrest, in which the crime is "solved" by arresting a suspect.

2. **Forensic Techniques**: This involves the use of science to aid in gathering physical evidence such as fingerprints, blood sample analysis, and DNA.

3. **Research on Investigation**: Police may have overrated the importance of investigation as a means of solving crimes and shows that most crimes are cleared because of arrests made by the patrol force at or near the scene. A key factor in crime clearance is identification of the offender by a victim or witness, and this can have very little to do with investigation. However, good detective work can help improve police-community relations as citizens see the police working to solve crime.

C. UUUUUSpecial Operations

1. **Traffic** work is highly discretionary and essentially proactive, and the level of enforcement can be considered a direct result departmental policies and norms. Traffic enforcement is one area in which departments enforce norms of productivity.

2. **Vice** officers work proactively to enforce laws against prostitution, gambling, and drug offenses. Because of the nature of the crimes, political influence is sometimes brought to bear to dampen enforcement. Police are increasingly using electronic surveillance and undercover work to clear vice crimes.

3. **Drug enforcement** is sometimes handled by separate drug bureaus within police departments. Departmental policy sometimes uses aggressive patrol to arrest a large number of drug dealers off the street. Some believe that the "war on drugs" is the wrong approach to take to combat drug-related crime.

V. ISSUES IN PATROLLING

Patrol officers utilize many different techniques to combat crime, typically defined by departmental policy. There is sometimes disagreement between researchers and police personnel about the most effective strategies for reducing crime.

A. Assignment of Patrol Personnel

It is important for departments to distribute officers geographically and by shift in a manner than is most effective in combating crime and keeping order. These decisions are usually made based on calls for service and crime problems.

1. **Preventive Patrol**: This method involves sending more police into neighborhoods to (1) actively look for criminal behavior, and (2) increase the visibility of the police. Unfortunately, research has indicated that preventive patrol does not seem to have a measurable effect on crime.

2. **Hot Spots**: Police can identify locations where crime is most likely to occur. These "hot spots" deserve more police attention given their higher than normal crime rates. This method of directed patrol can help to reduce crime, if that's where most crime is occurring. There are also seasonal and day/time variations in crime that can be used by police for directed patrol.

3. **Rapid Response Time**: Most believe rapid response time is important for controlling crime. Improvements in communication technology and the proliferation of cell phones have helped to decrease response time. However, there is little evidence that clearance rates increase if response time is decreased.

4. **Foot versus Motorized Patrol:** Most patrolling by police is done in cars, but sometimes it makes sense for police to patrol on foot or bicycle. Citizens feel better when officers are more "accessible", and patrol in police cars tends to distance police from citizens.

5. **One-Person versus Two-Person Patrol Units**: It is more cost-effective and efficient to place one officer in each police car, given that two officers in two police cars can cover twice as much area. However, it may be safer for two officers to ride together in one vehicle.

6. **Aggressive Patrol**: This proactive strategy involves the police aggressively attempting to reduce crime. There are many kinds of aggressive patrol, but most are targeted on specific types of crime. One strategy of aggressive patrol is based on the "broken windows theory", which advocates control of small crime problems that might encourage larger crime problems to flourish. Unfortunately, these policies can lead to poor police-community relations.

B. Community Policing
    Strategies for community policing involve problem-directed policing, in which officers are responsible for identifying community problems and working with community members to formulate solutions. The SARA strategy (Scanning, Analysis, Response, and Assessment) is often used for problem-solving in police work, and many departments train their officers to use these methods to reduce crime.

C. The Future of Patrol
    Improvements in technology, the shift to community policing, and the increasing importance of geographic crime analysis have changed the face of policing in the United States. In addition, the increased focus on fighting terrorism and the need for homeland security is currently changing American policing in many ways.

REVIEW OF KEY TERMS

Fill in the appropriate term for each statement.
socialization
subculture
working personality
reactive
proactive
incident-driven policing
differential response
clearance rate
line functions
sworn officers
preventive patrol
directed patrol
aggressive patrol
problem-oriented policing

90

1. _Problem oriented Policing_ is an approach in which officers seek to identify, analyze, and respond to the underlying circumstances that create the incidents that generate citizens' calls for police assistance.

2. The _clearance rate_ is used as a measure of officer success at solving crimes.

3. An officer's _working personality_ is developed through their experiences and interactions with citizens.

4. _Socialization_ is the process by which the rules, symbols, informal practices, and values of a group are learned by its members.

5. _Proactive_ policing strategies involve officers actively seeking out crime.

6. Officers who have taken an oath to uphold the law and protect society are called _Sworn officers_.

7. _line function_ are basic police operations performed by units such as patrol and traffic.

8. _Reactive policing_ policing is the typical American patrol strategy that involves officers responding to citizens' calls.

9. _incident driven policing_ emphasizes quick response to calls for service.

10. _directed patrol_ is a strategy designed to focus patrol resources in a proactive manner against known high crime areas

11. _differential response_ sets priorities for officer response to calls for service.

12. _subculture_ is a group with a shared system of beliefs. It is a smaller part of the larger society.

13. The goal of _preventive patrol_ is to make officer presence known in neighborhoods in order to deter crime.

14. _agressive patrol_ is a proactive patrol strategy which may involve greater numbers of on-street interrogations and traffic stops.

REVIEW OF KEY PEOPLE

George W. Bush
Lola Baldwin
Cristina Murphy

1. The first female police officer was _Lola Baldwin_ in 1905 in Portland, Oregon.

2. President _George W. Bush_ created a Department of Homeland Security that produced job changes within federal agencies, such as the movement of officers from various agencies into the expanded Sky Marshals program to provide security on airline flights.

3. Patrol Officer _Cristina Murphy_ stated that "women, they sometimes just can't stand the idea that a woman exists who can have power over them. They feel powerless and expect all women to feel that way too. As I said, everyone has an opinion."

GENERAL PRACTICE QUESTIONS

When police decide to allocate resources to crime "hot spots," they use 1. *directed patrol* , which is a form of 2. *proactive patrol* because it involves police initiative rather than reaction.

Police may directly address problems in a community through 3. *problem-oriented policing* , which involves in-depth examination recurring problems, and through 4. *foot patrol or* which will bring officers in closer contact with citizens in their neighborhoods. *community oriented policing*

5. *Response time* is not a particularly good measure of 6. *Productivity* because it is so heavily dependent on prompt reports from victims and witnesses and because impressive performance will not necessarily increase the rate of arrests.

There are two elements in the 7. *work personality* which affect police officers' views and interpretations of situation. One element, 8. *danger* , leads officers to be suspicious and cautious, and the other element, 9. *authority* , leads officers to feel isolated from a society in which people always see the officer as enforcer of the law, even in off-duty hours.

After many problems with police-community relations in inner-city neighborhoods, many departments sought to recruit 10. *minority police officers* in the hope that, among other things, officers' discretionary decisions would produce a reduction in the corrupt behavior classified as 11. *prejudice* in which groups of citizens are treated unequally.

SELF-TEST SECTION

MULTIPLE CHOICE QUESTIONS

6.1.   What bars state and local governments from discriminating in their hiring practices?
    a)   Equal Employment Opportunity Act of 1972
    b)   Civil Rights Act of 1866
    c)   Jim Crow laws
    d)   Equal Access Employment Act of 1987
    e)   Article V of the U. S. Constitution

6.2.   Which of the following is a line function?
    a)   patrol
    b)   investigation
    c)   traffic control
    d)   vice
    e)   all of the above

6.3.   Why do proactive responses to crime usually have a clearance rate of 100%?
    a)   these crimes are always reported to police
    b)   evidentiary problems usually reduce arrest rates
    c)   there are always witnesses to these kinds of events
    d)   these crimes are impossible to solve
    e)   because they are initiated in police, they usually result in arrest

6.4.   Which of the following is TRUE of police work?
   a)   working personality and occupational environment are closely linked and have a major impact on police work
   b)   working personality and occupational environment are closely linked and have a minor impact on police work
   c)   working personality and occupational environment are not linked and have no impact on police work
   d)   working personality and occupational environment are closely linked and have no impact on police work
   e)   working personality and occupational environment are not linked and have a major impact on police work

6.5.   What type of stress is produced by real threats and dangers?
   a)   external stress
   b)   organizational stress
   c)   personal stress
   d)   operational stress
   e)   none of the above

6.6.   What are the two elements that define a police officer's working personality?
   a)   Danger and uncertainty
   b)   Danger and authority
   c)   Weapons and uniform
   d)   Badge and gun
   e)   Discretion and platitudes

6.7.   When are police officers most likely to show disrespect to citizens?
   a)   When the citizen commits a crime in their presence
   b)   When the citizen strikes the officer physically
   c)   When the citizen first shows disrespect to the officer
   d)   When the citizen files a complaint
   e)   When the citizen flees the scene

6.8.   According to the chart below, which city has more officers per 1,000 people than crimes per 1,000 people?

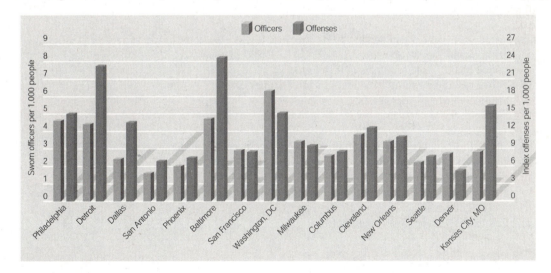

   a)   Kansas City
   b)   Baltimore
   c)   Detroit
   d)   Washington, DC
   e)   Dallas

6.9. What is TRUE about the profile of the American police officer in the 21st century?
    a) there are fewer women than in the past
    b) there are fewer nonwhites than in the past
    c) officers are better educated than in the past
    d) all of the above are TRUE
    e) all of the above are FALSE

6.10. In Baltimore, what is the system designed to reduce the number of nonemergency calls to 911?
    a) 211 system
    b) 311 system
    c) 411 system
    d) 007 system
    e) 611 system

6.11. What is the origin of the word "patrol"?
    a) from a Scottish word meaning "rolling police"
    b) from a German word meaning "police action"
    c) from a French word meaning "to tramp around in the mud"
    d) from a Spanish word meaning "to dance in the streets"
    e) from a Latin word meaning "walking with authority"

6.12. How many instances does rapid police response really make a difference?
    a) none
    b) a small fraction
    c) about one-half
    d) a great many
    e) all

6.13. Which of the following delays slow the process of calling the police?
    a) ambiguity delays
    b) coping delays
    c) conflict delays
    d) all of the above
    e) none of the above

6.14. In the past, patrols were organized by "beats" because it was assumed that...
    a) crime could happen anywhere
    b) police could "beat" criminals at their game
    c) police could use timing techniques to solve crimes
    d) criminals were all "deadbeats"
    e) all of the above

6.15. Which of the following is NOT a function of a well-organized police department?
    a) clear lines of authority
    b) division of labor
    c) each working separately to achieve goals
    d) unity of command
    e) link duties with appropriate authority

6.16. Urban police departments are divided into...
    a) units
    b) wards
    c) precincts
    d) classes
    e) categories

6.17. Which of the following is an example of a proactive strategy?
   a) responding to a citizens' call
   b) undercover work
   c) citizen approaching police on the street with information
   d) all of the above
   e) none of the above

6.18. Which of the following is an example of a reactive strategy?
   a) surveillance
   b) undercover work
   c) waiting for a citizen to approach police on the street with information
   d) all of the above
   e) none of the above

6.19. How can a police officer best handle stress?
   a) work harder
   b) keep to yourself
   c) seek counseling
   d) all of the above
   e) none of the above

6.20. Which of the following is a change in the profile of police in the past thirty years?
   a) more women are police officers
   b) more nonwhites are police officers
   c) police officers are better educated
   d) all of the above are examples of changes in the past thirty years
   e) none of the above are examples of changes in the past thirty years

6.21. Which of the following is TRUE about police work and stress?
   a) more police die by their own hands than are killed in the line of duty
   b) stress is not a problem today for police, but it was in the past
   c) police are less likely to commit suicide than a member of the general public
   d) all of the above are TRUE
   e) all of the above are FALSE

6.22. A police officer driving through a neighborhood spots a citizen waiving at her to stop. If the officer stops to talk with the citizen, this type of policing is considered to be:
   a) Proactive policing
   b) Reactive policing
   c) Informal policing
   d) Formal policing
   e) Occupational policing

6.23. What is the primary action by policing in incident-driven policing?
   a) Responding quickly to calls from citizens
   b) Driving around, looking for crime
   c) Gathering intelligence about criminal activity
   d) Cracking down on problem areas
   e) Identifying problems and generating solutions

6.24. Which of the following are measures of police productivity?
   a) Clearance rate
   b) Number of arrests
   c) Tickets issued
   d) Cars ticketed
   e) All of the above are measures of productivity

TRUE/FALSE QUESTIONS

6.1. **F** Women are prohibited from being patrol officers "on the street."

6.2. **T** Police often feel isolated from the public.

6.3. **T** Before the 1970s, many police departments did not hire nonwhites.

6.4. **F** Police officers are generally well paid.

6.5. **F** Policing is not a stressful job.

6.6. **T** Lola Baldwin was the first female police officer.

6.7. **T** Most police work generally is reactive.

6.8. **T** Patrol officers account for two-thirds of all sworn officers.

6.9. **T** Line functions are those that directly involve field operations.

6.10. **T** Police training affects the attitudes of the recruits.

6.11. **F** Police agencies are usually disorganized.

6.12. **F** Police do not use proactive strategies.

6.13. **T** Police assign priorities to calls for service.

6.14. **F** Most police action is initiated by an officer in the field.

6.15. **F** All police departments have vice squads.

6.16. **F** There have not been any attempts made to quantify police work.

6.17. **T** The clearance rate is the percentage of crimes solved through an arrest.

6.18. **T** Arrests for drug selling has a 100 percent clearance rate.

6.19. **T** Rapid response time is valuable for only a small fraction of police calls.

6.20. **T** Most calls to police involve service and order maintenance, not law enforcement.

ANSWER KEY

Key Terms
1. problem-oriented policing
2. clearance rate
3. working personality
4. socialization
5. proactive
6. sworn officers
7. line functions
8. reactive policing
9. incident-driven policing
10. directed patrol
11. differential response
12. subculture
13. preventive patrol
14. aggressive patrol

Key People
1. Lola Baldwin
2. George W. Bush
3. Cristina Murphy

General Practice Questions
1. directed patrol
2. proactive patrol
3. problem-oriented policing
4. foot patrol or community-oriented policing
5. response time
6. productivity
7. working personality
8. danger
9. authority
10. minority police officers
11. prejudice

Multiple Choice
6.1.   A
6.2.   E
6.3.   E
6.4.   A
6.5.   A
6.6.   B
6.7.   C
6.8.   D
6.9.   C
6.10.   B
6.11.   C
6.12.   B
6.13.   D
6.14.   A
6.15.   C
6.16.   C
6.17.   B
6.18.   C
6.19.   C

6.20.   D
6.21.   A
6.22.   B
6.23.   A
6.24.   E

<u>True/False</u>
6.1.   F
6.2.   T
6.3.   T
6.4.   F
6.5.   F
6.6.   T
6.7.   T
6.8.   T
6.9.   T
6.10.   T
6.11.   F
6.12.   F
6.13.   T
6.14.   F
6.15.   F
6.16.   F
6.17.   T
6.18.   T
6.19.   T
6.20.   T

WORKSHEET 6.1: RECRUITMENT AND TRAINING OF POLICE OFFICERS

1. What qualifications would you require for someone to be hired as a police officer? Why?

_____

_____

_____

_____

_____

_____

_____

2. What salary and benefits would you offer in order to attract the police officer-candidates that you described?

_____

_____

_____

_____

_____

3. What are the three most important subjects that should be taught to new police recruits? Why?

_____

_____

_____

_____

_____

4. Could you use training to combat any negative aspects of the police subculture and working personality? If so, how?

_____

_____

_____

_____

WORKSHEET 6.2: DETECTIVES

A study has raised questions about whether or not your police department should keep a separate investigation division containing detectives. There are questions about whether or not detectives solve many crimes because most arrests result from the work of patrol officers or the assistance of citizens. Pretend that you have to draft a report making recommendations about the future of the detective bureau. How would you address the following questions?

1. What is the job of the detectives? (write a job description)

_____

_____

_____

_____

_____

2. How are investigations conducted and what is the role of the detectives in investigations?

_____

_____

_____

_____

3. What is the relationship between detectives and patrol officers?

_____

_____

_____

_____

4. How would the police department be different if there were no detectives?

_____

_____

_____

_____

POLICING

Contemporary Issues and Challenges

OUTLINE

- Police Abuse of Power
- Civic Accountability
- Policing and New Technology
- Homeland Security
- Security Management and Private Policing

CHAPTER 7
POLICING: ISSUES AND TRENDS

LEARNING OBJECTIVES

After covering the material in this chapter, students should understand:

1.   police patrol activities, including issues of preventive patrol, response time, foot versus motorized patrol, aggressive patrol, and community-oriented policing

2.   police use of new technology and weapons in the fight against crime

3.   police abuse, including police brutality and corruption

4.   civic accountability, including internal affairs divisions, civilian review boards, standards and accreditation, and civil liability

5.   how homeland security has changed modern policing

6.   the issues and problems posed by the increase in private policing

CHAPTER SUMMARY

Police administrators must make decisions about possible patrol strategies, including directed patrol, foot patrol, and aggressive patrol. Community policing seeks to involve citizens in identifying problems and working with police officers to prevent disorder and crime. The development of new technologies has assisted police investigations through the use of computers, databases, surveillance devices, and methods to detect deception. Police departments are seeking to identify non-lethal weapons that can incapacitate suspects and control unruly crowds without causing serious injuries and deaths. The problems of police misuse of force and corruption cause erosions of community support. Internal affairs units, civilian review boards, standards and accreditation, and civil liability suits are four approaches designed to increase police accountability to citizens.   After September 11th, federal and local law enforcement have refocused their efforts on intelligence and keeping the public safe from terrorist attack. The expansion of security management and private policing reflects greater recognition of the need to protect private assets and plan for emergencies but it also produces new issues and problems concerning the recruitment, training, and activities of lower-level private security personnel.

CHAPTER OUTLINE

I.   POLICE ABUSE OF POWER

    A.   Use of Force
        Citizens use the term "police brutality" to describe a wide range of practices, from the use of profane or abusive language to physical force and violence. However, police use of deadly force often causes great emotional upheaval within a community. The typical victim of police force is an African-American male.

        In 1985, the Supreme Court ruled for first time that police use of deadly force to apprehend an unarmed, nonviolent, fleeing felony suspect violated the Fourth Amendment guarantee against unreasonable seizure (*Tennessee v. Garner*). Previously, police in many states followed common law principle that allowed the use of any force necessary to arrest a fleeing felon. The risk of significant lawsuits by victims of improper police shootings looms over contemporary police departments and creates incentives for administrators to set and enforce standards for the use of force.

B. Corruption
   Corruption is not easily defined. Can range from accepting free items from local businesses to murder.

   1. **"Grass Eaters" and "Meat Eaters"**: "Grass eaters" are officers who accept payoffs that circumstances of police work bring their way. This is the most common form of corruption. "Meat eaters" aggressively misuse their power for personal gain. Recent examples of officers getting actively involved in crimes related to illegal drug trafficking, either working with drug dealers or else robbing drug dealers.

      There are several types of "blue coat crime" committed by officers.   These include mooching, bribery, chiseling, extortion, shopping, shakedown, premeditated theft, favoritism, perjury, and prejudice.

      There are multiple effects from corruption: criminals are left free to pursue their illegal activities, departmental morale and supervision drop, and the public image of the police suffers.

   2. **Controlling Corruption**: The public needs to be involved by filing complaints about improper actions. To a great extent, the American political and legal systems have relied to police departments to keep their own houses in order. Police leadership must set the tone against corruption.

II. CIVIC ACCOUNTABILITY

   A. Internal Affairs
      These units investigate complaints against officers.   Investigations by Internal Affairs units do not often fit Hollywood model: frequently investigating allegations of sexual harassment, substance abuse problems, or misuse of physical force rather than grand corruption. Working in internal affairs offices an be stressful—it can be difficult for these officers to maintain relationships with other officers. It is often difficult to get officers to provide information about other officers.

   B. Civilian Review Boards
      There are political battles over creation of such boards because police oppose civilians evaluating of their actions. Such boards exist in 36 of the 50 largest cities and in 13 of the next 50 largest cities. Although officers believe such boards cannot understand and judge them fairly, the boards have not been harsh on police. Because of the low visibility of actions that result in complaints, most complaints cannot be substantiated.

   C. Standards and Accreditation
      Communities can gain greater accountability if they require that operations be conducted by nationally recognized standards. For example, the Commission on Accreditation of Law Enforcement Agencies includes the creation of standards for the use of discretion. Accreditation is voluntary. Certification may instill public confidence, provide management tool, and provide basis for educating officers about being accountable for their actions.

   D. Civil Liability Suits
      Civil lawsuits against departments for misconduct are another avenue for civic accountability. Lawsuits for brutality, false arrest, and negligence are increasingly common. Such suits first approved by the Supreme Court in 1961. Successful lawsuits and even the threat of lawsuits can affect the development of departmental policies. Insurance companies that provide civil liability coverage for police departments now give discounts to departments that achieve accreditation.

III. POLICING AND NEW TECHNOLOGY

Police rely on technology to investigate and solve crimes. As technology changes, investigative techniques also change. Questions about the accuracy of such technology are questioned, and some are concerned that police will rely on this technology too heavily. In addition, the use of some technology may violate citizens' constitutional rights.

A. <u>Investigative Tools</u>

1. **Computers** are used very frequently by police officers, especially in patrol cars. In addition, knowledge of computers is especially helpful in investigating cybercrimes.

2. **Databases** containing fingerprints, DNA, criminal histories and other information are vital to officers both on patrol and while conducting investigations.

3. **DNA testing** is a common event during criminal investigations, as offenders can be identified with precision. However, critics point out that DNA testing is only as good as the methods used to collect the evidence, and the likelihood that it will be contaminated prior to analysis.

4. A variety of **surveillance and identification** systems are used by police in public areas to apprehend criminals. These are sometimes used to find traffic offenders, but are also used to prevent theft and even terrorism. The newest types of surveillance systems use facial-recognition technology, but it is unknown if these methods are accurate enough to rely on them. Polygraph tests have been largely deemed unreliable, and police are examining other methods of judging someone's honesty.

B. <u>Weapons Technology</u>
Police are trying to develop alternative less-lethal weapons following needless citizen injury and lawsuits against officers and departments. Alternative weapons such as airguns, pepperballs or tasers can be used to incapacitate a person temporarily with minimal harm.

IV. HOMELAND SECURITY

The terrorist attacks of September 11th have changed the face of American policing. Policing has become more focused on international cooperation and intelligence gathering.

A. <u>Preparing for Threats</u>
The Department of Homeland Security (DHS) was created to help protect the United States from terrorist attacks. One of their main concerns is law enforcement intelligence, which is the information needed to preempt crime, including terrorism. Local police have increased their training in law enforcement intelligence, and have begun cross-jurisdiction cooperation to adequately fight threats from terrorism.

One consequence of the shift to homeland security-focused law enforcement is lack of funding for other programs, such as community policing. Experts warn that this shift needs to be planned carefully (such as using the Incident Command System) to avoid neglecting problems in other areas of law enforcement.

B. <u>New Laws and Controversies</u>

New laws and policies emerged following the terrorist attacks on September 11th. Some are concerned that our constitutional rights are at risk as the federal government attempts to prevent additional attacks. Laws such as the USA Patriot Act allow the government more liberty in searches and wiretaps, but some are concerned that the ability of the government to access library records (for example) is too intrusive.

V. SECURITY MANAGEMENT AND PRIVATE POLICING

Some private officers are merely watchmen who stand ready to call the police but others are deputized and granted arrest authority when a felony is committed in their presence. It is uncertain whether legal restrictions on police that protect individuals' constitutional rights also apply to actions by private police. There are indications that many private agencies are ready to assume increased responsibility for minor criminal incidents and that some governments are willing to consider letting private agencies handle some responsibilities (e.g. security at public buildings).

A. Functions of Security Management and Private Police
Top-level security managers have a range of responsibilities that call upon them to fulfill multiple roles that would be handled by a variety of separate individuals in the public sector. At lower levels, specific occupations in private security are more directly comparable to those of police officers. Many security personnel are the equivalent of private sector detectives. Other activities are more directly comparable to those of police patrol officers, especially for lower level security officers who must guard specific buildings, apartments, or stores.

B. Private Employment of Public Police
Many private agencies rely on public officers as employees. Off-duty police officers are frequently employed with private security firms, and there is a benefit of this to employers: off-duty police retain their full authority and powers to arrest, and stop and frisk while working for a private company.

1. **Conflict of Interest**: Police officers are banned from being process servers, bill collectors, repossessors, investigators for criminal defense attorneys and bail bondsmen, or employees at gambling establishments. Acting in these positions would create a conflict for them, as they may not be able to act in an unbiased way.

2. **Management Prerogatives**: departments require officers to gain permission to accept outside work, and department may deny permission if work degrading to department, physically exhausting, or dangerous.

   Some departments control officer's work through a *department contract model* in which department pays the officer directly for off-duty work and the private business reimburses the department. This helps to maintain departmental control and protect departmental needs and interests. The *officer contract model* allows officers to contract independently with businesses if they have permission of the department. Finally, the *union brokerage model* lets union set pay scale and working conditions for outside employment. Generally, the more closely a department controls its officers' off-duty employment, the more liability it assumes for officers' actions when they work for private firms.

C. The Public-Private Interface
Private employers' interests may not always coincide with the goals and policies of the local police department. Lack of communication between public and private agencies can lead to botched investigations, loss of evidence, and overzealousness by private officers. Some cooperative efforts and investigations have occurred between security and police.

Private agencies tend to report UCR index crimes, but do not report fraud, commercial bribery, employee theft, and other "white collar" type offenses in the companies for which they work. This tends to provide more lenient private justice for corporate employees caught in wrongdoing and is never reported to law enforcement authorities. Internal punishment through payroll deduction restitution or firing is usually much quicker than providing evidence for police and prosecutors.

D. Recruitment and Training
There are serious concerns on the part of law enforcement officials and civil libertarians about the recruitment and training of private officers, given that there is relatively little training provided in most places. Fewer than half of the states have licensing requirements. Because pay is low and many private officers work only temporarily, work is often done by the young or the retired, with few formal qualifications. Regulations that exist tend to be aimed at contractual private police (agencies that work for fees) rather than proprietary (officers hired by a company to provide security for that company).

REVIEW OF KEY TERMS

Fill in the appropriate term for each statement

Tennessee v. Garner (1985)
internal affairs units
Kyllo v. United States (2001)
Less-lethal weapons
Law enforcement intelligence
USA Patriot Act

1. _Internal affairs units_ are the divisions within police department responsible for investigating officers' misconduct.

2. In _Kyllo v United States_ the Supreme Court decided that thermal imaging devices could not be used for warrantless searches.

3. In order to reduce injury to citizens, police have been using _less-lethal weapon_ more often.

4. The _USA Patroit Act_ was enacted after September 11th in order to more easily conduct searches and wiretaps.

5. _Law enforcement intelligence_ is collected and analyzed to learn about illegal activities such as terrorism.

6. _Tennessee v Garner_ states important regulations for the use of force against fleeing suspects.

REVIEW OF KEY PEOPLE

Amadou Diallo
Abner Louima
James Q. Wilson and George L. Kelling
Rodney King
William Bratton

1. In "Broken Windows: The Police and Neighborhood Safety," _James Q. Wilson & George L. Kelling_ argue that disorderly behavior that is unregulated and unchecked is a signal to residents that the area is unsafe.

2. _Abner Louima_, a 32 year old Haitian immigrant, was arrested for disorderly conduct and brutally assaulted by New York City police officers.

3. The beating of _Rodney King_ by the LAPD sparked riots in which several citizens were killed.

4. Police Chief _Jerry Sandus_ believes that a significant amount of police corruption is caused by the drug trade.

5. _Amadou Diallo_, an unarmed West African immigrant, died in a fuselage of 41 bullets fired by four members of New York City's Street Crime Unit.

GENERAL PRACTICE QUESTIONS

Because of the power gained through the police union movement that has affected police departments in the past twenty years, police officers have greater input into policy decisions affecting law enforcement. In some cities, this power carries over into the organization of opportunities to gain extra income through 1. _Private policing_, because under the 2. _union brokerage model_, part-time jobs are secured by police unions.

Officers learn through on-the-job experience the informal practices of policing that constitute the
3. socialization process. Unfortunately, if a department has problems with 4. police brutality or
5. police corruption, new officers may learn harmful values and practices. Even if these officers do not engage
directly in these practices, they may participate in 6. prejury by creating alibis for fellow officers
because there are such strong pressures to remain loyal to fellow officers.

SELF-TEST SECTION

MULTIPLE CHOICE QUESTIONS

7.1.   Which of the following would NOT be considered a "hot time" in police work?
    a)   8 PM
    b)   10 PM
    c)   8 AM
    d)   2 AM
    e)   midnight

7.2.   What "remains the most influential test of the general deterrent effects of patrol on crime"?
    a)   Uniform Crime Report
    b)   National Crime Victimization Survey
    c)   The Mollen Commission Study
    d)   Kansas City Preventive Patrol Experiment
    e)   Robert Peel's "Bobbies on Patrol Analysis"

7.3.   When do rates of predatory crimes such as robbery and rape increase during the year?
    a)   fall months
    b)   spring months
    c)   summer months
    d)   winter months
    e)   rate is constant during the year

7.4.   When does domestic violence increase during the year?
    a)   fall months
    b)   spring months
    c)   summer months
    d)   winter months
    e)   rate is constant during the year

7.5.   According to a 1991 study of large cities, how many patrol cars are staffed by one officer?
    a)   25 percent
    b)   45 percent
    c)   70 percent
    d)   90 percent
    e)   99.9 percent

7.6.   What theory assert that disorderly behavior in public will frighten citizens and attract criminals, thus leading
    to more serious crime problems?
    a)   directed patrol
    b)   aggressive patrol
    c)   problem-oriented policing
    d)   private justice theory
    e)   broken windows theory

7.7.   What is the term used to describe a police officer accepting free coffee, cigarettes, meals, liquor, groceries, or other items, which are thought of as compensation either for receiving a low salary?
    a)   perjury
    b)   premeditated theft
    c)   mooching
    d)   bribery
    e)   stealing

7.8.   The term "police brutality" refers to which actions by police officers?
    a)   offensive language
    b)   physical force
    c)   violence
    d)   racial discrimination
    e)   all of the above

7.9.   Which of the following statements about police use of force is FALSE?
    a)   it is used infrequently
    b)   when used, it is less serious force
    c)   it is usually done in response to force
    d)   force usually involves an officer's weapon
    e)   excessive use of force is against policy

7.10.   What usually happens if an officer reports that another officer has done something unethical or illegal?
    a)   the reporting officer is given a promotion
    b)   the reporting officer is considered a snitch and ostracized
    c)   the reporting officer serves as a counselor for the offending officer
    d)   the reporting officer is given a job with internal affairs
    e)   the reporting officer is fired

7.11.   What is the term used to describe a police officer taking expensive items for personal use during an investigation of a break-in or burglary?
    a)   borrowing
    b)   chiseling
    c)   premeditated theft
    d)   mooching
    e)   shakedown

7.12.   In which community are officers most likely to use force?
    a)   in the suburbs
    b)   in rural areas
    c)   in communities with a mostly white population
    d)   in areas with low economic inequality
    e)   in communities that have a large minority population

7.13.   *Tennessee v. Garner*:
    a)   struck down the "feeling felon" rule
    b)   outlawed police use of force
    c)   holds officers accountable for their actions
    d)   legalized police brutality
    e)   banned weapons

7.14. What is the term used to describe a police officer lying in a court of law to provide an alibi for fellow officers engaged in unlawful activity?
a) perjury
b) premeditated theft
c) mooching
d) bribery
e) stealing

7.15. Why is the public image of the police important?
a) Racial disparities are reduced
b) A positive image helps the war on drugs
c) Homeland security
d) Police need citizen cooperation to investigate crime
e) A positive image increases officer salaries

7.16. Which of the following techniques are used to control the police?
a) internal affairs units
b) civilian review boards
c) standards and accreditation
d) civil liability lawsuits
e) all of the above

7.17. What is the size of an Internal Affairs Department?
a) ten officers
b) twenty officers
c) thirty officers
d) fifty officers
e) it may vary between one officer and an entire section of officers

7.18. According to the Supreme Court, in which situation can police use deadly force?
a) When a feeling suspect poses significant threat of death or serious injury to the public
b) When someone is running from the police who committed a felony
c) When someone is running from the police who committed a misdemeanor
d) When a citizen strikes an officer
e) When citizens are under the influence of drugs

7.19. "Grass Eaters" are police officers who:
a) actively use their power for personal gain
b) frequently use physical force against citizens
c) are vegetarians
d) regularly accept payoffs that the routines of police work bring their way
e) are not corrupt

7.20. In terms of costs and benefits, where are foot patrols most effective?
a) low density rural areas
b) high density urban neighborhoods
c) high density suburban areas
d) low density urban neighborhoods
e) foot patrols are not effective anywhere

7.21. In 1998, police officers in Cleveland were found guilty of:
a) prostitution
b) gambling
c) bad language
d) cocaine trafficking
e) accepting payoffs

7.22. What is the "blue wall of silence"?
   a) the belief that officers shouldn't rat on other officers
   b) the belief that corruption is acceptable, as long as no one gets hurt
   c) the belief that blue uniforms are more calming to hostile citizens
   d) the belief that citizens don't understand the value of police work
   e) the belief that officers should remain silent at all times

7.23. Why are results from DNA testing sometimes questioned in court?
   a) Because DNA is not very precise
   b) Because DNA cannot help to identify officers
   c) Because offenders must agree to DNA testing
   d) Because DNA can be contaminated by collection procedures
   e) Because DNA is not very scientific

7.24. The goal of the MATRIX database is to:
   a) Help local law enforcement coordinate intelligence efforts
   b) Keep track of offender's DNA
   c) Track corrupt police officials
   d) Trace routes for cocaine trafficking through South America
   e) Target juvenile offenders for selective incapacitation

TRUE/FALSE QUESTIONS

7.1. _____ Tasers can be used to incapacitate a person temporarily with minimum harm.

7.2. _____ Police accreditation is voluntary.

7.3. _____ Domestic violence crimes increase in the spring months.

7.4. _____ Rape crimes increase in the summer months.

7.5. _____ The service function is considered more important when police assume the crime fighting role.

7.6. _____ Disorder, such as a broken window, creates fear in a community and increases crime problems.

7.7. _____ The Violent Crime Control and Law Enforcement Act called for decreases in the numbers of officers assigned to community policing.

7.8. _____ Japanese policemen usually patrol in vehicles.

7.9. _____ "Crime mapping" databases provide updated information about crime trends.

7.10. _____ Most police departments are using the iris-recognition technology made famous by the movie, Minority Report.

7.11. _____ In *Kyllo v. United States (2001),* the use of a thermal imaging device by law enforcement was ruled to be an illegal search.

7.12. _____ Abuse of police power is a major issue on the public's agenda.

7.13. _____ Police may use "legitimate" force to do their job.

7.14. _____ Police scandals rarely have occurred in the last quarter-century.

7.15. _____ The use of new technology does not raise issues related to privacy.

7.16. _____ In regard to community policing, Rudolph Guliani argued that police officers engaged in too much social work and made too few arrests.

7.17. _____ A problem with community policing is that it does not reduce costs.

7.18. _____ The order maintenance function is considered less important when police assume the crime fighting role.

7.19. _____ The demands on the police differ according to the time of day, day of the week, and even season of the year.

7.20. _____ Internal Affairs officers usually have good relationships with officers outside of their department.

ANSWER KEY

Key Terms
1. internal affairs units
2. *Kyllo v. United States*
3. less-lethal weapons
4. USA Patriot Act
5. law enforcement intelligence
6. *Tennessee v. Garner*

Key People
1. James Q. Wilson and George L. Kelling
2. Abner Louima
3. James Q. Wilson
4. Jerry Sanders
5. Amadou Diallo

General Practice Questions
1. private policing
2. union brokerage model
3. socialization
4. police brutality
5. police corruption
6. perjury

Multiple Choice
7.1.   C
7.2.   D
7.3.   C
7.4.   D
7.5.   C
7.6.   E
7.7.   C
7.8.   E
7.9.   D
7.10. D
7.11. A
7.12. B
7.13. E
7.14. C
7.15. A
7.16. A
7.17. D
7.18. E
7.19. E
7.20. C
7.21. D
7.22. A
7.23. D
7.24. A

<u>True/False</u>

7.1.	T
7.2.	T
7.3.	F
7.4.	T
7.5.	F
7.6.	T
7.7.	F
7.8.	F
7.9.	T
7.10.	F
7.11.	T
7.12.	T
7.13.	T
7.14.	F
7.15.	F
7.16.	T
7.17.	T
7.18.	T
7.19.	T
7.20.	F

WORKSHEET 7.1: PATROL STRATEGIES

You are the police chief in medium-sized city. In one residential neighborhood, citizens are alarmed (and complaining to city hall) because there has been a rash of burglaries. In the downtown area, an increase in muggings has the merchants concerned about losing business. At a city council meeting, representatives from both groups ask you how you can adjust patrol strategies to address the problems in each area. Pretend that you are responding to their questions in explaining below how each patrol strategy might impact (or not impact) the two problems areas in the city.

1. Preventive Patrol_____

_____

_____

_____

_____

_____

_____

2. Foot Patrol_____

_____

_____

_____

_____

_____

3. Aggressive Patrol_____

_____

_____

_____

_____

Whether or not you would adopt any of the foregoing patrol strategies, describe how you would address the crime problems in each area in order to reduce the problem and/or make the citizens feel less concerned.

_____

_____

_____

_____

POLICE AND CONSTITUTIONAL LAW

OUTLINE

- Legal Limitations on Police Investigations
- Plain View Doctrine
- Warrantless Searches
- Questioning Suspects
- The Exclusionary Rule

CHAPTER 8
POLICE AND CONSTITUTIONAL LAW

LEARNING OBJECTIVES

After covering the material in this chapter, students should understand:

1.   police officers' responsibility to control crime under the rule of law

2.   search and seizure issues

3.   arrest and interrogation issues

4.   circumstances justifying warrantless searches

5.   the exclusionary rule, its application to the states, and exceptions to the rule

CHAPTER SUMMARY

The Supreme Court has defined rules for the circumstances and justifications for stops, searches, and arrests in light of the Fourth Amendment's prohibition on "unreasonable searches and seizures." Most stops must be supported by reasonable suspicion and arrests, like search warrants, must be supported by enough information to constitute probable cause. The plain view doctrine permits officers to visually examine and seize any contraband or criminal evidence that is in open sight when they are in a place that they are legally permitted to be. Searches are considered "reasonable" and may be conducted without warrants in a number of specific circumstances such as borders, airports, and other situations required by special needs beyond the normal purposes of law enforcement. Limited searches may be conducted without warrants when officers have reasonable suspicions to justify a stop-and-frisk for weapons on the streets, when officer make a lawful arrest, when exigent circumstances exist, when people voluntarily consent to searches of their persons or property, and in certain situations involving automobiles. The Fifth Amendment privilege against compelled self-incrimination helps to protect citizens against violence and coercion by police as well as to maintain the legitimacy and integrity of the legal system. The Supreme Court's decision in *Miranda v. Arizona (1966)* required officers to inform suspects of specific rights before custodial questioning, although officers have adapted their practices to accommodate this rule and several exceptions have been created. The exclusionary rule is a remedy designed to deter police from violating citizens' rights during criminal investigations by barring the use of illegally obtained evidence in court. The Supreme Court has created several exceptions to the exclusionary rule, including the inevitable discovery rule and the "good faith" exception in defective warrant situations.

CHAPTER OUTLINE

I.   LEGAL LIMITS OF POLICE INVESTIGATIONS

   In a democratic society, police are expected to control crime while complying with the rule of law as it protects the rights of citizens, including criminal suspects. Evidence used against suspects must be admissible in court.

   A.   Search and Seizure

The Fourth Amendment prohibits unreasonable searches and seizures. The Supreme Court defines searches as actions by law enforcement officials that intrude upon people's reasonable expectations of privacy. If people are not free to leave when officers' assert their authority to halt someone's movement, then a seizure has occurred and the Fourth Amendment requires that the seizure be reasonable

B. Arrest
An arrest is the seizure of an individual by government official who takes suspect into custody. Courts prefer arrest warrants for felonies, but have not required them. According to the Fourth Amendment, arrests must be based on probable cause.

C. Warrants and Probable Cause
An officer must show reliable information establishing *probable cause* to believe that a crime has been or is being committed. The particular premises and pieces of property to be seized must be identified and the officer must swear under oath that they are correct.

Search warrants can be obtained when officers present an affidavit that the information they present to obtain the warrant is believed to be correct.

II. PLAIN VIEW DOCTRINE

During a search, incident to arrest or with a warrant, officers can seize and examine items in plain view even if not listed on warrant, if those items may be evidence of illegal activity

A. Open Fields Doctrine
This doctrine states that property owners have no reasonable expectation of privacy in open areas on and around their property.

B. Plain Feel and Other Senses
Police officers can justify a warrantless search based upon smell or odor and also based upon feel

III. WARRANTLESS SEARCHES

A. Special Needs beyond the Normal Purpose of Law Enforcement
Officers do not need any suspicion to justify a search in specific contexts, such as airline passengers or border searches. U.S. Customs and Border Patrol agents (CBP) can use random searches at the Canadian and Mexican borders, and these agents can use the standard of "reasonable suspicion" to identify individuals to search.

Some states can use vehicle checkpoints to apprehend drunk drivers, but not every state allows this type of warrantless search due to differences in state statutes and court decisions.

B. Stop and Frisk on the Streets
Brief questioning and pat down searches (stop-and-frisk) are permitted based on reasonable judgment of police officers that a crime as occurred or is about to occur, and that the stopped person may have a weapon (*Terry v. Ohio*, 1968). However, an anonymous tip is insufficient justification for a stop-and-frisk search (*Florida v. J.L.*, 2000).

C. Search Incident to Lawful Arrest
Police can search people and areas in the immediate vicinity for weapons when a lawful arrest is made (*Chimel v. California*, 1969).

D. Exigent Circumstances
Officers might find themselves in the middle of an urgent situation where they must act swiftly and do not have time to request a warrant from the court.

E. Consent
A citizen may waive his or her Fourth Amendment and other rights and allow police to conduct a search. Police officers do not have to inform citizens of their right to decline a request to search (*United States v. Drayton*, 2002).

F. Automobile Searches
Automobiles differ from homes in terms of people's expectations of privacy and the risk that evidence may be contained in a mobile vehicle. Officers may search automobiles and containers in such vehicles if they have probable cause to do so.

IV. QUESTIONING SUSPECTS

Upon arrest, suspects must be informed of their rights. This is vitally important given the constitutional protection against self-incrimination in the Fifth Amendment.

A. *Miranda* Rules
In *Miranda v. Arizona* (1966), the Supreme Court stated that subjects in police custody must be notified of the following rights: (1) All suspects have the right to remain silent; (2) if they choose to make a statement, it can and will be used against them in court; (3) they have the right to have an attorney present during interrogation, or have an opportunity to consult with an attorney; and (4) if they cannot afford an attorney, the state will provide one.

In *Escobedo v. Illinois* (1964), the Court linked the Fifth and Sixth Amendments, stating that the right to counsel and the right against self-incrimination are interrelated.

B. The Consequences of *Miranda*
Police officers have adapted their techniques in various ways to question suspects and get information despite *Miranda* limitations. *Miranda* rights must be provided *before questions are asked* during custodial interrogations.

Departments train officers to read the *Miranda* warnings to suspects as soon as an arrest is made. This is done in order to make sure the warnings are not omitted as the suspect in processed in the system. The warnings may be read off a standard "Miranda card" to make sure that the rights are provided consistently and correctly. However, the courts do not require that police inform suspects of their rights immediately after arrest.

Officers are also trained in interrogation techniques that are intended to encourage suspects to talk despite *Miranda* warnings suspects of their rights immediately after arrest. The Supreme Court has ruled that officers may use tactics to encourage suspects to confess even if those tactics are dishonest.

V. THE EXCLUSIONARY RULE

If evidence used in criminal trials is obtained illegally, that evidence cannot be used against on offender in court. The Supreme Court created the exclusionary rule as a judicial remedy to guard against police corruption.

A. **Application of the Exclusionary Rule to the States**
One of the most important cases in the Warren Court, the case of *Mapp v. Ohio* (1961) applied the exclusionary rule to the states.

B. **Exceptions to the Exclusionary Rule**
As composition of the Supreme Court became more conservative in the 1970s and 1980s, a number of decisions limited or created exceptions to the exclusionary rule. Among the modifications created were exceptions for public safety, inevitable discovery (*Nix v. Williams*, 1984), and "good faith" exceptions.

REVIEW OF KEY TERMS

Fill in the appropriate term for each statement

search
reasonable expectation of privacy
seizure
stop
reasonable suspicion
probable cause
affidavits
totality of circumstances test
plain view doctrine
open fields doctrine
Terry v. Ohio (1968)
Stop-and-frisk search
Florida v. J.L. (2000)
Chimel v. California (1969)
exigent circumstances
United States v. Drayton (2002)
Miranda v. Arizona (1966)
Escobedo v. Illinois (1964)
"public safety" exception
Exclusionary rule
Mapp v. Ohio (1961)
"good faith" exception (??)
"inevitable discovery" exception
Nix v. Williams (1984)

1. _Terry v Ohio (1968)_ established the "stop and frisk" doctrine permitting pat-down searches during field interrogations.

2. In the case of _United States v Drayton (2002)_ the Supreme Court determined that officers are not required to inform suspects that they may decline a search by the police.

3. When suspects request an attorney, police officers cannot refuse access to counsel. This right was determined in _Escobedo v Illinois_

4. A _Search_ occurs when an official examines and hunts for evidence in or on a person or place in a manner that intrudes on reasonable expectation of privacy.

5. A court must use the _totality of circumstances test_ test before granting a search warrant.

6. _Chimel v California 1969_ established that a gun protruding from under seat is within the scope of the plain view doctrine.

7. The landmark case mandating that suspects must be informed of their rights prior to questioning is _Miranda v Arizona 1966_

8. When a government official interferes with an individual's freedom of movement, it is considered a _Stop_.

9. _Nix v Williams (1984)_ established the inevitable discovery exception to the exclusionary rule.

10. When officers have _reasonable suspicion_ to believe a crime has been committed, they are allowed to conduct a search.

11. The ___exclusionary rule___ prevents police and prosecutors from using evidence that has been obtained through improper procedures.

12. In *Terry v. Ohio*, the Supreme Court allowed police officers to conduct ___stop and frisk search___ if they have reasonable suspicion to believe a crime has occurred.

13. The standard used to determine whether an action actually constitutes a search is called ___reasonable expectation of privacy___

14. In the case of ___Florida v. J. L.___ , the Supreme Court decided that officers could not stop-and-frisk a suspect based on an anonymous tip.

15. ___good faith exception___ is based on the idea that evidence should not be excluded when police officers did everything that they thought they were supposed to do even though a mistake occurred.

16. If officers can see evidence of a crime on private property, they can seize it under the ___open field doctrine___.

17. ___Probable cause___ occurs when officers obtain reliable information indicating that evidence will be found somewhere or someone has committed a crime.

18. Officers may search, arrest, or question suspects when there is a threat to public safety or risk evidence will be destroyed when there are ___exigent circumstance___

19. ___"Public safety" exception___ allows courts to use evidence collected if officers took necessary actions to protect citizens, even if no warrant was issued.

20. ___inevitable discovery" exception___ permits the use of improperly obtained evidence that would have been found by the police eventually through proper means.

21. In ___Mapp v Ohio___ , the Supreme Court decided that evidence obtained illegally must be excluded at trial.

22. ___affidavits___ are sometimes used by police to obtain search warrants.

23. ___Seizure___ occurs when the police deprive people of their liberty or property in a reasonable manner.

24. ___Plainview doctrine___ is an exception to the warrant requirement because officers need not ignore illegal objects that are clearly visible.

REVIEW OF KEY PERSONS

Earl Warren
John Ashcroft
Warren Burger
O. J. Simpson

1. A warrantless search of football star ___O. J. Simpson___ 's house after his ex-wife was found murdered produced a bloody glove.

2. Under the direction of Attorney General ___John Ashcroft___ the government has jailed American citizens without charging them with any crimes, giving them access to court proceedings, or permitting them to meet with an attorney.

3. The appointment of _Earl Warren_ as Chief Justice in 1953 ushered in an era in which the Supreme Court expanded the definitions of constitutional rights affecting a variety of issues, including criminal justice.

4. Chief Justice _Warren Burger_, who served from 1969 to 1986, criticized the exclusionary rule as ineffective and misguided.

GENERAL PRACTICE QUESTIONS

Legal limitations are placed on the ability of the police to conduct searches of citizens and seizures of property. Warrants are usually necessary in order to search property, unless officers can see the evidence in 1. _plain view_. Sometimes called a "Terry stop", officers can stop citizens and frisk them under the Court's decision in the case of 2 _Terry v Ohio_. Officers are also allowed to search when 3. _exigent circumstance_ exist that indicates the public is at risk or evidence is about to be destroyed. Offenders must be read their Constitutional rights prior to any questioning in according with the case of 4. _Miranda v Arizona_

Oen of the most important Supreme Court decisions in the twentieth century was the finding that evidence obtained illegally cannot be used in court. This rule, called the 5. _Exclusionary Rule_, was later applied to the states in the court case 6. _Mapp v Ohio_. There are several exceptions to this rule—one allows a 7. _good faith_ exception when officers act honestly even if the warrant is later found to be in error.

SELF-TEST SECTION

MULTIPLE CHOICE QUESTIONS

8.1. How does the U. S. Supreme Court define a "search"?
   a) an action by a law enforcement official that creates tension between the official and a citizen
   b) an action by a law enforcement official that intrudes upon people's "reasonable expectations of privacy"
   c) when a law enforcement official speaks to a person
   d) when a law enforcement official informs a person that a search is taking place
   e) when a law enforcement official looks at a person

8.2. Which of the following statements is TRUE regarding courts and warrants?
   a) courts require arrest warrants for felonies, but do not prefer them
   b) courts prefer arrest warrants for felonies, but do not require them
   c) courts require arrest warrants for felonies and prefer them
   d) courts prefer arrest warrants for felonies, and require them
   e) courts require arrest warrants for felonies, but have no preference about them

8.3. All arrests must be supported by ...
   a) reasonable suspicion
   b) reasonable doubt
   c) preponderance of the evidence
   d) probable cause
   e) real evidence

8.4. What agency is responsible for security at the United States borders with Canada and Mexico?
   a) FBI
   b) CIA
   c) INS
   d) CBP
   e) IRS

8.5.   What is a written statement confirmed by oath or affirmation?
    a)   warrant
    b)   perjury
    c)   interrogatory
    d)   booking
    e)   affidavit

8.6.   If a judicial officer makes a generalized determination about whether the evidence is both sufficient and reliable enough to justify a warrant, this is called the standard of..
    a)   reasonable suspicion
    b)   reasonable doubt
    c)   preponderance of the evidence
    d)   the totality of the circumstances
    e)   real evidence

8.7.   Which of the following search does not require a warrant?
    a)   stop and frisk
    b)   border searches
    c)   exigent circumstances
    d)   consent
    e)   all of the above

8.8.   Which of the following would raise suspicion and justify a search of a person according to handbook of the U. S. Customs Service?
    a)   person has a beard
    b)   person has an earring
    c)   person shows signs of nervousness
    d)   person is alone
    e)   person is not smiling

8.9.   In what case did the U. S. Supreme Court rule that an unverified anonymous tip is not adequate as basis for a stop and frisk search?
    a)   *Maryland v. Wilson* (1997)
    b)   *Michigan v. Sitz* (1991)
    c)   *Minnesota v. Dickerson* (1993)
    d)   *New York v. Quarles* (1984)
    e)   *Florida v. J.L.* (2000)

8.10.   Critics concerned with violations of constitutional rights in the USA Patriot Act have argued:
    a)   It is not tough enough on terrorists
    b)   The use of 'sneak and peek' search warrants has focused too much on drug offenders
    c)   It has not ended conflict in the Middle East
    d)   'Sneak-and-peek' warrants violate the Fourth Amendment
    e)   The name should be changed to something more descriptive

8.11.   What is the name of the rule used when evidence is "thrown out" of court because it was obtained illegally?
    a)   The Patriot Act
    b)   The Miranda Rule
    c)   A Terry Stop
    d)   The Exclusionary Rule
    e)   The Probable Cause Rule

8.12. Which of the following are "good faith" exceptions to permit improperly obtained evidence?
a) Reliance on a warrant later found to be incorrect
b) Reliance on statutes later declared unconstitutional
c) Reliance on records maintained by justice system employees
d) Reasonable reliance on a consent to search provided by someone who lacked the authority to provide such consent
e) All of the above are good faith exceptions

8.13. Judges may rule that even when evidence was obtained improperly, it would have been found eventually. This is called:
a) The exclusionary rule
b) Inevitable discovery
c) Totality of circumstances
d) Exigent circumstances
e) Reasonable suspicion

8.14. If a citizens gives a police officer consent to search his or her property, then…
a) The officer no longer needs a search warrant
b) The officer still must obtain a search warrant
c) The officer must ask three times in order to search the property
d) The officers is violating the citizen's Fourth Amendment rights
e) The officer is in the wrong

8.15. Why does the Fifth Amendment contain the privilege against self-incrimination?
a) because suspects do not tell the truth and this infringes upon an investigation
b) because police officers often ask the wrong questions
c) because suspects can talk too much and this interferes with the investigation
d) to discourage police officers from using violent or coercive means to get suspects to confess
e) because police officers often fail to remember what suspects have to say

8.16. Which of the following movies is based on a true story in England in which police officers gain a confession from a bombing suspect whom they know to be innocent by placing a gun in the suspect's mouth and threatening to pull the trigger?
a) Minority Report
b) Clear and Present Danger
c) In the Name of the Father
d) The Sum of All Fears
e) Patriot Games

8.17. In what case did the U. S. Supreme Court rule that officers could forego Miranda warnings if there would be a threat to "public safety"?
a) *Minnesota v. Dickerson* (1993)
b) *Flippo v. West Virginia* (1999)
c) *Florida v. J.L.* (2000)
d) *Warden v. Hayden* (1967)
e) *New York v. Quarles* (1984)

8.18. Which of the following statements regarding automobile searches is true?
a) The trunk of a car can be treated the same as the rest of a car in a search
b) The trunk of a car must be treated differently as the rest of a car in a search
c) Police officers cannot open the hood of a car, even if they have a warrant to search the vehicle
d) Police officers must always have a warrant to search a car
e) Police officers cannot search a car, even if they arrest the driver for illegal behavior

8.19. Which of the following is FALSE regarding the Miranda warnings?
    a) police must inform suspects of their rights immediately after arrest
    b) the warnings do not have to be provided until the police begin to ask questions
    c) the warnings involve the Fifth and Sixth Amendments to the Constitution
    d) the warnings are designed to deter police misconduct
    e) all of the above are TRUE

8.20. Why must officers read suspects their *Miranda* rights prior to questioning?
    a) So the offender does not confess to the crime
    b) To make sure the offender gives an honest confession
    c) To force the offender to implicate a co-conspirator
    d) To make sure any information is provided voluntarily
    e) To force the offender to testify against himself in court

8.21. Which of the following exceptions to the exclusionary rule means that the officers acted with the honest belief that they were following the proper rules?
    a) inevitability of discovery exception
    b) public safety exception
    c) good faith exception
    d) "Honest Abe" exception
    e) mistaken identity exception

8.22. Under which exception can officers forgo using the Miranda warning and still question suspects?
    a) Inevitable discovery
    b) "public safety" exception
    c) "exigent circumstances" exception
    d) The Exclusionary rule
    e) "early warning" exception

8.23. In the image below, what is the officer most likely doing?

    a) Arresting the suspect
    b) Booking the suspect
    c) Searching the suspect
    d) Charging the suspect
    e) Adjudicating the suspect

8.24. In what case did the U. S. Supreme Court rule that improperly obtained statements can be used to impeach the credibility of defendants who take the witness stand and testify?
    a) *Harris v. New York* (1971)
    b) *Pennsylvania Board of Pardons and Parole v. Scott* (1998)
    c) *Flippo v. West Virginia* (1999)
    d) *Florida v. J.L.* (2000)
    e) *Immigration and Naturalization Service v. Lopez-Mendoza* (1984)

8.25. Which of the following is TRUE about the exclusionary rule?
  a) it is specifically mentioned in the Fourth Amendment
  b) it currently applies only to the federal courts
  c) the Rehnquist Court has expanded criminal defendants' rights by supporting the exclusionary rule
  d) it was created by the judiciary to prevent police misconduct
  e) all of the above are TRUE

TRUE/FALSE QUESTIONS

8.1. _T_ The U.S. Border Patrol regularly makes warrantless stops and searches.

8.2. _F_ An officer may NOT enter a vehicle to see the Vehicle Identification Number when a car has been validly stopped.

8.3. _T_ A warrant must be signed by a judicial officer.

8.4. _F_ Border searches without a warrant are an automatic violation of the Fourth Amendment.

8.5. _T_ The exclusionary rule applies to federal and state courts.

8.6. _F_ The American Bar Association is NOT concerned about the rights of defendants who are tried before military commissions.

8.7. _T_ Police can stop and frisk a person without a warrant if reasonable suspicion exists.

8.8. _T_ Chief Justice Earl Warren was a supporter of the exclusionary rule.

8.9. _T_ The Rehnquist Court has created a number of exceptions to the exclusionary rule.

8.10. _F_ The Fourth Amendment does not contain the word "warrant."

8.11. _F_ The Fifth Amendment contains the right against unreasonable search and seizure.

8.12. _T_ The Sixth Amendment contains the right to counsel.

8.13. _F_ The privilege against self-incrimination is found in the Fourth Amendment.

8.14. _T_ Evidence that was obtained illegally will not be thrown out if a police officer acted in good faith.

8.15. _T_ Warrantless searches are justified if exigent circumstances exist.

8.16. _T_ The handbook for the U. S. Customs Service advises agents to conduct a search if a person avoids eye-contact.

8.17. _F_ Sobriety checkpoints violate the Fourth Amendment rights of citizens.

8.18. _T_ If an officer smells marijuana, he or she has the ability to investigate further according to the Fourth Amendment.

8.19. _F_ Chief Justice William Rehnquist wrote the majority opinion in *Miranda v. Arizona* (1966).

8.20. _F_ Blood tests without a warrant violate the right against unreasonable search and seizure.

ANSWER KEY

Key Terms
1. *Terry v. Ohio*
2. *United States v. Drayton*
3. *Escobedo v. Illinois*
4. search
5. totality of circumstances
6. *Chimel v. California*
7. *Miranda v. Arizona*
8. stop
9. *Nix v. Williams*
10. reasonable suspicion
11. exclusionary rule
12. stop-and-frisk searches
13. reasonable expectation of privacy
14. *Florida v. J.L.*
15. "good faith" exception
16. open fields doctrine
17. probable cause
18. exigent circumstances
19. "public safety" exception
20. "inevitable discovery" exception
21. *Mapp v. Ohio*
22. affidavits
23. seizure
24. plain view doctrine

Key Persons
1. O. J. Simpson
2. John Ashcroft
3. Michael Irvin
4. Earl Warren
5. Warren Burger

General Practice
1. plain view
2. Terry v. Ohio
3. exigent circumstances
4. Miranda v. Arizona
5. exclusionary rule
6. Mapp v. Ohio
7. "good faith"

UUUUUMultiple Choice
8.1.   B
8.2.   B
8.3.   D
8.4.   D
8.5.   E
8.6.   D

8.7.   E
8.8.   C
8.9.   E
8.10. D
8.11. D
8.12. E
8.13. B
8.14. A
8.15. D
8.16. C
8.17. E
8.18. A
8.19. A
8.20. D
8.21. C
8.22. B
8.23. C
8.24. A
8.25. D

True/False
8.1.   T
8.2.   F
8.3.   T
8.4.   F
8.5.   T
8.6.   F
8.7.   T
8.8.   T
8.9.   T
8.10. F
8.11. F
8.12. T
8.13. F
8.14. T
8.15. T
8.16. T
8.17. F
8.18. T
8.19. F
8.20. F

WORKSHEET 8.1. THE JUSTIFICATION FOR WARRANTLESS SEARCHES

Warrantless searches are important for police officers in regard to gathering evidence that might otherwise be lost or endanger the safety of others in society. In the following exercise, students should list the basis for justifying the warrantless searches listed below. What purpose(s) are served by allowing law enforcement officers to conduct a search without a warrant? Are these searches justified in violating a person's rights based upon the purposes that you listed?

Stop and Frisk on the Streets _____

_____

_____

_____

Warrantless Search of Hispanics five miles from the Mexican border _____

_____

_____

_____

Search Incident to a Lawful Arrest _____

_____

_____

_____

Automobile Searches _____

_____

_____

_____

Searching through someone's luggage at the airport _____

_____

_____

_____

Consent searches_____

_____

_____

COURTS AND PRETRIAL PROCESSES

OUTLINE

- The Structure of American Courts
- Effective Management of the State Courts
- To Be a Judge
- From Arrest to Trial or Plea
- Bail: Pretrial Release
- Pretrial Detention

CHAPTER 9
COURTS AND PRE-TRIAL PROCESSES

LEARNING OBJECTIVES

After covering the material in this chapter, students should understand:

1. the dual court system, the hierarchy of courts (general jurisdiction, appellate etc.) and the fragmented nature of the organization of courts in the United States

2. the reform efforts to unify court systems and centralize court administration

3. the judge's functions and roles in the criminal court

4. the methods used for selecting judges and the results of those selection methods

5. defense attorneys' use of pretrial motions

6. the underlying purposes of bail

7. the actors who influence the bail decision

8. the consequences of being detained, especially for poor defendants, and the debate over preventive detention

9. mechanisms utilized to reform the bail system or as alternatives to money bail.

CHAPTER SUMMARY

The United States has a dual court system consisting of state and federal courts that are organized into separate hierarchies. Trial courts and appellate courts have different jurisdictions and functions. Despite resistance from local judges and political interests, reformers have sought to improve state court systems through centralized administration, state funding, and a separate personnel system. The judge is a key figure in the criminal justice process, who assumes the roles of adjudicator, negotiator, and administrator. State judges are selected through various methods, including partisan elections, nonpartisan elections, gubernatorial appointment, and merit selection. Merit selection methods for choosing judges have gradually spread to many states. Such methods normally use a screening committee to make recommendations of potential appointees who will, if placed on the bench by the governor, go before the voters for approval or disapproval of their performance in office. Pretrial processes determine the fates of nearly all defendants through case dismissals, decisions defining the charges, and plea bargains that affect more than 90% of cases. Defense attorneys use motions to their advantage to gain information and delay proceedings to benefit their clients. The bail process provides opportunities for many defendants to gain pretrial release, but poor defendants may be disadvantaged by their inability to come up with the money or property needed to secure release. Preventive detention statutes may permit judges to hold defendants considered dangerous or likely to flee. Bail bondsmen are private businesspeople who provide money for defendants' pretrial release for a fee. Their activities create risks of corruption and discrimination in the bail process, but they may help the system by reminding defendants about court dates and tracking down defendants who disappear. Although judges bear primary responsibility for setting bail, prosecutors are especially influential in recommending amounts and conditions for pretrial release. Initiatives to reform the bail process include release on own recognizance (ROR), police-issued citations, and bail guidelines. Pretrial detainees, despite the presumption of innocence, are held in difficult conditions in jails containing mixed populations of convicted offenders, detainees, and troubled people. The shock of being jailed creates risks of suicide and depression.

CHAPTER OUTLINE

I. THE STRUCTURE OF AMERICAN COURTS

Federal and state courts both have trial and appellate courts. Native Americans have tribal courts, with jurisdiction over crimes committed on tribal land. Both state and federal courts have trial and appellate courts.

Trial courts of limited jurisdiction handle less serious cases, while the more serious criminal cases and civil cases are handled by courts of general jurisdiction. Appellate courts hear appeals from the lower courts, and this occurs when defendants claim that errors were made in their original trial. While all jurisdictions use this system of courts, they do not always use the same names.

II. EFFECTIVE MANAGEMENT OF THE STATE COURTS

Recent court reform has focused on elimination of overlapping and conflicting jurisdictional boundaries (of both subject matter and geography); creating a hierarchical and centralized court structure, with administrative responsibility vested in a chief justice and court of last resort; financing of courts by state government; and creating a separate personnel system, centrally run by a state court administrator.

III. TO BE A JUDGE

A. <u>Who Becomes a Judge?</u>
    Judges enjoy high status and salaries well above the rates for most American workers, yet lower than pay for partners at large law firms. While this has changed in the past several years, judges are overwhelmingly white and male. In many cities, political factors dictate that judges be drawn from specific racial, religious, and ethnic groups.

B. <u>Functions of the Judge</u>
    1. **Adjudicator**: In the role of the adjudicator, judges are neutral actors between prosecution and defense in making decisions on bail, pleas, sentencing, and motions. They must avoid any appearance of bias.
    2. **Negotiator**: When in the negotiator role, judges spend much of their time talking to prosecutors, defense attorneys, and other court personnel. Judges may even provide informal advice to defense attorney or even defendant about what is likely to happen. Court rules in some states forbid judicial participation in plea bargaining, although judges participate behind the scenes in many other states.
    3. **Administrator**: As administrators, judges are responsible for managing the courthouse. In urban areas, there may be a professional court administrator. Judges, however, are still responsible for administration of their courtroom and staff. In rural areas, the administrative burdens on judges may be more substantial.

C. <u>How to Become a Judge</u>
    Quality of courts and justice depends on having judges with proper skills and qualities. Public confidence in courts is diminished by poor or impolite performance. There are five methods of selection for state trial judges: gubernatorial selection, legislative selection, merit selection, nonpartisan election and partisan election. Selection by public voting is most common.

    The transition from lawyer to judge can be difficult given the adversarial system used in American courts, in which the prosecution and defense attorneys engage in investigation. European courts use the inquisitorial system, in which the judge takes an active case in investigation.

    Merit selection is used in several states. Under this process, a nominating commission of lawyers and citizens sends the governor a list of three recommended names and the governor chooses one of them to fill a vacant seat. After one year, the citizens vote in a retention election on whether to approve the judge's continued service.

IV. FROM ARREST TO TRIAL OR PLEA

After arrest, the suspect is taken to the station for booking, including photographs and fingerprints. For warrantless arrests, a probable cause hearing must be held within forty-eight hours. At the subsequent arraignment, the formal charges are read and the defendant enters a plea. Prosecutors evaluate the evidence to make discretionary determinations about what charges to pursue or whether the charges should be dropped. Decisions to drop charges may be influenced by the defendant's age, prior record, seriousness of offense, or jail overcrowding. Such decisions may also be influenced by bias based on race or some other factor.

Large numbers of cases are filtered out of the court system through prosecutor's discretionary decisions. Approximately 90% of people arraigned on an indictment plead guilty and thus do not have a trial. Various factors influence how and when cases are filtered out of the system before trial. Most cases pass through a process that operates somewhat like an assembly line.

The defense attempts to use motions to its advantage by, for example, seeking to suppress evidence or to learn about the prosecutor's case. A motion is an application to a court requesting an order be issued to bring about a specified action. Motions are filed in only about 10% of felony cases and 1% of misdemeanor cases. They might be filed when a defense attorney believes that evidence was obtained illegally, or for a number of other reasons.

V. BAIL: PRETRIAL RELEASE

Bail is a sum of money or property specified by the judge that will be posted by the defendant as a condition of pretrial release and that will be forfeited if the defendant does not appear in court for scheduled hearings. Bail is a mechanism to permit presumptively innocent defendants to avoid loss of liberty pending the outcome of the case. The Eighth Amendment to the U.S. Constitution forbids excessive bail but does not establish a right to bail. Congress and some states have reformed bail's underlying purpose (i.e., return of the defendant) to allow preventive detention in order to permit holding some defendants in jail without bail, especially if they might pose a danger to the community upon release

A. The Reality of the Bail System
   The issue of bail may arise at the police station, during an initial court appearance (misdemeanor), or at the arraignment (felony). The amount of bail is normally based on the judge's perception of the seriousness of the crime and the defendant's record. Because bail is set within 24 to 48 hours after arrest, there is little time to seek background information about the defendant. Within particular localities, judges develop, in effect, standard rates for particular offenses.

   To post bail, a prisoner must give the court some form of monetary surety, usually cash, property, or bond from a bonding company. For lesser offenses, may be released on their own recognizance (ROR). The bail system favors affluent defendants who have enough money for bail and disadvantages poor defendants who may end up stuck in jail.

B. Bail Bondsmen
   Bondsmen provide bail for defendants for a fee, ranging from 5 to 10% of the bail amount. They typically use their own assets or those of an insurance company. Bondsmen are licensed by the state and choose their own clients, and may set their own collateral requirements. They may track down and return bail jumpers without extradition and by force if necessary.

   Bondsmen exert influence on the court through their ability to cooperate with police officers who recommend their services rather than those of other bondsmen. In return, bondsmen may refuse to provide bail for defendants whom the police would like to keep in jail. Bondsmen are private, profit-seeking actors with no official connection to the court who can, in effect, nullify a judge's decision that a defendant is eligible for release on bail.

Positive impact of bondsmen is to maintain social control over defendant during the pretrial period; remind clients about court dates; put pressure on defendant's friends and family to make sure defendant appears for court; bondsmen may help prepare defendants for ultimate outcome and may encourage and facilitate guilty pleas by using their experience to accurately predict how specific judges will sentence for particular crimes; help to relieve pressure on overcrowded jails by assisting with release of some defendants.

C. Setting Bail
Bail is sometimes set according to a set schedule for misdemeanors, but other factors such as severity of offense are usually taken into account for felonies. Judges also consider the characteristics of the defendant in setting bail. The police may be particularly active in attempting to influence the bail decision if they do not want to see a particular defendant released. Bail amounts also vary by race and class.

D. Reforming the Bail System
Reformers have been concerned that judges have too much discretion in setting bail, and the fact that the poor are discriminated against in setting bail. The following alternatives to bail have been suggested:

1. **Citation**: a citation or summons issued by a police officer. This method avoids booking, arrest, bail, and jailing. In some jurisdictions, only a small percentage of offenders fail to appear. Bail bondsmen have opposed this method as a threat to their livelihood.

2. **Release on Own Recognizance (ROR)**: Court personnel talk to defendants about their family ties and roots in the community (i.e., job, family, prior record, length of time in local area), then recommend ROR if sufficient contacts exist.

3. **Ten Percent Cash Bail**: many judges are unwilling to use ROR, so some states have instituted policy in which defendants deposit a percentage of bail as collateral. When they return to court, they receive 90% of this back.

4. **Bail Guidelines**: guidelines developed to establish criteria that will produce more consistency in bail decisions

5. **Preventive Detention**: called a basic threat to liberties by civil libertarians, but approved by Congress for federal court in Bail Reform Act of 1984. Judges can consider whether defendant poses a danger to community and decide not to set bail. The decision is made at a hearing, at which the prosecution contends that there is risk of flight, a risk that defendant will obstruct justice by threatening a witness or juror. The defendant must be accused of crime of violence or one punishable by life imprisonment or death. The Supreme Court has upheld the use of preventive detention as constitutional (*United States v. Salerno and Cafero*).

VI. PRETRIAL DETENTION

Defendants awaiting trial are typically held in jail. About half of the 600,000 people in jail at any given moment are in pretrial detention while the other half are serving short sentences; nearly all are poor. Conditions in jails may be much worse than those in prisons, given the transient population and constant overcrowding.

The ultimate outcome of a case is affected by whether the defendant was held in jail. Jailed defendants may look guiltier in the eyes of the judge and jury when escorted into court by guards rather than by friends and family. Some research shows a greater likelihood of conviction and incarceration for those jailed prior to trial, but it is difficult to know if the pretrial detention itself increases the severity of the outcome.

REVIEW OF KEY TERMS

Fill in the appropriate term for each statement

jurisdiction
trial court of limited jurisdiction
trial court of general jurisdiction
appellate court
drug courts
nonpartisan election
partisan election
adversarial system
inquisitorial system
merit selection
arraignment
motion
bail
citation
release on own recognizance (ROR)
preventive detention
United States v. Salerno and Cafero (1987)

1. _Partisan election_ is a judicial selection method in which the selection of candidates is controlled by the political parties.

2. _trial court of limited jurisdiction_ is the trial court that handles specific categories of less serious cases.

3. _drug court_ include drug testing and counseling requirements for substance abusers.

4. A court's _jurisdiction_ defines the boundaries of its authority over people, places, and types of legal actions.

5. _merit selection_ is a method of selecting judges that attempts to remove partisan politics, but merely replaces those politics with the political conflicts within the legal profession.

6. _appellate court_ is the level of the judicial hierarchy that looks for errors by trial judges.

7. The United States court system uses the _adversarial system_ to try cases.

8. _trial court of general jurisdiction_ is the trial court that handles felony cases.

9. _nonpartisan election_ is a method of selecting judges that attempts but fails to remove politics because, for example, so many judges initially gain their judgeships through gubernatorial mid-term appointments to fill vacancies created by deaths and retirements.

10. In an _inquisitorial system_, judges participate in investigation of cases.

11. _Arraignment_ is the stage in the criminal justice process in which formal charges are read in court and a plea is entered.

12. In _United States v Salerno and Cafero_, the Supreme Court decided that preventive detention is not a violation of constitutional rights.

13. _motion_ is a tactical tool employed by defense attorneys to challenge and discover aspects of the prosecution's case.

14. _Bail_ is to ensure that a defendant returns to court for subsequent proceedings.

15. _Citation_ is a method of summoning defendants to return to court without using the system's resources for arrests and jailing.

16. _release on own recognizance_ permits defendants to be freed from jail without paying bail and therefore reduces the harsh effects of bail upon the poor.

17. _prevention detention_ results when bail is not set and a defendant remains in jail because he or she has been determined to be a danger to the community.

GENERAL PRACTICE QUESTIONS

Although reformers hoped that 1. _merit selection_ would remove the influence of politics from the selection judges, there is still political maneuvering in the formation of the selection committee and there is the potential for politics in campaigning against judges who must stand for 2. _retention election_ during their terms on the bench.

After the 3. _Bail Reform Act of 1984_ permitted the federal courts to keep defendants in custody as a form of 4. _prevention detention_, the Supreme Court approved the constitutionality of the practice in the case of 5. _Bail Reform Act of 1984_ despite widespread concerns that the practice developed by the statute was a constitutional violation of the 6. _Eighth Amendment_.

Because they have a financial interest in the maintenance of the current bail system, 7. _bail bondsmen_ prefer not to see defendants freed without bail through 8. _Release on own recognizance_ and they especially object to reforms, such as 9. _ten percent cash bail_, which directly imitate their business practices and therefore cut them out of the system.

SELF-TEST SECTION

MULTIPLE CHOICE QUESTIONS

9.1.   What is CASA?
   a)   Court of Appeals for San Antonio
   b)   Court of Alabama State of Appeals
   c)   Court Appointed Special Advocates
   d)   Children Advocates Serving America
   e)   Counsel Appointed by Special Attorneys

9.2.   Which of the following is a goal of a unified court system?
   a)   eliminating overlapping and conflicting jurisdictional boundaries
   b)   creating a hierarchical and centralized court structure
   c)   having the courts funded by state government instead of local counties and cities
   d)   creating a separate civil service personnel system run by a state court administrator
   e)   all of the above

9.3.   Which of the following is NOT a reason to become a judge?
   a)   perform public service
   b)   gain political power
   c)   gain prestige
   d)   gain wealth
   e)   all of the above are reasons to become a judge

9.4.   Which of the following is a seldom-recognized function of most judges?
   a)   negotiating
   b)   managing the courthouse
   c)   adjudicating
   d)   all of the above
   e)   none of the above

9.5.   In Europe, how does a person become a judge?
   a)   special training in law school
   b)   elected to office
   c)   judicial lottery
   d)   appointed by the old boys network
   e)   inherit a judgeship

9.6.   Which statement best describes U. S. election campaigns for lower court judgeships?
   a)   low-key contests with great controversy
   b)   high-profile contests with little controversy
   c)   high-profile contests with great controversy
   d)   low-key contests with little controversy
   e)   there are no elections for lower court judgeships in the United States

9.7.   Which of the following U.S. Supreme Court decisions invalidated Minnesota's ethics rule that forbade judicial candidates from announcing their views on disputed legal or political issues?
   a)   *Buckley v. Valeo* (1976)
   b)   *Republican Party of Minnesota v. White* (2002)
   c)   *Rutan v. Republican Party* (1990)
   d)   *FEC v. Ventura* (2000)
   e)   *Minnesota Republican Party v. Wellstone* (2001)

9.8.   How often do acquittals occur in urban felony cases?
   a)   frequently
   b)   sometimes
   c)   rare
   d)   never
   e)   almost always

9.9.   How often are decisions made quickly about bail?
   a)   never
   b)   not very often
   c)   often
   d)   almost always
   e)   always

9.10.   Which of the following is a TRUE statement about courts in the United States?
   a)   courts are under pressure to limit the number of cases going to trial
   b)   courts are under pressure to limit the number of plea bargains
   c)   courts are under pressure to limit the number of persons releases on bail
   d)   all of the above are TRUE
   e)   all of the above are FALSE

9.11. What was the name of the two wealthy young brothers in California who were convicted of murdering their parents?
a) Gonzalez
b) Menendez
c) Arias
d) Hernandez
e) Gomez

9.12. What is the rate of conviction for offenses that a prosecutor decides to pursue?
a) very low rate of conviction
b) average rate of conviction
c) low rate of conviction
d) high rate of conviction
e) 100% rate of conviction

9.13. Which of the following is NOT a purpose of bail?
a) to ensure that the defendant appears in court for trial
b) to protect the community from further crimes that some defendants may commit while out on bail
c) to punish the defendant
d) all of the above are purposes of bail
e) none of the above are purposes of bail

9.14. When does the question of bail arise?
a) at the police station
b) at the initial court appearance
c) at the arraignment
d) all of the above
e) none of the above

9.15. When does the question of bail arise in most misdemeanor cases?
a) at the police station
b) at the initial court appearance
c) at the arraignment
d) at the opening arguments of the trial
e) in chambers between the attorney and the judge

9.16. When does the question of bail arise in most felony cases?
a) at the police station
b) at the initial court appearance
c) at the arraignment
d) at the opening arguments of the trial
e) in chambers between the attorney and the judge

9.17. Who usually sets bail for serious offenses?
a) police officer
b) prosecutor
c) public defender
d) judge
e) jury

9.18. Who usually sets bail for minor offenses?
a) police officer
b) prosecutor
c) public defender
d) judge
e) jury

9.19. Where is the right to representation by an attorney at bail hearings found in the Bill of Rights?
   a) Fifth Amendment
   b) Sixth Amendment
   c) Seventh Amendment
   d) Eighth Amendment
   e) there is no constitutional right to representation by an attorney at bail hearings

9.20. In 1998, how many felony suspects in the largest U. S. counties were unable to make bail or utilize the services of a bail bondsman to gain release?
   a) none
   b) 1,500
   c) 9,000
   d) 16,000
   e) 27,000

9.21. What is the usual fee charged by a bail bondsperson?
   a) 1 percent of the bail amount
   b) 5 to 10 percent of the bail amount
   c) 20 to 30 percent of the bail amount
   d) 40 to 50 percent of the bail amount
   e) 90 percent of the bail amount

9.22. What is the requirement for becoming a bail bondsperson?
   a) high school education
   b) college degree
   c) state license
   d) $100,000 cash as collateral
   e) there are no formal requirements

9.23. Which of the following is NOT true about bail bondspersons?
   a) they usually act in their own self-interest
   b) they usually have close relationships with police and correctional officials
   c) they slow the processing of cases
   d) they are required to be licensed by the state
   e) all of the above are TRUE

9.24. What determines the amount of bail set by the judge?
   a) the interactions of the judge, prosecutor, and defense attorney
   b) the interactions of the bailiff, jury, and defense attorney
   c) the interactions of the judge, clerk, and defendant
   d) the interactions of the judge, court reporter, and defense attorney
   e) the interactions of the judge, probation officer, and bail bondsperson

TRUE/FALSE QUESTIONS

9.1. __T__ Most criminal cases are heard at the state level.

9.2. __T__ Native Americans have their own court systems in the United States.

9.3. __F__ State court systems do not have appellate courts.

9.4. __T__ The United States Supreme Court has the power to decide which cases it wants to hear.

9.5. __F__ The American state court systems are centralized.

9.6. __T__ The larger a state's population, the lower the portion of court funds that come from the state government.

9.7. __F__ The American Bar Association has prohibited the control of court jobs by political parties and judges.

9.8. __T__ Under the adversary system of justice in the U. S., each side (prosecution and defense) is represented by an attorney.

9.9. __F__ Under the inquisitorial system, the judge takes a very passive role in deliberations.

9.10. __F__ The work of a judge is limited to presiding at trials.

9.11. __T__ Judges are given considerable discretion in performing their duties throughout the judicial process.

9.12. __T__ Some judges are responsible for managing the administrative affairs at their courthouses.

9.13. __F__ The selection process of judges is nonpolitical.

9.14. __F__ Judicial elections are characterized by high voter turnout.

9.15. __F__ The bail bondsperson does not profit from his position.

9.16. __F__ The Eighth Amendment created the bail bondsperson as a key actor within the criminal justice system.

9.17. __F__ A person cannot be denied bail.

9.18. __T__ The bail bondsperson is a private businessman.

9.19. __F__ Bail is always set by a judge.

9.20. __F__ A person cannot be deprived of their freedom until they are found guilty in a court of law.

ANSWER KEY

Key Terms
1. partisan election
2. trial court of limited jurisdiction
3. drug courts
4. jurisdiction
5. merit selection
6. appellate court
7. adversarial system
8. trial court of general jurisdiction
9. nonpartisan election
10. inquisitorial system
11. arraignment
12. *United States v. Salerno and Cafero*
13. motion
14. bail
15. citation
16. release on own recognizance (ROR)
17. preventive detention

Key People
1. John Rigas
2. Ricardo Armstrong
3. Hernando Williams

General Practice Questions
1. merit selection
2. retention election
3. Bail Reform Act of 1984
4. preventive detention
5. Bail Reform Act of 1984
6. Eighth Amendment
7. bail bondsmen
8. release on own recognizance
9. ten percent cash bail

Multiple Choice
9.1.	C
9.2.	E
9.3.	D
9.4.	B
9.5.	A
9.6.	D
9.7.	B
9.8.	C
9.9.	C
9.10.	A
9.11.	B
9.12.	D
9.13.	C
9.14.	D
9.15.	B
9.16.	C
9.17.	D
9.18.	A

9.19.   E
9.20.   D
9.21.   B
9.22.   C
9.23.   C
9.24.   A

<u>True/False</u>
9.1.   T
9.2.   T
9.3.   F
9.4.   T
9.5.   F
9.6.   T
9.7.   F
9.8.   T
9.9.   F
9.10.   F
9.11.   T
9.12.   T
9.13.   F
9.14.   F
9.15.   F
9.16.   F
9.17.   F
9.18.   T
9.19.   F
9.20.   F

WORKSHEET 9.1: BAIL

Imagine that you are a judge responsible for setting bail. For each of the following cases, indicate whether you would order Release on Own Recognizance (ROR), set bail at some specific amount [state the amount], or deny bail and order preventive detention. Provide brief comments that explain each decision.

1. Jane Williams is a new assistant professor of literature at the local university. She is twenty-six years old. She has no relatives in the area and her family lives 500 miles away in the city where she went to college for the eight years it took to earn her undergraduate and graduate degrees. She is charged with fraud in obtaining $50,000 in student loans during the previous three years by lying about her income and assets on student loan application forms. Seven years earlier she pleaded guilty in her hometown to a misdemeanor charge of underage drinking.

_____

_____

_____

_____

_____

2. Karl Schmidt is charged with attempted rape. He is accused of attacking a woman in his car while giving her a ride home from the bar where he met her. He is a twenty-two year old, rookie police officer [now suspended from the force] who has lived in the city for his entire life and has no prior record.

_____

_____

_____

_____

3. Susan Claussen is charged with theft for ordering and eating dinner at an expensive restaurant, and then leaving without paying the bill. She has been charged with and entered guilty pleas to the offense on five previous occasions over the past three years. She has been placed on probation several times and served one thirty-day jail sentence. She is unemployed and a life-long resident of the city. She lives with her parents.

_____

_____

_____

_____

WORKSHEET 9.2: JUDICIAL SELECTION

Respond to the following questions in light of the text's discussion of the importance of judicial selection methods. Think about the implications and consequences of each selection methods (Gubernatorial Appointment, Legislative Appointment, Partisan Election, Nonpartisan Election, Merit Selection)

1. What are the four most important qualities that we should look for in the people we select to be judges?

_____

_____

_____

_____

2. How do we know which people possess these qualities?

_____

_____

_____

3. Which judicial selection method would provide the best means to identify and select the people who possess these qualities?

_____

_____

_____

_____

4. What are the drawbacks to this judicial selection method?

_____

_____

_____

_____

5. Which judicial selection method is used in the state where you live or go to school? Why do you think that this state uses this selection method instead of one of the other methods?

_____

_____

_____

PROSECUTION AND DEFENSE

OUTLINE

- The Prosecutorial System
- The Defense Attorney: Image and Reality

CHAPTER 10
PROSECUTION AND DEFENSE

LEARNING OBJECTIVES

After covering the material in this chapter, students should understand:

1.   the decentralized organization of prosecution in the United States

2.   the significant discretionary power of prosecutors to make unsupervised, low visibility decisions that shape criminal justice outcomes

3.   the exchange relations between prosecutors and other actors that affect prosecutors' decisions (e.g., police, victims, court, community)

4.   the prosecutor's dilemma of seeking to win cases for the state while also ensuring that justice is served

5.   the role conceptions of prosecutors (trial counsel for police, house counsel for police, representative of the court, and elected officials)

6.   the nature of the accusatory process and the models for prosecutorial decision making: Legal Sufficiency, System Efficiency, and Trial Sufficiency

7.   the Supreme Court's requirement for the appointment of defense counsel for indigent defendants facing incarceration

8.   the role of the defense attorney as client-counselor and agent-mediator, and the environment of criminal defense work

9.   the characteristics and weaknesses of the three systems for indigent defense: assigned counsel, contract counsel, and public defender; and comparison of effectiveness of private versus public defense

10.   the issue of attorney competence and standards for assessing the ineffective assistance of counsel.

CHAPTER SUMMARY

American prosecutors at all levels have considerable discretion to determine how to handle criminal cases. There is no higher authority over most prosecutors that can overrule a decision to decline to prosecute (*nolle prosequi*) or to pursue multiple counts against a defendant. The prosecutor can play a variety of roles, including trial counsel for the police, house counsel for the police, representative of the court, and elected official.

Prosecutors' decisions and actions are affected by their exchange relationships with many other important actors and groups, including police, judges, victims and witnesses, and the public. Three primary models of prosecutors' decision-making policies are legal sufficiency, system efficiency, and trial sufficiency. The image of defense attorneys portrayed in the media as courtroom advocates is often vastly different from the reality of pressured, busy negotiators constantly involved in bargaining with the prosecutor over guilty plea agreements. Relatively few private defense attorneys make significant incomes from criminal work, but larger numbers of private attorneys accept court appointments to handle indigent defendants' cases quickly for relatively low fees. Three primary methods for providing attorneys to represent indigent defendants are appointed counsel, contract counsel, and public defenders. Defense attorneys must often wrestle with difficult working conditions and uncooperative clients as they seek to provide representation, usually in the plea negotiation process. The quality of representation provided to criminal defendants is a matter of significant concern, but U.S. Supreme Court rulings have made it difficult for convicted offenders to prove that their attorneys did not provide a competent defense.

CHAPTER OUTLINE

I. THE PROSECUTORIAL SYSTEM

United States attorneys are federal prosecutors, appointed by the President in each of 94 districts around the country. They are responsible for prosecuting federal crimes. Attorneys General are elected in most states. In Alaska, Delaware, and Rhode Island, they direct all local prosecutions as well as state prosecutions. County Prosecutors have a total of 2,341 offices in the country. These are the primary locations of prosecutions, and these posts are elected (except in Connecticut and New Jersey) and therefore heavily involved in local politics. The number of assistant prosecutors will vary by size of office (as many as 500 in Los Angeles). Assistants usually young attorneys who use their position to gain trial experience.

A. Politics and Prosecution
The process and organization of prosecution is inescapably political. For example, the appointment of deputies may serve the political party's purposes. In addition, the decision about whether to prosecute may include consideration of prosecutor's or political party's electoral interests. Historically, some groups (e.g., racial minorities) received harsher treatment when prosecutors used their discretion to pursue their cases while not pursuing others' cases.

B. The Prosecutor's Influence
The low visibility of prosecutors' decisions increases their power in making discretionary decisions—voters cannot easily hold elected prosecutors accountable because they do not know the range and nature of prosecutors' decisions. State statutes generally state that all crimes shall be prosecuted, but it is really up to the prosecutor to decide if and how that will really happen. Prosecutors may decline to prosecute crimes if they believe that the local community no longer considers such behavior worthy of punishment, even if the law is still on the books. Because most prosecutors are in smaller counties, they can be highly influenced by local public opinion—especially with respect to the discretionary enforcement of such things as victimless crimes (such as gambling and drug use).

C. The Prosecutor's Roles
"Prosecutor's Dilemma": as lawyers for the state, prosecutors are expected to do everything in their power to win the public's case, but as officers of the court and members of the local legal profession, they are also obligated to see that justice is done. This environment can create a "prosecution complex": prosecutors can come to consider themselves instruments of law enforcement although they are supposed to represent all people, including the accused. Prosecutors sometimes make mistakes, but they are immune from lawsuits if they prosecute innocent people.

The prosecutor's role is defined by a variety of factors in addition to formal professional responsibilities—individual prosecutor's personality, the political and social environment in which the prosecutor operates, the individual prosecutor's expectations concerning the attitudes of other actors. There are four role conceptions found among prosecutors: Trial counsel for the police, house counsel for the police, representative of the court, and elected official.

D. Discretion of the Prosecutor
Autonomy, lack of supervision, and low visibility of decisions give prosecutors broad discretionary authority to make decisions at each step of the criminal justice process. Prosecutors have the discretion to: file or not file charges, determine the type of charge, and determine the number of charges for an offender.

Discovery is the legal requirement that information be made available to the defense attorney. It is part of the prosecutor's obligation to act impartially in seeking justice rather than in seeking only convictions on behalf of the state. Prosecutors may also drop charges (*nolle prosequi* or nol. pros.), which essentially dismisses the criminal case against an offender.

E. Key Relationships of the Prosecutor
The decisions made by the prosecuting attorney's office reflect the personal and organization clients with whom it interacts. Precise decisions and procedures will vary with each environment.

1. **Police**: Prosecutors are dependent on the police to bring them cases that are strong enough to prosecute. They depend on the investigative function of the police, and they can affect police workload by returning cases for further investigation or by refusing to approve arrest warrants. Police requests to prosecute may be turned down by the prosecutor's office based on caseload or due to poor evidence.

2. **Victims and Witnesses**: Victims and witnesses are vital components of evidence in prosecuting criminal cases. Prosecutors must make important decisions about the credibility of victims and witnesses, as that affects the likelihood that cases will be prosecuted.

   The relationship between the victim and offender can sometimes play a part in the decision to prosecute. There are significantly higher conviction rates in stranger crimes than in non-stranger crimes, in which the victim may decide not to cooperate with the prosecution. Some victim advocates want victim input to be weighted more heavily in prosecutions.

3. **Judges and Courts**: Sentencing history of each judge may influence prosecutors' decisions about which charges to file and whether to prosecute. The sentencing behavior of judges must be predictable in order for plea bargaining to run smoothly. Prosecutors can often control the timing and flow of cases, and they can seek delays if it suits their interests (it may help to let public attention of the case diminish prior to prosecution).

4. **The Community**: Like other elected officials, prosecutors cannot remain unresponsive to public opinion—otherwise, they may risk losing their jobs. The public is especially influential in "gray areas" of law in which full enforcement is not expected (e.g., does community want prostitution, gambling, and pornography to be fully prosecuted, or is there public toleration for many activities that are ostensibly illegal?). In general, however, public attention to the criminal justice system is low. Prosecutors are often concerned with avoiding decisions that will generate public reactions. Prosecutors' decisions are also affected by their relationships with news media, state and federal officials, legislators, and political party officials.

F. Decision-Making Policies

1. **Implementing Prosecution Policy**: There are three policy models used by prosecutors: the legal sufficiency model, in which prosecutors must determine if there is enough evidence for prosecution; the system efficiency model, in which prosecutors aim for speedy and early disposition of a case (possibly through plea bargaining); and the trial sufficiency model, in which cases are accepted only when there is enough evidence to ensure conviction.

2. **Case Evaluation**: The accusatory process consists of the series of activities that take place from the moment of arrest and booking through formal charging. This process involves the activities of police, grand jury, bail agency, and the court linked with the activities of the prosecuting attorney. Formal charges filed with the court through an indictment (if issued by a grand jury), or an information if the prosecutor files the charges directly. The prosecutor's decision may be influenced by the office's charging policies as well as the prosecutor's sense of individualized justice in a particular case.

II. THE DEFENSE ATTORNEY: IMAGE AND REALITY

The defense attorney represents individuals accused of committing a crime. Defense attorneys typically handle a large caseload and process them quickly with low pay. They are sometimes considered 'partners' with the prosecutor because of the bargaining that usually takes place with the prosecutor to arrive at plea bargains.

A. The Role of the Defense Attorney

Criminal defense lawyers are essential advocates on behalf of defendants through the application of pretrial investigative skills, verbal skills in plea negotiations and courtroom proceedings, and ability to creatively question prosecution witnesses. In addition to advocacy functions, defense counsel provides psychological support to the defendant and the defendant's family.

B. The Realities of the Defense Attorney

The provision of defense counsel does not automatically create the adversarial nature assumed by the due process model. Defense attorneys' actual behavior will depend on exchange relations and organizational setting of the court. Defense attorneys may, in fact, act as mediators between the defendant, judge, and prosecutor. By facilitating the smooth processing of cases, the defense counsel may be able to bargain for a better deal for his client.

C. The Environment of Criminal Practice

Much of the service provided by defense counsel involves preparing clients and relatives for possible negative outcomes of cases. Defense counsel's "guilty knowledge" may be psychological burden—the defense counsel is the only judicial actor to view the defendant in the context of social environment and family ties.

The low pay for such work is a key factor in the environment: defense attorneys must make every effort to obtain payment ahead of time, including trying to get payment from defendant's relatives if defendant does not pay. This problem creates incentives to negotiate quick pleas, since they may pay the same as a three-day trial.

1. **Relationship to Court Officials**: Defense attorneys work hard to negotiate pleas. They maintain close relationships with police, prosecutors, judges, and other officials, which compromises their independence. Many expect the defense counsel and prosecutor to be 'enemies', but they must work together to resolve cases.

2. **Relationship with Clients**: Realistically, the goals of the defense attorney focus on settling cases, not necessarily protecting their clients' due process rights or trying to get their charges dropped.

D. Counsel for Indigents

The Supreme Court requirement that counsel be appointed early in criminal process for all defendants facing incarceration has drastically raised the percentage of defendants relying on publicly supported criminal defense lawyers. In some jurisdictions, 90 percent of accused must be provided with counsel. Unfortunately, the quality of representation for the poor is often questioned.

1. **Ways of Providing Indigents with Counsel**
    a. *Assigned Counsel*: the court appoints a private practice attorney to represent indigent defendants. This is widely used in small cities and rural areas, but also used in some urban areas. Courts may use an ad hoc system to assign counsel, in which a judge selects lawyers at random from a prepared list or appoints lawyers who are present in the courtroom; or a coordinated system, in which a court administrator oversees the appointment of counsel.

    Attorney competence is sometimes questionable. Lawyers seeking appointments may be recent law school grads who need income or else attorneys who were not successful in more lucrative areas of legal practice. Fee schedules may be so low as to lead assigned counsel to encourage their clients to plead guilty; spares attorney from prospect of working hard on a case for very little money. Profitability comes from doing a large number of cases as quickly as possible.

b. *Contract System*: currently in use in about 200 counties, the government enters into a contract with a law firm, individual attorney, or non-profit organization that will provide representation for all indigent defendants. The terms of each contract may vary, but commonly there is a set amount that a law firm receives under the contract. It is also common to have fixed-price contracts that pay a certain amount for each case.

c. *Public Defender*: Public defenders are salaried government employees who handle indigents' criminal cases. Public defender systems predominate in large cities, and are typically overburdened with cases.

Public defenders may tend to routinize decision-making in the face of overwhelming caseloads. They may have little time to investigate cases or to interview clients. They may negotiate with prosecutors concerning pleas in groups of cases simultaneously.
Public defenders often assigned to a "zone" or stage in the criminal process rather than assigned to one-on-one representation. One public defender may handle preliminary hearings, another may handle arraignments, and another may handle trials (if there is a trial). The dispersion of responsibility may create a routinization of defense work and lose the special elements of individualized representation.

E. Private Versus Public Defense

Recent studies have cast doubt on previous assumptions that public defenders enter more guilty pleas than did privately retained and assigned counsel. Difficult to compare with retained counsel because they may serve only upper-income clients charged with white-collar crime, drug dealing, or involvement in organized crime. Findings from research indicate that the types of pleas negotiated, case dispositions, and length of sentences by different types of attorneys.

F. Attorney Competence

The right to counsel may be meaningless if the attorney is incompetent or ineffective. It is difficult to define inadequate representation, especially when many defense attorneys struggle with high caseloads or make tactical decisions which turn out to be unsuccessful.

The Supreme Court has decided that attorneys must demonstrate "reasonable competence" if issues of inadequate representation arise. Poor performance can only be considered legally defective if a reasonably competent attorney would not have acted as the trial counsel did, and specific errors resulted in an unfair proceeding and an unreliable result.

REVIEW OF KEY TERMS

Fill in the appropriate term for each statement

United States Attorney
state attorney general
prosecuting attorney
count
discovery
nolle prosequi
legal sufficiency
system efficiency
trial sufficiency
accusatory process
defense attorney
assigned counsel
contract counsel
public defender

1. _public defender_ is a salaried government employee who represents indigent criminal defendants in most large cities.

2. _defense attorney_ is the lawyer who represents the accused in the criminal justice process.

3. _assigned counsel_ is a private attorney among a list of attorneys appointed to represent an indigent defendant for a relatively small fee.

4. _contract counsel_ is a private attorney who successfully submits a bid to represent all indigent defendants in a county for one year.

5. _United States attorney_ is the prosecutor responsible for federal crimes in each federal district court.

6. _accusatory process_ is the series of activities from arrest through the filing formal charges.

7. _Court_ is an individual charge filed against a defendant.

8. _legal sufficiency model_ involves the pursuit of charges in any cases for which there is the minimum legal evidence against a defendant.

9. _trial sufficiency model_ involves considerations of whether the prosecutor can win the case in front of a judge and jury.

10. _nolle prosequi_ is the discretionary decision to decline to initiate a prosecution.

11. _attorney general_ is an elected official who is responsible for the legal duties of a state.

12. _discovery_ is the process that permits defense attorneys to gain access to information possessed by the prosecutor.

13. _prosecuting attorney_ is regarded as the most powerful figure in the criminal justice system.

14. _system efficiency model_ involves case screening and other decision making that emphasizes the limited resources possessed by the prosecutor and the criminal justice system generally.

GENERAL PRACTICE QUESTIONS

In many counties and cities that use the 1. assigned counsel system for representing 2. indigent defendants, virtually any attorney can have the opportunity to participate. By contrast, in some other countries, attorneys are carefully selected because of the emphasis on quality. In the United States, there is quality control in some locations such as in Detroit, Michigan, where a panel of judges approves only a select list of applicants to participate in the 75% of cases handled in this manner.

Larger cities tend to use the 3. public defender system, and some places have a state-wide system in place to use this mechanism. Although many observers believe this approach provides the highest quality representation because of the attorneys' interest and expertise, 4. low pay can lead to personnel turnover and 5. large caseloads can prevent careful attention to individual cases.

Because prosecutors depend on the police for 6. investigative resources, prosecutors must maintain positive relationships with the police and therefore use organizational considerations when making decisions about charging defendants.

Prosecutors who are sensitive to 7. community values may decide not to pursue some kinds of crimes because their role as 8. elected official leads them to seek to please the voters.

Prosecutors who adopt the role of 9. _trial counsel for police_ run the greatest risk of having a 10. _prosecution complex_ (or a prosecutor's bias) that leads them to ignore their obligation to see that justice is done in each case.

Prosecutors who apply pragmatic considerations can use their 11. _discretionary power_ in order to move defendants out of the criminal justice system through 12. _diversion_ .

Because 13. _exchange relation_ influence a prosecutor's decisions about charging and plea bargaining, victims who refuse to cooperate in providing testimony against defendants can lead prosecutors to end the case by entering a notation of 14. _nolle prosequi_ .

Prosecutors have adopted the 15. _Trial Sufficiency Model_ when their decisions are based on whether or not they can win the case in front of a judge or jury. They are unlikely to use this decision-making model if they view their role as 16. _trial counsel for police_ by primarily reflecting law enforcement views in the courtroom and therefore being less discriminating about which cases to push forward.

SELF-TEST SECTION

MULTIPLE CHOICE QUESTIONS

10.1. Federal criminal laws are prosecuted by:
    a)   the state attorney general
    b)   the United States Attorney
    c)   the local police
    d)   the prosecuting attorney
    e)   the Federal Bureau of Investigation

10.2. In all states except Connecticut and New Jersey, prosecutors are:
    a)   elected
    b)   appointed
    c)   represented
    d)   prosecuted
    e)   regurgitated

10.3. The vast majority of criminal cases are handled in...
    a)   city level offices of the prosecuting attorney
    b)   state level offices of the prosecuting attorney
    c)   township level offices of the prosecuting attorney
    d)   county level offices of the prosecuting attorney
    e)   federal offices of the prosecuting attorney

10.4. How does each state obtain an attorney general?
    a)   gubernatorial appointment
    b)   state legislative appointment
    c)   state bar appointment
    d)   state supreme court appointment
    e)   election by the voters

10.5. Which of the following best describes the role of prosecutors within the criminal justice system?
    a)   prosecutors are involved in every aspect of the criminal justice system
    b)   prosecutors are only involved with adjudication
    c)   prosecutors are concerned with pre-trial processes and adjudication
    d)   prosecutors define their own roles for themselves
    e)   state law defines the role of a prosecutor

10.6. Which of the following is TRUE concerning prosecutors in Germany?
- a) they always act against a criminal suspect
- b) they are immune from public opinion
- c) they are elected
- d) all of the above are TRUE
- e) all of the above are FALSE

10.7. When are prosecutors less inclined to drop charges?
- a) if the damage (monetary value or physical injuries) was considerable
- b) if the suspect had previously been convicted
- c) if the evidence is strong
- d) all of the above
- e) none of the above

10.8. What type of relationship exists between the prosecutor and police?
- a) conflictual relationship
- b) informal relationship
- c) exchange relationship
- d) no relationship at all
- e) unethical relationship

10.9. Which of the following traits of a victim will affect whether a prosecutor pursues charges?
- a) criminal record of the victim
- b) victim's role in his or her own victimization
- c) credibility of the victim
- d) all of the above
- e) none of the above

10.10. If a prosecutor decides not to prosecute a case, this is known as a:
- a) *means rea*
- b) *actus rea*
- c) *nolo contendere*
- d) *e pluribus unum*
- e) *nolle prosequi*

10.11. How can victim characteristics affect a criminal case?
- a) if the victim is poor, they might not be able to afford paying the prosecutor for his or her services
- b) if the victim is wealthy, the prosecutor may ask for a bribe
- c) if the victim has a bad reputation, they may not be taken seriously by the judge/jury
- d) if the victim did not witness the crime, they cannot testify
- e) if the victim was not injured, no crime has been committed

10.12. What is the name given to the proposed constitutional amendment that would require prosecutors to keep victims informed on the progress of criminal cases?
- a) Informed Progress Amendment
- b) Victims' Rights Amendment
- c) Victims' Due Process Amendment
- d) Anti-Defendants' Rights Amendment
- e) Criminal Rights for Victims Amendment

10.13. What did this woman do (pictured below) to receive national media attention as well as the attention of the criminal justice system?

   a) Forged checks for wedding supplies
   b) Sent out stolen wedding invitations
   c) Tried to marry more than one man
   d) Lied about being kidnapped to avoid her wedding
   e) Told her fiancé she killed a man

10.14. According to studies, what is the public's level of attention on the criminal justice system?
   a) extremely high
   b) high
   c) moderate
   d) low
   e) the public does not pay attention at all

10.15. Which of the following is TRUE about most defense attorneys?
   a) defense attorneys usually earn high fees from wealthy clients
   b) defense attorneys work in a pleasant environment
   c) defense attorneys work very hard
   d) all of the above are TRUE
   e) all of the above are FALSE

10.16. What model involves prosecutors aiming at speedy and early disposition of a case?
   a) legal sufficiency model
   b) system efficiency
   c) trial sufficiency
   d) due control model
   e) crime process model

10.17. How many assistant prosecutors serve in a prosecutor's office?
   a) two
   b) five
   c) ten
   d) twenty
   e) it varies based upon the size of the office

10.18. At what stage is evidence presented to a grand jury made up of citizens who determine whether to issue a formal charge?
   a) arrest
   b) booking
   c) c)sentencing
   d) appeal
   e) indictment

10.19. What is the main reason for declining to prosecute a case?
    a)   lack of resources
    b)   insufficient evidence
    c)   politics
    d)   lack of prison space
    e)   defendant's lack of a criminal record

10.20. Based upon a study in Los Angeles County, which of the following is most likely to be prosecuted?
    a)   white female
    b)   African American female
    c)   Hispanic male
    d)   white male
    e)   Hispanic female

10.21. Which of the followings is NOT a basic duty of the defense attorney?
    a)   to save criminals from punishment
    b)   to protect constitutional rights
    c)   keep the prosecution honest in preparing and presenting cases
    d)   prevent innocent people from being convicted
    e)   all of the above are basic duties

10.22. Most criminal defense attorneys interact with...
    a)   upper class clients
    b)   middle class clients
    c)   lower class clients
    d)   upper and middle class clients
    e)   upper and lower class clients

10.23. The right to an attorney is found in the _____ Amendment.
    a)   First
    b)   Second
    c)   Fourth
    d)   Fifth
    e)   Sixth

10.24. When does the U. S. Supreme Court require that attorneys be appointed to defend suspects?
    a)   early in the criminal justice process
    b)   immediately prior to jury selection
    c)   immediately prior to a trial
    d)   immediately prior to sentencing
    e)   the Court has no such requirement

10.25. In the past three decades, the portion of defendants who are provided with counsel because they are indigent has...
    a)   remained constant
    b)   increased greatly
    c)   increased slightly
    d)   decreased slightly
    e)   decreased greatly

TRUE/FALSE QUESTIONS

10.1. ___F___ Prosecutors in America have very little discretion.

10.2. ___F___ Prosecutors in America are active only at the adjudication stage of the criminal justice process.

10.3. ___T___ Most prosecutors in America are elected officials.

10.4. ___T___ Prosecutors might not file charges if a victim is dressed shabbily.

10.5. ___T___ German prosecutors are civil servants who do not face the same public pressures as Americans.

10.6. ___T___ Most charges are filed by county prosecutors in the United States.

10.7. ___F___ The Fifth Amendment contains the right to counsel.

10.8. ___F___ Most criminal defense attorneys have wealthy clients.

10.9. ___T___ The public defender system started in Los Angeles in 1914.

10.10. ___T___ Studies show significantly higher conviction rates in stranger crimes than in non-stranger crimes.

10.11. ___T___ The main reason that charges are dropped by prosecutors is insufficient evidence.

10.12. ___F___ It is easy for convicted offenders to prove that their attorneys did not provide a competent defense.

10.13. ___T___ The system efficiency model emphasizes the speedy and early disposition of cases.

10.14. ___F___ Defense attorneys rarely have to visit jails.

10.15. ___T___ The sentencing history of a judge may influence prosecutors' decisions about which charges to file.

10.16. ___T___ Prosecutors are immune from lawsuits if they prosecute innocent people.

10.17. ___F___ The service provided by defense counsel usually involves preparing clients for positive outcomes of cases.

10.18. ___T___ Federal law enforcement maintains priority in prosecuting cases.

10.19. ___T___ Prosecutors may reduce charges in exchange for a plea bargain.

10.20. ___F___ If a person is too poor to pay for legal counsel, the state will not provide an attorney.

ANSWER KEY

Key Terms
1.   public defender
2.   defense attorney
3.   assigned counsel
4.   contract counsel
5.   United States Attorney
6.   accusatory process
7.   count
8.   Legal Sufficiency Model
9.   Trial Sufficiency Model
10.   *nolle prosequi*
11.   attorney general
12.   discovery
13.   prosecuting attorney
14.   System Efficiency Model

General Practice Questions
1.   assigned counsel
2.   indigent
3.   public defender
4.   low pay
5.   large caseloads
6.   investigative resources
7.   community values
8.   elected officials
9.   trial counsel for police
10.   prosecution complex
11.   discretionary power
12.   diversion
13.   exchange relations
14.   *nolle prosequi*
15.   Trial Sufficiency Model
16.   trial counsel for police

Multiple Choice
10.1.   B
10.2.   A
10.3.   D
10.4.   E
10.5.   A
10.6.   C
10.7.   D
10.8.   C
10.9.   D
10.10.   E
10.11.   C
10.12.   B
10.13.   D
10.14.   D
10.15.   C
10.16.   B
10.17.   E
10.18.   E
10.19.   B

10.20.   C
10.21.   A
10.22.   C
10.23.   E
10.24.   A
10.25.   B

True/False
10.1.   F
10.2.   F
10.3.   T
10.4.   T
10.5.   T
10.6.   T
10.7.   F
10.8.   F
10.9.   T
10.10.   T
10.11.   T
10.12.   F
10.13.   T
10.14.   F
10.15.   T
10.16.   T
10.17.   F
10.18.   T
10.19.   T
10.20.   F

WORKSHEET 10.1: PROSECUTION POLICIES

A man and a woman were brutally murdered with a knife. A bloody glove was found near the bodies. A second bloody glove with blood samples matching those of the victims was found two miles away outside the home of the woman's ex-husband. The ex-husband claims that he was at home preparing to leave for the airport at the time of the killings, but testimony from his driver indicates that he may not have been at his house until after the time that the killings occurred. The husband behaved erratically when he came under suspicion for the killing by disappearing for a day and then threatening to kill himself before surrendering to the police. He claims that he is innocent. The trial court in Los Angeles is backlogged with thousands of cases awaiting disposition.

Imagine that you are the prosecutor. Tell whether or not (and why) you would decide to prosecute based on the following prosecution policies. How would the facts of the case fit with each model?

LEGAL SUFFICIENCY _____

_____

_____

_____

_____

_____

_____

SYSTEM EFFICIENCY

_____

_____

_____

_____

_____

_____

TRIAL SUFFICIENCY

_____

_____

_____

_____

_____

WORKSHEET 10.2: COUNSEL FOR INDIGENTS

If you were given the responsibility for selecting the method of providing counsel for indigent defendants within your local courthouse, which method would you choose? For each method listed below, state whether you would select that method and explain why or why not?

ASSIGNED COUNSEL_____

_____

_____

_____

_____

CONTRACT COUNSEL_____

_____

_____

_____

_____

PUBLIC DEFENDER_____

_____

_____

_____

_____

Is there some other feasible alternative?_____

_____

_____

_____

_____

DETERMINATION OF GUILT

Plea Bargaining and Trials

OUTLINE

- The Courtroom: How It Functions
- Plea Bargaining
- Trial: The Exceptional Case
- Appeals

CHAPTER 11
DETERMINATION OF GUILT:
PLEA BARGAINING AND TRIALS

LEARNING OBJECTIVES

After covering the material in this chapter, students should understand:

1.   the impact of local legal culture on the courts

2.   the development and impact of courtroom workgroups

3.   the central role of plea bargaining and prosecutor' discretion in determining the outcomes of 90 percent of criminal cases

4.   the difference between implicit and explicit plea bargaining

5.   the role of exchange relationships in plea bargaining, the actors who influence plea negotiations, and the tactics used by those actors

6.   the justifications for and criticisms of plea bargaining

7.   the stages of the trial process

8.   the nature and prevalence of jury trials

9.   the functions of the jury

10.   the selection of juries and the experience of being a juror

CHAPTER SUMMARY

The outcomes in criminal cases are largely influenced by a court's local legal culture, which defines the "going rates" of punishment for various offenses. Courtroom workgroups composed of judges, prosecutors, and defense attorneys who work together to handle cases through cooperative plea bargaining processes. Most convictions are obtained through plea bargains, a process that exists because it fulfills the self-interest of prosecutors, judges, defense attorneys, and defendants. Plea bargaining is facilitated by exchange relations between prosecutors and defense attorneys. In many courthouses, there is little actual bargaining, as outcomes are determined through the implicit bargaining process of settling the facts and assessing the "going rate" of punishment according to the standards of the local legal culture.

The U.S. Supreme Court has endorsed plea bargaining and addressed legal issues concerning the voluntariness of pleas and the obligation of prosecutors and defendants to uphold agreements. Plea bargaining has been criticized for pressuring defendants to surrender their rights and reducing the sentences imposed on offenders. Through the dramatic courtroom battle of prosecutors and defense attorneys, trials are presumed to provide the best way to discover the truth about a criminal case. Less than 10 percent of cases go to trial, and half of those are typically bench trials in front of a judge, not jury trials. Cases typically go to trial because they involve defendants who are wealthy enough to pay attorneys to fight to the very end, they involve charges that are too serious to create incentives for plea bargaining. The U.S. Supreme Court has ruled that juries need not be made up of twelve members, and twelve-member juries can, if permitted by state law, convict defendants by a majority vote instead of a unanimous vote. Juries serve vital functions for society by preventing arbitrary action by prosecutors and judges, educating citizens about the justice system, symbolizing the rule of law, and involving citizens from diverse segments of the community in judicial decision making.

The jury selection process, especially in the formation of the jury pool and the exercise of peremptory challenges, often creates juries that do not fully represent all segments of a community. The trial process consists of a series of steps: jury selection, opening statements, presentation of prosecution's evidence, presentation of defense evidence, presentation of rebuttal witnesses, closing arguments, judge's jury instructions, and the jury's decision. Rules of evidence dictate what kinds of information may be presented in court for consideration by the jury. Types of evidence include are real evidence, demonstrative evidence, testimony, direct evidence, and circumstantial evidence.

Convicted offenders have the opportunity to appeal, although defendants who plead guilty--unlike those convicted through a trial--often have few grounds for an appeal.

Appeals focus on claimed errors of law or procedure in the investigation by police and prosecutors or the decisions by trial judges. Relatively few offenders win their appeals, and most of those simply gain an opportunity for a new trial, not release from jail or prison. After convicted offenders have used all of their appeals, they may file a habeas corpus petition to seek federal judicial review of claimed constitutional rights violations in their cases. Very few petitions are successful.

CHAPTER OUTLINE

I. THE COURTROOM: HOW IT FUNCTIONS
    Guilt or innocence determined in much the same fashion in every state, although the definitions of crimes and practices in setting punishments may vary significantly. The local legal culture, or the shared beliefs, attitudes, and norms of a court community, greatly influences events. This is why courts operate differently even though they have the same formal rules and procedures. The norms of a court community define the going rate, or the typical expected sentence for a crime.

    A. The Courtroom Workgroup
        Although our court system is adversarial, the actors in the courtroom (judge, prosecutor, defense attorney) tend to act more like a workgroup. They work together to process cases quickly while also trying to use fairness in sentencing. Judges tend to lead the workgroup, ensuring that everyone follows procedure. Different judges tend to define their roles differently in the workgroup.

    B. The Impact of Courtroom Workgroups
        Some research has indicated that felony cases tend to be handled differently in specific courts, but dispositions were remarkably similar once defendants reached the trial court (for those who did not plea bargain). Workgroups tend to have informal processes for screening cases, and dismissal rates can be high.

II. PLEA BARGAINING

    Plea bargaining is the most important step in the criminal justice process: generally 90% of felony defendants plead guilty. Plea bargaining helps to reduce heavy caseloads, moves cases along quickly, and reduces the time that pretrial detainees spend in jail. In addition, offenders who are processed quickly can move to treatment very quickly. Supporters of plea bargaining also note that plea bargaining helps to individualize punishment, and allows the punishment to "fit the crime".

    A. Exchange Relationships in Plea Bargaining

        Plea bargaining is a process that can sometimes take surprising amounts of time. One benefit of this process is that the prosecutor or defense attorney may find evidence that helps their respective cases.

B. Tactics of Prosecutor and Defense

One common tactic used by prosecutors is the multi-count indictment. Even when they cannot prove all of the charges in the indictment, it puts greater pressure on defendant to plead guilty and gives prosecutor more items to negotiate away. On the other hand, defense attorneys may threaten to move ahead with a jury trial or threaten delays, during which witnesses' memories may fade. However, other defense attorneys feel more effective bargaining on friendly basis rather than trying to pin down or threaten the prosecutor.

Both prosecutors and defense attorneys are dependent on cooperation from defendants and judges. Judges may be reluctant to interfere with plea agreements to avoid jeopardizing future exchange relationships. Prosecutors and defense attorneys often consult with judges to be sure about what sentence will result from a guilty plea, but judges possess the power to reject the recommended sentence.

C. Pleas without Bargaining

Guilty pleas may not result from formal negotiations. In some courthouses, prosecutor, defense attorney, and sometimes judge talk simply to settle the facts in the case. (i.e., was it really an assault or just a pushing and shoving match?); when they agree on what kind of crime it was, then the local "going rate" punishment for such crimes is clear to all actors and the defense attorney can know what the punishment will be upon entering a guilty plea.

Both prosecutor and defense attorney may be members of the same local legal culture with shared values and understandings about the punishments for particular offenses. Implicit plea bargaining may be less likely to occur when there is personnel turnover in a court community that inhibits recognition of shared values.

Process may differ from courthouse to courthouse; some courts may use "slow plea of guilty" as defendant pleads to lesser charge as case progresses through trial; prosecutors may use diversion or dropping cases to reduce caseload in other courts.

D. Legal Issues in Plea Bargaining

Questions exist concerning the voluntariness and sanctity of plea bargains. Many judges now more open about admitting in court that they are aware of plea bargains struck in particular cases. In *Boykin v. Alabama* (1969), the Court decided that the defendant must make affirmative statement that plea was voluntary before judge accepts the plea. In *North Carolina v. Alford* (1970), it was decided that courts can accept guilty pleas entered by defendants who maintain their innocence, but is willing to accept punishment for lesser charge to avoid risk of maximum penalty. *Santobello v. New York* (1971) assures that the prosecutor's promises of leniency must be kept. *Ricketts v. Adamson* (1987) found that defendants must keep their part of the bargain if they agree to testify against others as part of the plea bargain. Finally, in *Bordenkircher v. Hayes* (1978) the Supreme Court decided that prosecutors can threaten defendants with additional charges if they do not agree to plead guilty

E. Criticisms of Plea Bargaining

The biggest criticisms of plea bargaining focus on due process violations and leniency in sentencing. Those concerned with due process believe that bargaining does not provide procedural fairness because defendants forfeit the constitutional rights designed to protect them . Critics concerned with leniency express concerns that offenders are "getting off" with sentences that are too lenient. Some are also worried that the plea bargaining process coerces innocent people into admitting crimes they did not commit.

III. TRIAL: THE EXCEPTIONAL CASE

Thanks to plea bargaining, judge and jury trials are unusual in the United States. They are usually reserved for more serious cases. The trial process is based on the adversarial system, a symbolic combat between prosecution and defense. Trials are also biased processes, because of vagaries in the criminal law and the fact that human error also enters into courtroom decisions. While defendants have the right to a jury trial, these are less common than a bench trial over which a judge presides.

A. Going to Trial
Trials are based on the idea that the adversarial process and laws of criminal procedure and evidence will produce the truth. The judge must make sure that rules are followed, and the jury must impartially evaluate the evidence and reflect the community's interests. The jury is the sole evaluator of the facts in the case.

Juries provide several important functions in the criminal justice system, including safeguarding citizens against arbitrary law enforcement, determining guilt or innocence, and representing diverse community interests. In addition, citizens who serve on juries learn about the criminal justice system. Juries are usually made up of 12 citizens, but smaller jury sizes are allowed under the United States Constitution (Williams v. Florida (1970))

B. The Trial Process
There are several steps in the trial process:

1. **Jury Selection**: Juries should be made up of a cross-section of the community, but until the mid-twentieth century many states excluded women and members of minority groups. A jury pool is used to select members of the jury from the greater community.

   Voir dire is the process of questioning potential jurors to ensure a fair trial. Attorneys for both sides and the judge may question each juror about background, knowledge of the case, or acquaintance with people involved in the case. If a juror says something to indicate that he or she may be unable to make a fair decision, then he or she may be challenged for cause.

   Attorneys can also make peremptory challenges, in which they can dismiss a juror without providing cause. Although the Supreme Court has said that peremptory challenges cannot be based on the race or gender of potential jurors, the Court also permits trial judges to accept flimsy excuses when it appears that race or gender is being improperly applied.

2. **Opening Statements** are made by attorneys. Lawyers use this opportunity to establish themselves with the jurors and to emphasize points they intend to make during the trial.

3. **Presentation of the Prosecution's Evidence.** The prosecution must prove the accused is guilty beyond a reasonable doubt. They can present real evidence, demonstrative evidence, testimony, direct evidence, or circumstantial evidence. The rules of evidence govern which pieces of evidence the judge will exclude or permit.

4. **Presentation of Defense's Evidence**: this evidence is usually presented to rebut the states' case, offer an alibi for the defendant, or to present an affirmative defense (such as self-defense or insanity). The defense also must consider whether or not the defendant will take the stand and thereby be subject to impeachment and cross-examination.

5. **Presentation of Rebuttal Witnesses**: the prosecution calls witnesses to rebut the defense's case.

6. **Closing Arguments by Each Side**: this is an opportunity to tie the cases together and to make impassioned, persuasive presentation to the judge or jury.

7. **Judge's Instructions to the Jury**: the judge instructs the jury on the manner in which the law bears on their decision. The judge may discuss the standard of proof (beyond a reasonable doubt), the necessity of the prosecution proving all of the elements of a crime, and the rights of the defendant. Judges will explain the charges and the possible verdicts.

8. **Decision by the Jury**: jurors deliberate in private room after instructions from the judge. They may request that the judge reread to them portions of the instructions, they may ask for additional instructions, or for portions of the trial transcript. The trial will end with a hung jury if they cannot reach a verdict. When a verdict is reached, it is ready aloud to the courtroom.

C. Evaluating the Jury System

Social relationships outside the courtroom tend to be reflected in the jury. Men, white jury members, and those with more education are generally more active in jury deliberations. It is important to note that juries may be more likely to make judgments based on personal characteristics about defendants than judges.

IV. APPEALS

Appeals are made when the defendant believes an error was made in his or her trial. Appeals from state court go through the state appeals system, but sometimes appeals go through the federal system if they involve a constitutional issue.

A. Habeas Corpus

This writ asks a judge to determine whether an individual is being property detained. A successful habeas corpus writ can result in a defendant being released from custody or order a new trial.

There has been a tremendous increase in habeas corpus petitions although only about 1% are successful—this causes an increase in caseloads for federal judges. There is no right to counsel for habeas corpus petitions, so most prisoners must attempt to present their own cases. They generally lack sufficient knowledge to identify and raise constitutional issues effectively.

Since the 1980s, the Supreme Court has made decisions imposing more difficult procedural requirements on prisoners seeking to file habeas corpus petitions. In 1996, Congress created further restrictions on petitions by passing a new statute affecting habeas corpus procedures.

B. Evaluating the Appellate Process

Some conservatives argue that appeals should be limited. Appeals can be regarded as a burden on the system and an impediment to swift punishment of convicted offenders. However, since 90% of accused persons plead guilty and relatively few of these people have any basis for appeal, the actual number of appeals (as a percentage of total cases) seems less significant.

Appeals can serve the function of correcting errors. Even if a defendant wins an appeal, there is no automatic release from prison. A successful appeal may simply lead to a new trial or provide the basis for a new plea bargain.

REVIEW OF KEY TERMS

Fill in the appropriate term for each statement

local legal culture
going rate
workgroup
Boykin v. Alabama (1969)
North Carolina v. Alford (1970)
Santobello v. New York (1971)
Ricketts v. Adamson (1987)
Bordenkircher v. Hayes (1978)

Williams v. Florida (1970)
voir dire
challenge for cause
peremptory challenge
real evidence
demonstrative evidence
testimony
direct evidence
circumstantial evidence
reasonable doubt
appeal
habeas corpus

1. The typical sentence for a crime in a jurisdiction is known as the ___going rate___ among courtroom staff.

2. ___peremptory challenge___ permits defense attorneys and prosecutors to exclude jurors without providing a reason.

3. ___circumstantial evidence___ requires the jurors to draw inferences.

4. ___appeal___ creates the opportunity for reviews to determine whether trial judges made errors or constitutional rights were violated.

5. ___voir dire___ is the process of questioning and selecting jurors.

6. ___habeas corpus___ provides the basis for incarcerated people to challenge the legal basis for their detention.

7. ___testimony___ is evidence presented by witnesses.

8. ___challenge for cause___ permits, with the judge's approval, the exclusion of jurors who demonstrate a particular bias.

9. ___reasonable doubts___ is the standard of proof in criminal cases.

10. ___William v Florida___ stands for the proposition that juries can have fewer than twelve members.

11. ___real evidence___ is presented by the prosecutor and includes concrete objects, such as fingerprints and stolen property.

12. ___direct evidence___ includes eye witness accounts of what happened.

13. ___courtroom workgroup___ is the organizational entity that can process cases quickly, efficiently, and consistently in a particular courthouse if the relevant actors remain in their positions for a sufficient length of time.

14. ___local legal culture___ is the shared norms and values within a court community that helps to shape the speed and content of case processing.

REVIEW OF KEY PEOPLE

John Walker Lindh
Helen "Holly" Maddux
Ira Einhorn
Bill Clinton

1. In 1977, _Helen "Holly" Maddux_ , a 30-year-old woman from a wealthy Texas family, disappeared. She had been living in Philadelphia with her boyfriend, _Ira Einhorn_ , a former hippie leader was charged with her murder.

2. President _Bill Clinton_ signed the Antiterrorism and Effective Death Penalty Act, which placed additional restrictions on habeas corpus petitions, because prisoners' cases were a burden on the courts.

3. _John Walker Lindh_ was a twenty-one-year-old American captured while fighting with the Taliban in Afghanistan in 2002.

GENERAL PRACTICE QUESTIONS

In order to obtain a jury containing a 1._cross-section of community_ , many reformers have advocated the use of drivers' license lists and other lists in addition to the usual 2._voter registration_ that have traditionally been used to create the jury pool.

During the process of 3._voir dire_ , attorneys can use 4._challenge for cause_ to seek exclusion of potential jurors who make prejudicial statements before deciding strategically which remaining potential jurors to remove through the use of 5._peremptory challenge_

The 6._appeals_ court examines arguments concerning errors that occurred during the trial. It may also consider 7._habeas corpus_ petitions from prisoners challenging the basis for their incarceration.

SELF-TEST SECTION

MULTIPLE CHOICE QUESTIONS

11.1. Which of the following is true about the trial process?
   a) the selection of the jury occurs after the opening statements by the prosecution and the defense
   b) the defense presents evidence and witnesses before the prosecution
   c) the judge offers instructions to the jury after a decision is reached in a case
   d) the selection of jurors is never bias toward the defendant
   e) retired persons and homemakers are overrepresented on juries

11.2. The courtroom process of questioning prospective jurors in order to screen out those who might be incapable of being fair is called...
   a) mala in se
   b) habeas corpus
   c) voir dire
   d) ex post facto
   e) demonstrative evidence

11.3. In the elimination of jurors from the jury pool, what is the difference between a peremptory challenge and challenge for cause?
    a) peremptory challenges cannot be used in felony cases
    b) challenge for cause cannot be used in felony cases
    c) a judge must rule on a peremptory challenge, but attorneys control a challenge for cause
    d) a judge must rule on a challenge for cause, but attorneys generally control a peremptory challenge
    e) peremptory challenges and challenge for cause are the same

11.4. The prosecution must prove that a defendant is guilty beyond...
    a) probable cause
    b) all doubt
    c) reasonable doubt
    d) a preponderance of the evidence
    e) reasonable suspicion

11.5. In a trial, fingerprints submitted as evidence would be considered...
    a) circumstantial evidence
    b) reasonable evidence
    c) real evidence
    d) direct evidence
    e) probable evidence

11.6. In a trial, eyewitness accounts submitted as evidence would be considered...
    a) circumstantial evidence
    b) reasonable evidence
    c) real evidence
    d) direct evidence
    e) probable evidence

11.7. In a trial, what type of evidence requires the jury to infer a fact from what a witness observed?
    a) circumstantial evidence
    b) reasonable evidence
    c) real evidence
    d) direct evidence
    e) probable evidence

11.8. Which of the following is true concerning Fifth Amendment rights?
    a) defendants must take the stand and face cross examination
    b) defendants do not have to testify against themselves, but a prosecutor can criticize a defendant for this strategy
    c) defendants do not have to testify against themselves and a prosecutor cannot criticize a defendant for this strategy
    d) defendants must take the stand, but the Fifth Amendment prevents cross-examination by the prosecution
    e) all of the above are TRUE

11.9. In criminal cases, the majority of states require that a twelve person jury reach ...
    a) at least a seven to five vote to convict
    b) at least an eight to four vote to convict
    c) at least a nine to three vote to convict
    d) at least a ten to two vote to convict
    e) a unanimous vote to convict

11.10. Who is absent if a trial is conducted "in absentia"?
    a) judge
    b) jury
    c) defense attorney
    d) defendant
    e) prosecutor

11.11. Social scientists who wish to study jury deliberations...
    a) can observe or film after getting permission from the judge
    b) can ask to become a member of the jury
    c) are barred because jury deliberations are secret
    d) must stay behind a two-way mirror
    e) can watch the videos that the courts takes of all jury meetings

11.12. According to social scientists, who is more likely to be active and influential during jury deliberations?
    a) white women who are less educated
    b) minority women who are less educated
    c) white men who are less educated
    d) minority men who are better educated
    e) white men who are better educated

11.13. Who are the key participants in a plea bargain?
    a) bailiff and clerk
    b) probation officer and bail bondsperson
    c) prosecutor and defense attorney
    d) jury and the judge
    e) all of the above are key participants

11.14. Which of the following is NOT a function of a jury?
    a) safeguarding citizens against arbitrary law enforcement
    b) determining whether the accused is guilty
    c) representing the interests of the prosecutor
    d) educating citizens selected for jury duty about the criminal justice system
    e) symbolizing the rule of law

11.15. Who was the American citizen who was captured in 2002 fighting with the Taliban in Afghanistan?
    a) John Walker Lindh
    b) Andrew Goldstein
    c) Ira Einhorn
    d) Roger Hanson
    e) Bill Clinton

11.16. What is the strategy called when police file charges for selling a drug when they know they can probably convict only for possession?
    a) voir dire
    b) multiple-offense indictment
    c) intimidation
    d) habeas corpus
    e) peremptory challenge

11.17. Who is the former hippie leader who had developed a network of friends among prominent people that allowed him to flee the U. S. after being charged with murder in the 1970s?
a) John Walker Lindh
b) Roger Hanson
c) Ira Einhorn
d) Andrew Goldstein
e) Michael Irvin

11.18. What is it called when the judge, the public, and sometimes even the defendant do not know for sure who got what from whom in exchange for what?
a) bargain justice
b) multiple-offense indictment
c) implicit plea bargaining
d) voir dire
e) challenged for cause

11.19. In a study of the nation's seventy-five largest counties, how many murder cases went to trial?
a) 10 percent
b) 17 percent
c) 26 percent
d) 37 percent
e) 50 percent

11.20. How many felony cases go to trial?
a) fewer than two percent
b) fewer than five percent
c) fewer than 10 percent
d) more than 20 percent
e) more than 40 percent

11.21. How many constitutional amendments mention the right to a trial?
a) one
b) two
c) three
d) four
e) none

11.22. How many percent of jury trials worldwide take place in the United States?
a) 20
b) 40
c) 60
d) 80
e) 90

11.23. Which of the following is a function of a jury?
a) to prevent government oppression
b) to determine whether the accused is guilty on the basis of the evidence presented.
c) to represent diverse community interests
d) to serve as a buffer between the accused and the accuser
e) all of the above

11.24. How many percent of adult Americans have ever been called to jury duty?
- a) 5 percent
- b) 15 percent
- c) 25 percent
- d) 40 percent
- e) 75 percent

TRUE/FALSE QUESTIONS

11.1. __T__ Juries serve as a buffer between the accused and the accuser.

11.2. __F__ Juries in the United States must always be comprised of twelve members.

11.3. __T__ The prosecution presents evidence and witnesses before the defense presents its case.

11.4. __F__ Among all occupational groups, lawyers are mostly likely to be chosen to serve on juries because of their knowledge about law.

11.5. __F__ A judge has a final ruling on all peremptory challenges made by attorneys.

11.6. __T__ Racial discrimination has been a problem in lawyers' use of peremptory challenges.

11.7. __F__ Circumstantial evidence is always sufficient to convict a defendant.

11.8. __T__ Juries decide the facts of case, but judges determine the law.

11.9. __F__ Judges in France handle only civil cases.

11.10. __T__ Research indicates that jurors' deliberations often include their perceptions of the trial process rather than just the facts of the case.

11.11. __F__ Jury duty rarely involves personal and financial hardship.

11.12. __F__ A defendant who wins an appeal must be set free and cannot be tried again.

11.13. __F__ The vast majority of jury trials worldwide take place in Europe.

11.14. __F__ Courts apply rules and procedures in exactly the same way across the nation.

11.15. __T__ The "going rate" is the opinion of the local jurisdiction regarding the proper sentence for a crime.

11.16. __F__ Television shows, such as *Law and Order*, provide a realistic view of the courtroom.

11.17. __T__ In a workgroup, each participant has a specified role.

11.18. __F__ Plea bargaining has always been discussed publicly

11.19. __T__ Plea bargaining reduces the time that people must spend in jail.

11.20. __F__ Plea bargaining always occurs in a single meeting between prosecutor and defense attorney.

ANSWER KEY

Key Terms

1. going rate
2. peremptory challenge
2. circumstantial evidence
3. appeal
4. *voir dire*
5. *habeas corpus*
6. testimony
7 challenge for cause
8 reasonable doubt
9 *Williams v. Florida*
10. real evidence
11. direct evidence
12. courtroom workgroup
13. local legal culture

Key People

1. Helen "Holly" Maddux; Ira Einhorn
2. Bill Clinton
3. John Walker Lindh

General Practice Questions

1. cross-section of the community
2. voter registration lists
3. *voir dire*
4. challenges for cause
5. peremptory challenges
6. appeals
7. *habeas corpus*

Multiple Choice

11.1.	E
11.2.	C
11.3.	D
11.4.	C
11.5.	C
11.6.	D
11.7.	A
11.8.	C
11.9.	E
11.10.	D
11.11.	C
11.12.	E
11.13.	C
11.14.	C
11.15.	A
11.16.	B
11.17.	C
11.18.	A
11.19.	C
11.20.	C
11.21.	C
11.22.	D
11.23.	E
11.24.	B

<u>True/False</u>

11.1.	T
11.2.	F
11.3.	T
11.4.	F
11.5.	F
11.6.	T
11.7.	F
11.8.	T
11.9.	F
11.10.	T
11.11.	F
11.12.	F
11.13.	F
11.14.	F
11.15.	T
11.16.	F
11.17.	T
11.18.	F
11.19.	T
11.20.	F

WORKSHEET 11.1. COURTROOM WORKGROUP

A newly elected prosecutor has hired you as a consultant. She wants to know whether she should assign assistant prosecutors to single courtrooms to handle all cases before a specific judge or, alternatively, rotate assistant prosecutors to different courtrooms and other assignments every week. She says, "I've heard that these 'courtroom workgroups,' whatever they are, form if you keep assistant prosecutors in one courtroom. What should I do?"

1. Define the concept of "courtroom workgroup."

_____

_____

_____

2. Describe how courtrooms will work if an assistant prosecutor is permanently assigned to one courtroom. What are the consequences?

_____

_____

_____

_____

_____

_____

3. How will courtrooms work if assistant prosecutors are rotated? What are the consequences?

_____

_____

_____

_____

_____

_____

4. Which approach do you recommend? Why?

_____

_____

_____

_____

_____

WORKSHEET 11.2: PLEA BARGAINING

Imagine that you are the prosecutor who has been responsible for investigating and prosecuting the case of a suspected serial killer. Over the span of a few years, eight hunters, fishermen, and joggers have been found dead in isolated areas of a three-county rural area. Each one had been shot by a sniper from a great distance. Two bits of evidence led you to arrest a suspect. First, among the many tips you received about possible suspects, one informant described the employee of a nearby city water department who owned many guns and frequently drove out into the country to shoot at random animals he encountered, including farmers' cows and pet dogs. Second, you knew that one of the victims was shot with a rifle that was made in Sweden and was not commonly available in local gun stores. You learned from a second informant that the city employee sold one of these unusual Swedish rifles to another gun enthusiast shortly after the time that a hunter was killed by a shot from such a rifle. You located the gun and ballistics tests indicated a high probability that it was the weapon used in that particular murder. You charged the suspect with five of the eight murders and you scrambled to find evidence to link him with these and the remaining three murders. You have spoken publicly about seeking the death penalty. Now, after months of heavy publicity about the case, you announce that the defendant will plead guilty to one count of murder and be sentenced to life in prison. (Based on a real case in Canton, Ohio).

When giving a guest lecture in a criminal justice course at a nearby university, a student asks you to explain how the plea bargain in this case can be viewed as a "good" or "fair" result in light of the number of victims and the fact that you could have pursued the death penalty. Whether or not you personally agree with the plea bargain, in your role as the prosecutor, how would you explain the benefits of the plea bargain with respect to various interested actors and constituents listed below.

BRIEFLY EXPLAIN IF AND HOW THE PLEA BARGAIN BENEFITS THE:

PROSECUTOR_____

_____

JUDGE_____

_____

COURT SYSTEM_____

_____

DEFENSE ATTORNEY_____

_____

DEFENDANT_____

_____

SOCIETY_____

_____

VICTIMS' FAMILIES_____

_____

WORKSHEET 11.3: JURY SELECTION

Imagine that a thirty-year-old African-American woman is facing trial for the murder of her Hispanic husband. He was shot while standing in the doorway of the house soon after he returned home from work. There are no eyewitnesses. The murder weapon had the wife's fingerprints on it. On the advice of her lawyer, she never answered any questions from the police. Several defense witnesses will testify that the deceased husband used to beat his wife frequently.

1. If you are the prosecutor in this case, what is the demographic profile of your ideal juror (e.g., age, race, education, occupation, gender, political party affiliation, religion, etc.)? Why?

_____

_____

_____

_____

_____

2. If you are the defense attorney in this case, what is the demographic profile of your ideal juror? Why?

_____

_____

_____

_____

_____

3. If you were the prosecutor, what questions would you want to ask the potential jurors during *voir dire*? Why?

_____

_____

_____

_____

_____

_____

4. If you were the defense attorney, what questions would you want to ask the potential jurors during *voir dire*?

_____

_____

_____

WORKSHEET 11.4: JURY PROCESSES

There are many debates about changing the jury system How would you address the following issues?

1. Should peremptory challenges be abolished? What would be the consequences of excluding potential jurors only for cause and not through attorneys' discretionary decisions?

_____

_____

_____

_____

_____

_____

_____

2. Should juries have twelve members or should we use six-member juries for criminal cases? What are the consequences of using small juries?

_____

_____

_____

_____

_____

_____

_____

3. Should guilty verdicts be unanimous? What would be the consequences of permitting people to be convicted of crimes by non-unanimous jury decisions?

_____

_____

_____

_____

_____

_____

_____

PUNISHMENT AND SENTENCING

OUTLINE

- The Goals of Punishment
- Forms of the Criminal Sanction
- The Sentencing Process

CHAPTER 12
PUNISHMENT AND SENTENCING

LEARNING OBJECTIVES

After completing the material in this chapter, students should understand:

1.   the philosophical basis for criminal punishment

2.   the goals and weaknesses of retribution

3.   the goals and weaknesses of deterrence

4.   the goals and weaknesses of incapacitation

5.   the goals and weaknesses of rehabilitation

6.   the nature and extent of the various forms of criminal sanctions, including incarceration, intermediate sanctions, probation, and death

7.   the constitutional and policy debates concerning the application of capital punishment

8.   the influences on sentencing, including administrative context, attitudes and values of judges, presentence report, and sentencing guidelines

9.   the debates about who receives the harshest punishment.

CHAPTER SUMMARY

The four goals of the criminal punishment in the United States are 1) retribution, 2) deterrence, 3) incapacitation, and 4) rehabilitation. The U.S. system is experimenting with restoration is a new approach to punishment. These goals are carried out through a variety of punishments such as incarceration, intermediate sanctions, probation, and death. Penal codes vary as to whether the permitted sentences are indeterminate, determinate, or mandatory. Each type of sentence makes certain assumptions about the goals of the criminal sanction. Good time allows correctional administrators to reduce the sentence of prisoners who live according to the rules and participate in various vocational, educational, and treatment programs. The death penalty is allowed as a form of punishment by the U.S. Supreme Court if the judge and jury are allowed to take into consideration mitigating and aggravating circumstances. The death penalty can be used by the states against juveniles, but not against the mentally retarded or the mentally insane. The U. S. Supreme Court led by Chief Justice William Rehnquist (1986-2005) is attempting to limit the number of appeals for defendants on death row in multiple courts within the United States criminal justice system. Judges have considerable discretion in handing down sentences. Judges consider such factors as the seriousness of the crime, the offender's prior record, and mitigating and aggravating circumstances. The sentencing process is influenced by the administrative context of the courts, the attitudes and values of the judges, and the presentence report. Since the 1980s, sentencing guidelines have been formulated in federal courts and seventeen states as a way of reducing disparity among the sentences given offenders in similar situations. Severe or unjust punishments may result from racial discrimination or wrongful convictions.

CHAPTER OUTLINE

I. THE GOALS OF PUNISHMENT
Beliefs about appropriate punishments differ over time. The public has supported many different themes of sentencing, depending on the social climate of the time.

A. Retribution—Deserved Punishment
Retribution is the idea that those who do wrong should be punished in proportion to the gravity of the offense or to the extent to which others have been made to suffer ("an eye for an eye"). Retribution is sometimes seen as an expression of the community's disapproval of crime. It is sometimes referred to as "just deserts" or "deserved punishment".

B. Deterrence
Deterrence is based on the idea that criminals weigh the pros and cons of offending before committing a crime. If the "cons" can be made strong enough so as to deter crime, the crime rate will be reduced. There are two types of deterrence: general deterrence, which focuses on keeping society at large from committing crime; and specific deterrence, which focuses on the individual being punished. Many question that philosophy has any affect on crime rates.

C. Incapacitation
The assumption of incapacitation is that a crime may be prevented if criminals are physically restrained (i.e., incarcerated). Prison is the typical mode of incapacitation, since offenders can be kept under control so that they cannot violate the rules of society. Capital punishment is the ultimate method of incapacitation. Selective incapacitation methods attempt to identify the most severe criminals and incarcerate them for long periods of time. Incapacitation is criticized for being unduly severe, and that our predictions about who will be most likely to reoffend are often incorrect.

D. Rehabilitation
Rehabilitation focuses on treating and "curing" criminal offenders. It assumes that techniques are available to identify and treat the causes of the offender's behavior. Because rehabilitation is oriented solely toward the offender, no relationship can be maintained between the severity of the punishment and the gravity of the crime. There is currently public support for rehabilitation, but the current political climate in the United States supports more punitive techniques.

E. New Approaches to Punishment
Recent approaches in punishing offenders focus on restoration. Using restorative justice philosophy, offenders are encouraged to return victims to the state they were prior to the crime. Monetary losses to the victim are restored, and victim/offender mediation is sometimes used to help victims feel safer.

II. FORMS OF THE CRIMINAL SANCTION

A. Incarceration
Incarceration is the most visible punishment used by the courts. It is generally believed to be a deterrent, but it is very expensive and does not serve to rehabilitate offenders. There are several different types of sentences that result in incarceration.

1. **Indeterminate sentences** allow correctional personnel to make decisions about when to release inmates. Judges sentence offenders to a range of months in prison, and the offender is released when the parole board determines they have served a sufficient amount of time.

2. **Determinate sentences** are set sentences that do not vary. Offenders are sentenced to a specific period of time and typically serve the entire sentence. Some states use presumptive sentences, in which the state legislature sets the expected sentence for specific crimes. These sentences reduce the discretion of the judge in setting sentences.

3. **Mandatory sentences** stipulate some minimum period of incarceration that must be served by persons convicted of selected crimes. No regard may be given to the circumstances of the offense or the background of the individual—the judge has no discretion and is not allowed to suspend the sentence. Mandatory prison terms are most often specified for violent crimes, drug violations, habitual offenders, or crimes where a firearm was used. Plea bargaining can undercut the intentions of the legislature by negotiating for a different charge.

4. **Sentence versus actual time served**: in all but four states, days are subtracted from prisoners' minimum or maximum term for "good time". This time is meant to reflect good behavior in prison, or for participation in various types of vocational, educational, and treatment programs.

5. **"Truth in Sentencing"** is the requirement that offenders serve a substantial portion of their sentences before release on parole (usually 85% of their sentence) for a violent crime. This policy can increase imprisonment costs.

B. Intermediate Sanctions
Punishments such as fines, home confinement, intensive probation supervision, restitution and community service, boot camp, and forfeiture are among the sentencing forms that fit this category. These sentences are expanding in response to the expense and overcrowding of prisons, and it has been recommended that they be used in combination to sentence offenders.

C. Probation
This is the most frequently used criminal sanction. Probation is generally advocated as a way of rehabilitating offenders with less serious offenses or clean prior records. It is less expensive than prison and may avoid prison's embittering effects on young offenders. Shock probation is sometimes used to "shock" offenders into refraining from future criminal activity. In this method, offenders receive a short jail period followed by a period of probation.

D. Death
Most other Western democracies have abolished the death penalty but the United States continues to use it. The Supreme Court has decided the death penalty is not cruel and unusual punishment, although there was a moratorium on the death penalty from 1968 to 1976.

1. **The Death Penalty and the Constitution**: Several important Supreme Court cases have spoken to the constitutionality and implementation of the death penalty.

2. **Key Supreme Court Decisions**
   Furman v. Georgia (1972): the Supreme Court ruled that the death penalty, as administered, constituted cruel and unusual punishment, thereby voiding the laws of thirty-nine states and the District of Columbia. Only two of the justices argued that capital punishment per se was cruel and unusual, in violation of the Eighth Amendment.

   McCleskey v. Kemp (1987): McCleskey's attorneys cited research that showed a disparity in the imposition of the death sentence in Georgia based on the race of the murder victim and, to a lesser extent, the race of the defendant. McCleskey would have had to prove that the decision makers in his case had acted with a discriminatory purpose toward McCleskey himself and not the generalized statistical study.

   In *Atkins v. Virginia (2002),* Justice John Paul Stevens wrote for the majority in ruling that it was unconstitutional for states to execute the mentally retarded.

   Roper v. Simmons (2005): The Court finds that individuals who committed crimes as juveniles cannot be executed, since such action violates the Eighth Amendment.

   In *Ring v. Arizona* (2002), the Supreme Court decided that the decision to sentence an offender to death must be made by juries rather than judges.

3. **Continuing Legal Issues**:
   a. *Execution of the Insane*: the U. S. Supreme Court has stated that states cannot execute the insane. However, there are problems with defining and identifying insanity.

   b. *Effective Counsel*: Defendants charged with capital offenses have the right to effective counsel. Issues about the adequacy of defense lawyers' efforts. Some very public cases have provided evidence that some defense attorneys have literally fallen asleep during trial, and others have been incompetent.

   c. *Death-Qualified Juries*: There is much debate about whether citizens opposed to the death penalty should be excluded from capital cases. Currently, jurors opposed to the death penalty may be excluded, but some argue that these juries do not represent a cross-section of the community.

   d. *Methods of Execution*: Most states (except Nebraska) use lethal injection as the preferred form of execution because it is more "humane" than other methods. There are critics who state that even lethal injection can be extremely painful.

   e. *Appeals*: the average length of time inmates sit on death row awaiting execution is about 11 years. During this time sentences are reviewed by the state courts and through the writ of habeas corpus by the federal courts. Innocent citizens are sometimes sentences to death, and the appeals process makes it very difficult for them to obtain release. It is impossible to know how many innocent citizens are executed in the United States.

   f. *International Law*. The United States has come under fire for sentencing foreign citizens to death without consulting their home countries. Several countries have filed complaints against the United States for violating the Vienna Convention.

4. The Death Penalty: A Continuing Controversy
   While public support for the death penalty remains high, few offenders are actually executed each year. Several states have imposed moratoria on the death penalty, but there is much dissention over the issue.

III. THE SENTENCING PROCESS
   Judges have responsibility for sentencing after conviction, whether the conviction was by judge, jury, or plea bargain. Initial definitions of punishments are defined by legislatures. There may be room under the law for judges to use discretion in shaping individuals sentences.

   A. The Administrative Context of the Courts

   1. **Misdemeanor Courts: Assembly Line Justice**. Limited jurisdiction courts have limits on the punishments that can be meted out for specific offenses, usually a maximum of one year in jail. These courts handle over 90% of criminal cases for arraignment and preliminary hearing before referring case to a general jurisdiction trial court or for completion through dismissal or sentence.

      Most lower courts are overloaded and the time allotted for each case is minimal. Judicial decisions are mass produced because the actors in the system work together. Most offenders in misdemeanor courts receive lenient sentences.

   2. **Felony Courts**: in courts of general jurisdiction, sentencing is influenced by organizational considerations and community norms, including interactions and relationships between judges, prosecutors, and defense attorneys.

   B. Attitudes and Values of Judges
      Sentencing differences among judges can be ascribed to a number of factors. The individual characteristics of the judges, the blameworthiness of the offender, and other factors can affect judicial decisions.

C. The Presentence Report

The Presentence report is based on the investigation of the probation officer. In some states, the probation officer makes an actual recommendation; in others, the probation officer merely provides information. Report can be based on hearsay. The presentence report helps judges to ease the strain of decision making; helps to shift responsibility to the probation department.

D. Sentencing Guidelines

Guidelines have emerged in the federal system and some state systems as a means to limit the discretion of judges and to reduce sentencing disparities for offenders convicted of the same offense. Sentencing ranges in the guidelines are based on seriousness of offense and criminal history of the offender.

Guidelines appear in a grid constructed on the basis of two scores, seriousness of offense and offender's history/prior record or other offender characteristics. The grid provides an offender score which indicates the sentencing range for the particular offender who commits a specific offense. Judges are expected to provide a written explanation if they depart from the guidelines/grid.

E. Who Gets the Harshest Punishment?
1. **Racial Disparities**. Some studies have shown that members of racial minorities and the poor are treated more harshly by the system. Other studies show no clear link between harshness of sentence and the offender's race or social status.

2. **Wrongful Convictions**: While much public concern is expressed over those who "beat the system" and go free, comparatively little attention is paid to those who are innocent, yet convicted. Each year several such cases of persons convicted but innocent come to national attention.

REVIEW OF KEY TERMS

Fill in the appropriate term for each statement.

retribution
general deterrence
special deterrence
incapacitation
selective incapacitation
rehabilitation
restoration
indeterminate sentence
determinate sentence
presumptive sentence
mandatory sentence
good time
intermediate sanctions
probation
shock probation
Furman v. Georgia
McCleskey v. Kemp
Atkins v. Virginia
Roper v. Simmons
Ring v. Arizona
Witherspoon v. Illinois
presentence report
sentencing guidelines

1. _Selective incapacitation_ is the careful selection of offenders who will receive long prison sentences that will prevent them from committing additional crimes.

2. _indeterminate sentence_ is a term of incarceration based on a minimum and maximum amount of time; the actual amount to be served will be based on the judgment of the parole board.

3. _Special deterrence_ is punishment inflicted on criminals with the intent to discourage them from committing any future crimes.

4. _Shock probation_ is a sentence in which the offender is released after a short incarceration and placed in the community under supervision.

5. _restoration_ aims to obtain justice for victims by "making them whole" and restoring their original state before the crime was committed.

6. _mandatory sentence_ is a type of sentence determined by statutes which require that a certain penalty shall be imposed and executed upon certain convicted offenders.

7. _intermediate sanctions_ is a variety of punishments that are more restrictive than traditional probation but less stringent and costly than incarceration.

8. _Probation_ is a punishment involving conditional release under supervision.

9. _retribution_ is the underlying goal of punishment in which the offender is considered deserving of punishment and the punishment fits the seriousness of the crime.

10. _incapacitation_ is the deprivation of the ability to commit crimes against society, usually through means of detention in prison.

11. _McCleskey v Kemp_ is a case in which the Supreme Court rejected a claim that systematic racial discrimination made the death penalty unconstitutional.

12. _determinate sentence_ is a sentence that fixes the term of imprisonment at a specified period of time.

13. _Sentencing guidelines_ are a reform designed to reduce the disparities in sentences for people who have committed the same or similar crimes.

14. _rehabilitation_ is the goal of restoring a convicted offender to a constructive place in society.

15. _Furman v Georgia_ is the Supreme Court case that temporarily halted executions in the United States.

16. _general deterrence_ is the punishment of criminals that is intended to serve as an example to the public and discourage others from committing crimes.

17. _presentence report_ is submitted by the probation officer to the judge.

GENERAL PRACTICE QUESTIONS

Among the purposes of punishment, 1. _retribution_ and 2. _rehabilitation_ focus on the specific offender by, respectively, focusing the seriousness of the offense committed and seeking to turn the offender into a productive citizen. By contrast, 3. _general deterrence_ and 4. _incapacitation_ focus on society by, respectively, seeking to discourage others from crime and protecting society from acts by repeat offenders.

The underlying purpose of 5. <u>*immediate sanction*</u> is to identify sentencing options that will save money while giving the offender a punishment more harsh than 6. <u>*probation*</u>, in which the restrictions and supervision may not drastically change the offender's behavior while living in the community.

The 7. <u>*administrative context*</u> of misdemeanor courts includes the assumption that police and prosecutors have filtered out the innocent people. This assumption contrasts sharply with capital punishment cases in which jurors must carefully way mitigating and 8. <u>*aggravating factors.*</u> in deciding whether to impose the death penalty.

SELF-TEST SECTION

MULTIPLE CHOICE QUESTIONS

12.1. The U. S. Supreme Court declared that the death penalty did not violate the Constitution through imposition in a racially discriminatory manner in the case of...
   a) *Furman v. Georgia* (1972)
   b) *Gregg v. Georgia* (1976)
   c) *McCleskey v. Kemp* (1987)
   d) *Payne v. Tennessee* (1991)
   e) *Ford v. Wainwright* (1986)

12.2. Which of the following is true concerning the current majority on the Rehnquist Court and the appeal process for death penalty cases?
   a) the Rehnquist Court majority is satisfied with the appeals process
   b) the Rehnquist Court majority wants to provide more appeals across multiple courts for death row inmates
   c) the Rehnquist Court majority wants to limit the opportunities for capital punishment defendants to have their appeals heard by multiple courts
   d) the Rehnquist Court majority wants to abolish the death penalty so it won't have to deal with the issue of appeals
   e) the Rehnquist Court majority wants to end all state and federal appeals for capital punishment defendants

12.3. Punishments that are less severe and costly than prison, but more restrictive than traditional probation, are called...
   a) indeterminate sentences
   b) mandatory sentences
   c) "good time" sentences
   d) presumptive sentences
   e) intermediate sanctions

12.4. Which is the most frequently applied criminal sanction?
   a) probation
   b) the death penalty
   c) life in prison
   d) indeterminate sentences
   e) presumptive sentences

12.5. The U. S. Supreme Court declared that the death penalty is illegal in the case of the mentally retarded in the case of...
   a) *Payne v. Tennessee* (1991)
   b) *Ring v. Arizona* (2002)
   c) *McCleskey v. Kemp* (1987)
   d) *Stanford v. Kentucky* (1989)
   e) *Atkins v. Virginia* (2002)

12.6. In what case did the U. S. Supreme Court rule that juries, rather than judges, must make the crucial factual decisions as to whether a convicted murderer should receive the death penalty?
  a) *Payne v. Tennessee* (1991)
  b) *Ring v. Arizona* (2002)
  c) *McCleskey v. Kemp* (1987)
  d) *Stanford v. Kentucky* (1989)
  e) *Atkins v. Virginia* (2002)

12.7. According to the chart below, in which year was the largest gap between the number of offenders sentenced to death and the actual number of executions carried out?

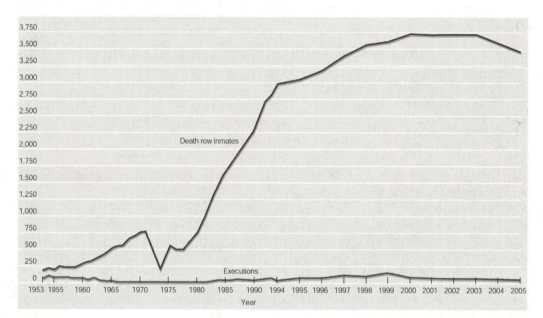

  a) 2000
  b) 1973
  c) 1970
  d) 1996
  e) 2005

12.8. In what case did the Supreme Court rule that the Eighth Amendment prohibited the state from executing the insane?
  a) *Furman v. Georgia* (1972)
  b) *Gregg v. Georgia* (1976)
  c) *McCleskey v. Kemp* (1987)
  d) *Payne v. Tennessee* (1991)
  e) *Ford v. Wainwright* (1986)

12.9. Which of the following justices supports the use of the death penalty?
  a) William Rehnquist
  b) Antonin Scalia
  c) Clarence Thomas
  d) all of the above
  e) none of the above

12.10. Which of the following justices opposed the use of the death penalty?
   a) Sandra Day O'Connor
   b) Antonin Scalia
   c) Clarence Thomas
   d) Thurgood Marshall
   e) Warren Burger

12.11. Which of the following countries allows for the execution of juveniles?
   a) United States
   b) Nigeria
   c) Iran
   d) Yemen
   e) all of the above

12.12. The U. S. Supreme Court declared that the death penalty did not violate the Constitution in the case of juveniles in the case of...
   a) *Furman v. Georgia* (1972)
   b) *Gregg v. Georgia* (1976)
   c) *Stanford v. Kentucky* (1989)
   d) *Payne v. Tennessee* (1991)
   e) *Ford v. Wainwright* (1986)

12.13. The U. S. Supreme Court ruled that defendants in capital cases had the right to representation that meets an "objective standard of reasonableness" in the case of...
   a) *Furman v. Georgia* (1972)
   b) *Gregg v. Georgia* (1976)
   c) *Stanford v. Kentucky* (1989)
   d) *Payne v. Tennessee* (1991)
   e) *Strickland v. Washington* (1984)

12.14. In what case did the U. S. Supreme Court hold that potential jurors who have general objections to the death penalty cannot be automatically excluded from jury service in capital cases?
   a) *Witherspoon v. Illinois* (1968)
   b) *Ring v. Arizona* (2002)
   c) *McCleskey v. Kemp* (1987)
   d) *Apprendi v. New Jersey* (2000)
   e) *Atkins v. Virginia* (2002)

12.15. What is the average amount of time that a death row inmate is under the sentence of the death before the execution?
   a) one year
   b) six years
   c) eleven years
   d) twenty-one years
   e) six months

12.16. Which chief justice has actively sought to reduce the opportunities for capital punishment defendants to have their appeals heard by multiple courts?
   a) Earl Warren
   b) Warren Burger
   c) Earl Burger
   d) William Rehnquist
   e) John Paul Stevens

12.17. Which of the following factors influence the sentencing process?
    a) the administrative context of the courts
    b) the attitudes and values of judges
    c) the presentence report
    d) sentencing guidelines
    e) all of the above

12.18. What type of jurisdiction do misdemeanor, or lower courts, maintain in the American system?
    a) general
    b) limited
    c) intermediate
    d) all of the above
    e) none of the above

12.19. What type of jurisdiction do felony courts, maintain in the American system?
    a) general
    b) limited
    c) intermediate
    d) all of the above
    e) none of the above

12.20. Which goal of punishment is based upon the biblical expression, "An eye for an eye, a tooth for a tooth?"
    a) retribution
    b) deterrence
    c) incapacitation
    d) rehabilitation
    e) all of the above

12.21. Who is responsible for the presentence report?
    a) bailiff
    b) police
    c) clerk
    d) judge
    e) prosecutor

12.22. Which of the following is TRUE about presentence reports?
    a) they are scientific
    b) they are not stereotypical
    c) they are largely determined by the present offense and the prior criminal record
    d) all of the above are true
    e) none of the above are true

12.23. If a person believes that techniques are available to identify and treat the causes of criminal behavior, then which goal of punishment would that person support?
    a) retribution
    b) deterrence
    c) incapacitation
    d) rehabilitation
    e) all of the above

12.24. Legislatures construct sentencing guidelines as a grid of two scores. What are the two scores?
    a) seriousness of the offense and likelihood of recidivism
    b) race and age
    c) judges' attitudes and values
    d) age and status of employment
    e) community ties and family history

12.25. Which of the following is a goal of punishment in the American system of criminal justice?
    a) retribution
    b) deterrence
    c) incapacitation
    d) rehabilitation
    e) all of the above

TRUE/FALSE QUESTIONS

12.1. _T_ Virtually all states and the federal government have some types of mandatory sentences.

12.2. _F_ It is legal for states to execute the mentally retarded.

12.3. _F_ "Good time" refers to the amount of a time that a judge allows a jury to deliberate a decision.

12.4. _F_ The majority of industrialized democracies in the world use the death penalty as a form of punishment.

12.5. _T_ Intermediate sanctions are punishments that are less severe and financially burdensome than prison.

12.6. _T_ The most frequently employed criminal sanction is probation.

12.7. _T_ Jeremy Bentham supported the deterrence approach toward punishment.

12.8. _F_ In recent years less attention has been paid to the concept of selective incapacitation, whereby offenders who repeat certain kinds of crimes are sentenced to long prison terms.

12.9. _F_ At sentencing, judges rarely give reasons for the punishments imposed.

12.10. _F_ Rehabilitation is focused upon the victim of a crime.

12.11. _T_ The country of Singapore offers harsh punishment for a wide range of crimes.

12.12. _T_ Less than 30 percent of persons under correctional supervision are in prisons and jails.

12.13. _T_ Truth-in-sentencing refers to laws that require offenders to serve a large proportion of their prison sentence before being released on parole.

12.14. _F_ Most states do not use the death penalty as punishment in the United States.

12.15. _T_ It is illegal to execute the mentally insane.

12.16. _F_ Offenders can have their prison sentence increased by earning good time for bad behavior.

12.17. _F_ Felony cases are processed and offenders are sentenced in courts of limited jurisdiction.

12.18. _T_ Presentence reports are not scientific and can reflect stereotypes.

12.19. _F_ Since the 1980s sentencing guidelines have been established in the federal courts and in all fifty states.

12.20. _T_ Sentencing guidelines are constructed on the basis of past sentences.

ANSWER KEY

Key Terms
1.   selective incapacitation
2.   indeterminate sentence
3.   special deterrence
4.   shock probation
5.   restoration
6.   mandatory sentence
7.   intermediate sanctions
8.   probation
9.   retribution
10. incapacitation
11. *McCleskey v. Kemp*
12. determinate sentence
13. sentencing guidelines
14. rehabilitation
15. *Furman v. Georgia*
16. general deterrence
17. presentence report

General Practice Questions
1.   retribution
2.   rehabilitation
3.   general deterrence
4.   incapacitation
5.   intermediate sanctions
6.   probation
7.   administrative context
8.   aggravating factors

Multiple Choice Questions
12.1.   C
12.2.   C
12.3.   E
12.4.   A
12.5.   E
12.6.   B
12.7.   A
12.8.   E
12.9.   D
12.10. D
12.11. E
12.12. C
12.13. E
12.14. A
12.15. C
12.16. D
12.17. E
12.18. B
12.19. A
12.20. C
12.21. A
12.22. C
12.23. D
12.24. A
12.25. C

<u>True/False</u>
12.1.   T
12.2.   F
12.3.   F
12.4.   F
12.5.   T
12.6.   T
12.7.   T
12.8.   F
12.9.   F
12.10.   F
12.11.   T
12.12.   T
12.13.   T
12.14.   F
12.15.   T
12.16.   F
12.17.   F
12.18.   T
12.19.   F
12.20.   T

WORKSHEET 12.1   FORMS OF THE CRIMINAL SANCTION

Discuss whether and how the underlying purposes of the criminal sanction fit with various forms of punishment. Ask yourself: Does this form of punishment effectively advance any or all of the underlying purposes? For each punishment, comment on the pros and cons of all of the following: rehabilitation, deterrence, incapacitation, retribution.

1. INCARCERATION:_____

_____

_____

_____

_____

_____

_____

2. PROBATION:

_____

_____

_____

_____

3. FINES: _____

_____

_____

_____

_____

4. CAPITAL PUNISHMENT:_____

_____

_____

_____

_____

5. COMMUNITY SERVICE:_____

_____

_____

_____

_____

WORKSHEET 12.2   SENTENCING

Imagine that you are a judge deciding on sentences for individuals who have entered guilty pleas in the following situations. What sentence would you impose?

1. A nineteen-year-old high school dropout pleads guilty to burglary. He broke into a home and was caught carrying a VCR out the window when the homeowners awoke from the noise of someone in their living room. He has one previous felony conviction for burglary.

SENTENCE:_____

2. A college senior who was caught copying copyrighted computer software from a university computer system onto his own diskette without permission. The value of the software was $700. The student entered a guilty plea to a simple theft charge with an agreement that the prosecutor would recommend leniency. The student has been suspended from college for one year by the school's disciplinary board.

SENTENCE:_____

3. A man who recently completed a prison sentence for armed robbery killed a man during an argument at a bar. The defendant claimed that the victim owed him money so he went to the bar with a knife in order to scare the victim. A confrontation between the two developed into a fight and the victim was stabbed to death. The defendant entered a guilty plea to the charge of second-degree murder. He has served prior prison terms for two armed robbery convictions.

SENTENCE:_____

Now look at the Minnesota sentencing guidelines in the chapter. What would be the sentence for each offender under the guidelines?

1. _____

2. _____

3. _____

Do you think the guidelines are too harsh, too lenient, or just right? Explain.

_____

_____

_____

CORRECTIONS

OUTLINE

- Development of Corrections
- Organization of Corrections in the United States
- Jails: Detention and Short-Term Incarceration
- The Law of Corrections
- Correctional Policy Trends

CHAPTER 13
CORRECTIONS

LEARNING OBJECTIVES

After covering the material in this chapter, students should understand:

1.   the history of corrections, from the development of the penitentiary to reformatories to the rise and fall
        of rehabilitation, including the Pennsylvania and New York systems and community corrections

2.   the nature of prisons by classification and the fragmented organization of corrections nationally

3.   the nature of and problems facing local jails

4.   which constitutional rights are afforded to prisoners

5.   recent trends toward community corrections in correctional policy

CHAPTER SUMMARY

From the colonial days to the present, the methods of criminal punishments that are considered appropriate have
variety. The development of the penitentiary ended corporal punishment. The Pennsylvania and New York
systems competed with different ideas about the penitentiary. In 1870, the Declaration of Principles was written
in Cincinnati and it contained critical ideas about reform and rehabilitation for prisoners. The administration of
corrections in the U. S. is decentralized and scattered across all levels of government. Jails are distinct from
prisons and usually to hold persons awaiting trial and persons who have been sentenced for misdemeanors to
terms of less than one year. Prison populations have increased dramatically during the last ten years and there
has also been a great increase in facilities and staff to administer them.

While prisoners lose many of their constitutional rights while incarcerated, the courts have guaranteed them
freedom to practice their religion, protection against cruel and unusual punishment, due process rights with
regard to discipline and equal protection under the law. Community corrections involves monitoring of
offenders post-release through parole, which can be revoked if offenders fail to live up to the conditions of
release. Increasing use of incarceration has also led to increasing use of parole, straining caseloads and making
regular monitoring a difficult undertaking.

CHAPTER OUTLINE

The correctional system includes prisons, probation, parole, work camps, Salvation Army facilities, medical
facilities, and other types of facilities. The correctional system is authorized by all levels of government and
administered by both public and private organizations, and with a total cost of over $50 billion yearly.

I. DEVELOPMENT OF CORRECTIONS

    A. The Invention of the Penitentiary
        Prior to the year 1800, the most commonly used method of punishment was torture. This was changed
        during the Enlightenment and punishment shifted to houses of hard labor. John Howard (sheriff of
        Bedfordshire, England in the late 18th century) was a strong proponent of the penitentiary. This type of
        facility provided a place for prisoners to work and reflect on their misdeeds. Prisoners were kept in solitary
        cells to allow time for reflection and penitence.

B. Reform in the United States
In the first decades of the nineteenth century, the creation of penitentiaries in Pennsylvania and New York attracted the attention of legislators in other states and also investigators from Europe.

1. **The Pennsylvania System**: The Walnut Street Jail in Philadelphia (1790) was modeled on European penitentiaries. It used solitary confinement, with each small cell, dark holding one inmate. No communications of any kind were allowed. It was from this limited beginning that the Pennsylvania system of separate confinement evolved based on premise of rehabilitation. Other states soon followed in building penitentiaries similar to the Pennsylvania model.

   Critics of these early facilities charged that physical punishment was sometimes used, and the use of isolation was emotionally damaging to prisoners, who suffered mental breakdowns.

2. **The New York System**: In 1819 the Auburn penitentiary opened. They used the congregate system, in which prisoners were kept in individual cells at night but congregated in workshops during the day. However, inmates were forbidden to talk to one another or even to exchange glances while on the job or at meals.

   This system reflected some of the growing emphases of the Industrial Revolution. The men were to have the benefits of labor as well as meditation. They were to work to pay for a portion of their keep. Advocates of both the separate confinement and the congregate systems agreed that the prisoner must be isolated from society and placed on a disciplined routine. By the middle of the nineteenth century, reformers had become disillusioned with the results of the penitentiary movement. There was no evidence these systems deterred or rehabilitated offenders.

3. **Prisons in the South and the West**: In the South, the lease system was developed. This allowed businesses in need of workers to negotiate with the state for the labor and care of prisoners. Prisoners were leased to firms that used them in milling, logging, cotton picking, mining, and railroad construction. Except in California, the prison ideologies of the East did not greatly influence penology in the West. Prior to statehood, prisoners were held in territorial facilities or federal military posts and prisons.

B. Reformatory Movement
Prisons quickly became overcrowded and understaffed by the middle of the 19th century. Discipline, brutality, and corruption were common—Sing Sing Prison in New York was but one example of declining conditions.

1. **Cincinnati, 1870**: In 1870 the newly formed National Prison Association (predecessor of today's American Correctional Association) met in Cincinnati and issued a Declaration of Principles, which asserted that prisons should be operated in accordance with a philosophy of inmate change that would reward reformation with release.

2. **Elmira Reformatory**: Opened in 1876, the first reformatory (run by Zebulon Brockway) regarded education the key to reform and rehabilitation. Elmira used the "mark" system of classification in which prisoners earned their way up (or down) by following rules.

C. Improving Prison Conditions for Women
Elizabeth Gurney Fry, led reform efforts in England after visiting London's Newgate Prison in 1813. Reform took longer in the United States, where recommended changes for female prisoners were sometimes thwarted by male leadership.

During this period, three principles guided prison reform: the separation of women prisoners from men; the provision of care in keeping with the needs of women; and the management of women's prisons by female staff.

D. Rehabilitation Model

In 1930s, attempts were made to implement fully what became known as the rehabilitation model of corrections. Penologists using the newly prestigious social and behavioral sciences helped shift the emphasis of the post-conviction sanction to treatment of criminals, whose social, intellectual, or biological deficiencies were seen as the causes of their illegal activities.

The medical model worked under the assumption that the causes of crime were biological or psychological in nature. Under this approach, correctional institutions were to be staffed with persons who could diagnose the causes of an individual's criminal behavior, prescribe a treatment program, and determine when a cure had been affected so that the offender could be released to the community.

The failure of these new techniques to stem crime, the changes in the characteristics of the prison population, and the misuse of the discretion required by the model prompted another cycle of correctional reform, so that by 1970s rehabilitation fell out of favor with the public.

E. Community Model

Community corrections are based on the assumption that the goal of the criminal justice system should be to reintegrate the offender into the community. This model arose from a sense of social disorder in turbulent 1960s and 1970s. It was argued that corrections should turn away from an emphasis upon psychological treatment to programs that would increase the opportunities for offenders to be successful citizens, e.g., vocational and educational programs. While the community model fell out of favor as the punitive philosophy reigned in the 1970s and 1980s, there has been a resurgence of interest in community corrections.

F. Crime Control Model

The popularity of the crime control model for punishing offenders dominated corrections in the late 1970's through the end of the century. This punitive model attacked rehabilitation as too "lenient" on crime. Incarceration became the dominant form of punishment.

II. ORGANIZATION OF CORRECTIONS IN THE UNITED STATES

A. The Federal Corrections System

1. **Federal Bureau of Prisons**: The U.S. Bureau of Prisons was created by Congress in 1930. Facilities and inmates are classified in a security-level system ranging from Level 1 (the least secure) through Level 6 (the most secure). The federal prison population contains many inmates who have been convicted of white-collar crimes, although drug offenders are increasing. There are fewer offenders who have committed crimes of violence than are found in most state institutions.

2. **Federal probation and parole supervision** for federal offenders are provided by the Division of Probation, a branch of the Administrative Office of the United States Courts. Officers are appointed by the federal judiciary and serve at the pleasure of the court. The Pretrial Services Act of 1982 required pretrial services to be established in each judicial district. Pretrial services officers must collect, verify, and report to the judge concerning information relevant to the pretrial release of defendants.

B. State Correctional Systems

Wide variation exists in the way correctional responsibilities are divided between the state and local governments. Every state has a centralized department of the executive branch that administers corrections, but the extent of these departments' responsibility for programs varies.

1. **Community Corrections**: Community corrections include probation, parole, and other intermediate sanctions. Probation and intermediate sanctions are typically handled by local and/or county jurisdictions, while parole is typically handled by the state.

2. **State Prison Systems**: Most state prisons are generally old and large. Most inmates are in very large "megaprisons" that are antiquated and often in need of repair. State correctional institutions are classified according to the level of security: usually maximum, medium, and minimum.

   Maximum security prisons (where 36% of state inmates are confined) are built like fortresses, surrounded by stone walls with guard towers and designed to prevent escape. Medium security prisons (holding 48% of state inmates) resemble the maximum security prison in appearance, but are less rigid and tense. There is a greater emphasis on rehabilitative programs in medium security institutions. Minimum security prisons (with 16% of state inmates) houses least violent offenders, principally white-collar criminals. The minimum security prison does not have the guard towers and walls usually associated with correctional institutions.

3. **State Institutions for Women**: Women only make up 6.9% of those incarcerated, so there are few facilities designed solely for them. In part, the low percentage of women incarcerated reflects the fact that women are less likely than men to commit violent crimes. Because there are few institutions for women, they usually find themselves far away from family, their children, and other mechanisms of social support.

C. Private Prisons

Private corporations have argued that they can run prisons more cheaply and efficiently than states. The largest providers of private correctional services are the Corrections Corporation of America and Wackenhut Corrections Corporation.

Critics argue that private corporations cut corners while attempting to maximize profits. Several high profile cases of inmate injury as well as facilities cutting back on staff and basic needs for inmates have led some to question the ability of corporations to provide adequate correctional services.

III. JAILS: DETENTION AND SHORT-TERM INCARCERATION

Prisons are at the federal or state level and house inmates with sentences of one year or more. Jails are local facilities for person awaiting trial.

A. Origins and Evolution

Jails in the United States derived from feudal practices in twelfth-century England. The colonists brought the idea of the jail to America.

B. The Contemporary Jail

The U.S. jail has been called the "poorhouse of the twentieth century". They serve partly as a detention center for people awaiting trial, partly as a penal institution for sentenced misdemeanants, and partly as a holding facility for transients taken off the street. Local jails and short-term institutions in the United States are generally regarded as poorly managed custodial institutions. Small jails are becoming less numerous because of new construction and new regional, multi-county facilities.

C. Who Is in Jail?

There are an estimated 11 million jail admissions every year. Nationally, about 600,000 people are in any given day. Many people are held for less than twenty-four hours, others may reside in jail as sentenced inmates for up to one year, a few may await their trials for more than a year. Ninety percent of jail inmates are men and under thirty years old. More than half are of color and most are low income with little education.

D. Managing Jails

1. **Role of the Jail**: Jails are usually run by law enforcement agencies, mostly often the county Sheriff. They hold accused offenders awaiting trial and convicted offenders serving terms of less than one year.

2. **Inmate Characteristics**. The inmate population is made up of inmate of different races, ages, and economic backgrounds. These differences can cause problems for administrators and it can be difficult to keep order, especially in light of the transient nature of this population of offenders.

3. **Fiscal Problems**. Jails can be a financial drain on the jurisdictions that administer them. Resources are often limited given overcrowding, and some jails do not have a strong focus on rehabilitative programming.

IV. THE LAW OF CORRECTIONS

Until the 1960s, the courts, with few exceptions, took the position that the internal administration of prisons was an executive, not a judicial, function. Judges maintained a hands-off policy with regard to prisoner's rights. This changed in the 1960's with the prisoner's rights movement.

A. Constitutional Rights of Prisoners

In 1964, the Supreme Court ruled in *Cooper v. Pate* that prisoners may sue state officials over the conditions of their confinement such as brutality by guards, inadequate nutritional and medical care, theft of personal property, and the denial of basic rights. These changes had the effect of decreasing the custodian's power and the prisoners' isolation from the larger society.

The prisoner rights cases involved prison abuses: brutality and inhuman physical conditions. Gradually, however, prison litigation has focused more directly on the daily activities of the institution, especially on the administrative rules that regulate inmates' conduct.

1. **First Amendment**
   Prisoner litigation has been most successful with respect to many of the restrictions of prison life--access to reading materials, censorship of mail, and some religious practices--have been successfully challenged by prisoners in the courts.

   Generally, prisoners have freedom of speech in prisons. Of course, there are restrictions in order to maintain control in correctional facilities. Freedom of religion has been a major part of prison litigation, and prisoners have been granted the right to worship. In addition, inmates have the right to be served meals that meet their religious dietary laws as well as other religious freedoms.

2. **Fourth Amendment**
   The Fourth Amendment prohibits "unreasonable" searches and seizures and the courts have not been active in extending these protections to prisoners. Thus regulations are viewed as reasonable in light of the institutions' needs for security and order. *Hudson v. Palmer* (1984) upheld the right of officials to search cells and confiscate any materials found. Body searches have been harder for administrators to justify than cell searches, for example, but they have been upheld when they are part of a clear policy demonstrably related to an identifiable legitimate institutional need and when they are not intended to humiliate or degrade.

3. **Eighth Amendment**
   The Eighth Amendment's prohibition of cruel and unusual punishments leads to claims involving the failure of prison administrators to provide minimal conditions necessary for health, to furnish reasonable levels of medical care, and to protect inmates from assault by other prisoners.

   The "totality of conditions" may be such that life in the institution may constitute cruel and unusual punishment. Specific institutions in some states and the entire prison system in other states have been declared to violate the Constitution.

4. **Fourteenth Amendment**
   Two clauses of the Fourteenth Amendment are relevant to the question of prisoners' rights-- those requiring (procedural) due process and equal protection--and have produced a great amount of litigation in the 1970s.

a. *Due Process in Prison Discipline*: Administrative discretion in determining disciplinary procedures can usually be exercised within the prison walls without challenge. *Wolff v. McDonnell* (1974) extended certain procedural rights to inmates: to receive notice of the complaint, to have a fair hearing, to confront witnesses, to be assisted in preparing for the hearing, and to be given a written statement of the decision. Yet the Court also said that there is no right to counsel at a disciplinary hearing.

b. *Equal Protection*: Institutional practices or conditions that discriminate against prisoners on the basis of race or religion have been held unconstitutional. In 1968 the Supreme Court firmly established that racial discrimination may not be official policy within prison walls. Racial segregation is justified only as a temporary expedient during periods when violence between the races is demonstrably imminent.

5. **A Change in Judicial Direction?**
The implementation of the Prison Reform Litigation Act (1996) has made it difficult for prisoners to file suit against the state. Following this act, the number of lawsuits was cut in half.

6. **Impact of the Prisoners' Rights Movement**
Conditions have improved for inmates since the prisoner's rights movement began. Law libraries and legal assistance are now generally available; communication with the outside is easier; religious practices are protected; inmate complaint procedures have been developed; and due process requirements are emphasized.

B. Law and Community Corrections

1. **Conditions of Probation and Parole**
Offenders serving terms of probation or parole must abide by specific conditions of their punishment. These conditions usually interfere with an offender's constitutional rights.

2. **Revocation of Probation and Parole**
Revocation of probation can result from a new arrest or conviction or from failure to comply with a condition of probation. In *Mempa v. Rhay* (1967), the Supreme Court determined that a state probationer had the right to counsel at a revocation proceeding, but nowhere in the opinion did the Court refer to any requirement for a hearing. The Court established due process for parolees facing revocation in Morrissey v. Brewer (1972). Finally, in *Gagnon v. Scarpelli* (1973), the Supreme Court ruled that revocation of probation and parole requires a preliminary and a final hearing.

C. Law and Correctional Personnel
Laws also define the relationship between inmates and personnel. Because prison guards are employees of the state, they are bound by certain regulations and are also able to be sued.

1. **Civil Service Laws**
These laws regulate the hiring and firing of government employees. They are also important with regard to labor unions and how employees are treated by their employers.

2. **Liability of Correctional Personnel**
Under the civil service laws, inmates can sue correctional officials if they feel their civil rights have been violated.

V. CORRECTIONAL POLICY TRENDS

A. Community Corrections
The number of offenders on probation and parole has increased dramatically. This has occurred for a number of reasons, and there are significant implications for the future of community corrections.

1. **Probation**: People on probation make up over seventy percent of the correctional population but resources such as money and staff have not risen accordingly.

2. **Parole**: The number of persons on parole has also grown rapidly. Over one-half million felons are released from prison each year and allowed to live within a community under supervision. Many of these individuals have difficulty finding work and there are few programs to assist them. The average parolee has a 50/50 chance of returning to prison.

B. Incarceration

Since 1973, the incarceration rate has quadrupled but crime levels have stayed the same. In 2001, the nation's prison population rose only 1%, which is the lowest since 1979. It is difficult to predict if this trend will continue. This increase has not occurred "evenly" throughout the United States. Much of the increase is due to the southern region of the U.S. Why the increase in incarceration rates?

1. **Increased Arrests and More Likely Incarceration:** Both the number of arrests and the probability of incarceration has increased in recent years.

2. **Tougher Sentences**: A hardening of public attitudes toward criminals during the past decade has been reflected in longer sentences, in a smaller proportion of those convicted being granted probation, and in fewer being released at the time of the first parole hearing. In addition, the move toward determinate sentencing in many states means that many offenders are now spending more time in prison.

3. **Prison Construction**: The increased rate of incarceration may be related to the creation of additional space in the nation's prisons. Again, public attitudes in favor of more punitive sentencing policies may have influenced legislators to build more prisons. If serious offenses are less common, judges will be inclined to use prison space for less harmful offenders.

4. **War on Drugs**: The crusade against illegal narcotics has produced stiff mandatory sentences by federal government and states.

5. **State Politics**: The election of "law and Order" governors is associated with increases in prison populations, even in states with lower crime rates than neighboring states. Because of public attitudes, crime rates, and the expansion of prison space, incarceration rates are likely to remain high. A policy shift may occur if taxpayers begin to object to the high costs.

REVIEW OF KEY TERMS

Fill in the appropriate term for each statement

corrections
Enlightenment
penitentiary
separate confinement
congregate system
contract labor system
lease system
reformatory
mark system
rehabilitation model
medical model
community corrections
crime control model of corrections
prison
jails

hands-off policy
Cooper v. Pate (1964)
Hudson v. Palmer (1984)
Wolff v. McDonnell (1974)
Mempa v. Rhay (1967)
Morrissey v. Brewer (1972)
Gagnon v. Scarpelli (1973)

1. In the _contract labor system_ , inmates' labor was sold to private employers and inmates made goods to be sold in the prison.

2. Increased use of incarceration and other strict punishments dominate the _crime control model of correction_ .

3. The _hands-off_ is the policy that judges should not interfere with correctional management.

4. In _Cooper v Pate_ , the Supreme Court decided that prisoners may challenge the conditions of their confinement in court.

5. _Enlighten_ was a philosophical movement that emphasized the individual, limitations on government, and rationalism.

6. The _medical model_ assumes that offenders have biological or psychological irregularities and they need to be "cured" in order to stop offending.

7. According to _Wolff v McDonnell_, prisoners have the right to procedural due process when decisions are made regarding the discipline of prisoners.

8. _Corrections_ is the body of programs, services, and organizations responsible for managing people who have committed crimes.

9. A _Congregate system_ is a penitentiary system developed in New York in which prisoners worked together silently during the day before being held in isolation at night.

10. A _penitentiary_ is an institution intended to isolate prisoners from society and from one another so that they could reflect on their misdeeds and repent.

11. The _lease system_ involves inmates leased to contractors, who gave prisoners food and clothing in exchange for their labor.

12. Offenders who are sentenced to one year or more of incarceration serve their sentence in a _prison_ .

13. According to the finding in _Hudson v Palmer_ , prisoners do not have the same protections against search and seizure as non-incarcerated citizens.

14. _Separate confinement_ is a penitentiary system developed in Pennsylvania by the Quakers involving isolation in individual cells.

15. In the case of _Morrisey v Brewer_, parolees are entitled to a hearing prior to revocation of probation.

16. A _reformatory_ is an institution for young offenders emphasizing training and reformation.

17. _Community corrections_ is a model of corrections based on the assumption that the reintegration of the offender into society should be the goal of the criminal justice system.

18. The case of ___Mempa v Rhay___ determined that prisoners have the right to counsel at sentencing and revocation hearings.

19. When institutions use a ___mark system___, offenders receive points for good behavior and negative points for bad behavior.

20. ___rehabilitation model___ is a model based on behavioral and social sciences that emphasized treatment of criminals' deficiencies which caused them to commit crimes.

21. ___JAILS___ are usually under the administration of local, elected law enforcement officials rather than corrections specialists.

22. The Supreme Court decided in ___Gagnon v Scarpelli___ that in order to parole to be revoked, parolees are entitled to an official inquiry.

REVIEW OF KEY PEOPLE

Zebulon Brockway
Elizabeth Gurney Fry
John Howard
Robert Martinson

1. ___Elizabeth Gurney Fry___ was the English reformer who is associated with sparking reform for women offenders.

2. ___John Howard___ was the English reformer whose investigation of prison conditions led Parliament to enact reforms and sparked reform movements in England and the United States.

3. ___Zebulon Brockway___ was the American corrections specialist who advanced his ideas about reformatories while serving many decades as a corrections administrator.

4. Opponents of rehabilitation frequently cite the "nothing works" research findings by ___Robert Martinson___.

GENERAL PRACTICE QUESTIONS

The 1. ___Quaker___ led the reform movement which led to the establishment of 2. ___Walnut Street Jail___, the first institution to implement the 3. ___PA system___ of 4. ___Separate confinement___ as a means to encourage offenders to repent.

5. ___Zebulon Brockway___ served as the warden of 6. ___Elmira Reformatory___ in which he tried to put into practice his ideas for gearing the length and nature of incarceration to the reform of prisoners. Because of the emphasis on indeterminate sentences, these nineteenth century practices shared a similarity with the so-called 7. ___medical model___ of the 8. ___rehabilitation model___, which relied on science to determine when a prisoner had been cured.

9. ___jails___ are short-term holding facilities that contain both 10. ___misdemeanants___ serving short sentences and 11. ___pretrial detainees___ awaiting completion of their cases.

SELF-TEST SECTION

MULTIPLE CHOICE QUESTIONS

13.1. How many adults are under some form of correctional control in The United States?
   a) 1 million
   b) 3.5 million
   c) 6.5 million
   d) 10.9 million
   e) 20 million

13.2. The Enlightenment was the main intellectual force behind:
   a) the civil rights movement
   b) the women's rights movement
   c) the American Revolution
   d) the Crusades
   e) the Louisiana Purchase

13.3. The Penitentiary Act of 1779 called for the creation of:
   a) special facilities for women
   b) educational programs in prison
   c) special courts to hear cases regarding prisoner's rights
   d) rehabilitative programs
   e) houses of hard labor

13.4. Why was isolation an important part of the penitentiary?
   a) Reformers didn't like foul language being used in prison
   b) Reformers wanted inmates to have time to reflect upon their behavior
   c) Reformers wanted inmates to enter the monastery upon release
   d) Reformers didn't want the inmates to file lawsuits
   e) Reformers believed that inmates didn't need human companionship

13.5. How did prisons in New York in the mid-1800's attempt to cover expenses associated with running a prison?
   a) Contracting labor to private companies
   b) Selling prisoner's blood and organs
   c) Using inmates to provide legal services to other inmates
   d) Asking inmates for cash payments to run the prison
   e) Telling guards and staff they would have to accept cuts in pay

13.6. How much money is spent on corrections annually?
   a) $1 billion
   b) $3 billion
   c) $10 billion
   d) $50 billion
   e) $100 billion

13.7. Which countries spawned a movement in the eighteenth century known as the Enlightenment?
   a) U. S. and Canada
   b) England and France
   c) Spain and Italy
   d) Sweden and Denmark
   e) Japan and China

13.8. Prior to 1800, who did Americans copy in using physical punishment as the main criminal sanction?
   a) Europeans
   b) Japanese
   c) Africans
   d) Mexicans
   e) Chinese

13.9. As sheriff of Bedfordshire, England, who was especially influential in promoting the reform of corrections?
   a) John Howard
   b) Michel Foucault
   c) Zebulon Brockway
   d) Benjamin Rush
   e) Elizabeth Fry

13.10. What law passed by Parliament called for the creation of a house of hard labor where offenders would be imprisoned for up to two years?
   a) English Prison Association Act of 1870
   b) Penitentiary Act of 1779
   c) English Bureau of Prisons Act of 1930
   d) London Newgate Prison Act of 1813
   e) Walnut Street Jail Act of 1790

13.11. Who inspired the Philadelphia Society for Alleviating the Miseries of Public Prisons, which formed in 1787?
   a) John Howard
   b) Michel Foucault
   c) Zebulon Brockway
   d) Benjamin Rush
   e) Elizabeth Fry

13.12. What was the first penitentiary created by the Pennsylvania legislature in 1790?
   a) Philadelphia Jail Institute
   b) Pittsburgh Prison House
   c) Auburn House
   d) Walnut Street Jail
   e) Sing Sing Prison

13.13. Who was the warden at the Auburn Penitentiary who was convinced that convicts were incorrigible and that industrial efficiency should be the overriding purpose of the prison?
   a) John Williams
   b) John Howard
   c) Elizabeth Fry
   d) Benjamin Rush
   e) Elam Llynds

13.14. Which system rented prisoners to firms that used them in milling, logging, cotton picking, mining and railroad construction?
   a) New York system
   b) Pennsylvania system
   c) lease system
   d) Auburn system
   e) loan system

13.15. The prison ideologies of the East did not greatly influence penology in the West, except for the state of…
   a) Arizona
   b) California
   c) New Mexico
   d) Oregon
   e) Nevada

13.16. Which law passed by Congress restricted the employment of federal prisoners?
   a) Federal Bureau of Prisons Act of 1930
   b) Anticontract Law of 1887
   c) Hatch Act of 1940
   d) Pendleton Act of 1883
   e) The Prisoners Services Act of 1982

13.17. What system based prisoner release on performance through voluntary labor, participation in educational and religious programs, and good behavior?
   a) enlightenment system
   b) congregate system
   c) lease system
   d) mark system
   e) Walnut Jail system

13.18. What is a release under supervision that could be revoked if the offender did not live up to the conditions of his release?
   a) mere lapse of time
   b) corporal punishment
   c) mark system
   d) ticket-of-leave
   e) lease system

13.19. When did the reformatory system start to decline?
   a) around the Civil War
   b) around World War I
   c) around World War II
   d) around the Korean conflict
   e) around the Vietnam conflict

13.20. When and where was the Women's Prison Association was formed?
   a) 1804 in Boston
   b) 1844 in New York
   c) 1903 in Cleveland
   d) 1925 in Kansas City
   e) 1987 in Las Vegas

13.21. Who was the head matron of the women's wing at Sing Sing (1844 to 1848), sought to implement Elizabeth's Fry's ideas but was thwarted by the male overseers and legislators and was forced to resign?
   a) John Williams
   b) John Howard
   c) Elizabeth Farnham
   d) Benjamin Rush
   e) Zebulon Brockway

13.22. What was NOT addressed in the Cincinnati Declaration of Principles?
    a) rewarding reformed prisoners with release
    b) fixed sentences should be replaced with indeterminate sentences
    c) the treatment of criminals through moral regeneration
    d) the problems of female offenders
    e) all of the above were addressed

13.23. This cell is most likely to be found in this type of facility:

    a) work farm
    b) group home
    c) super max prison
    d) minimum security prison
    e) local jail

13.24. In the late nineteenth century, which of the following principles guided female prison reform?
    a) the separation of women prisoners from men
    b) the provision of care in keeping with the needs of women
    c) the management of women's prisons by female staff
    d) all of the above
    e) none of the above

13.25. Based on the chart below, which correctional population has experienced the most growth since 1980?

    a) jail
    b) parole
    c) prison
    d) probation
    e) parole

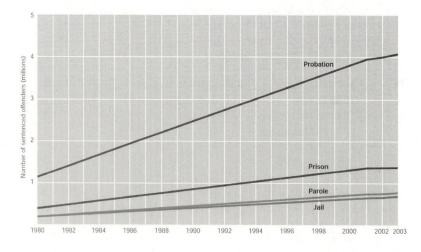

TRUE/FALSE QUESTIONS

13.1. _____ The Quakers played a large role in developing the Pennsylvania system.

13.2. _____ The Declaration of Principles did NOT deal with the problems of female offenders.

13.3. ___F___ Since the 1700s, Women and men have been treated differently in prison.

13.4. ___T___ Group therapy became part of rehabilitation after World War II.

13.5. ___F___ John Howard was the first prisoner executed at Sing Sing prison.

13.6. ___T___ From 1776-1826, the emphasis shifted to a belief that crime was a result of forces operating in the environment.

13.7. ___F___ Corrections cost less than one billion dollars a year.

13.8. ___F___ The Enlightenment focused upon increasing the powers of government, group behavior, and irrationalism.

13.9. ___T___ The Crime Control Model emphasized incarceration as a way to solve the crime problem.

13.10. ___F___ The U. S. Bureau of Prisons was created by executive order in 1990.

13.11. ___T___ Community corrections focuses on reintegrating the offender into society.

13.12. ___T___ There are fewer adults under federal correctional supervision because fewer activities constitute federal crimes.

13.13. ___F___ Women comprise roughly 35 percent of the incarcerated population.

13.14. ___F___ Private run prisons do not exist anymore in the U. S.

13.15. ___F___ Private prisons provide better security than government-operated prisons.

13.16. ___F___ Private prisons are more expensive than government-operated prisons.

13.17. ___T___ There is a difference between prisons and jails within the U. S. system.

13.18. ___T___ Jails in the United States descend from feudal practices in twelfth-century England.

13.19. ___T___ The primary function of jails is to hold persons awaiting trial and persons who have been sentenced for misdemeanors to terms of less than one year.

13.20. ___T___ Most jails are at the county level.

ANSWER KEY

Key Terms
1. contract labor system
2. crime control model of corrections
3. hands-off policy
4. *Cooper v. Pate*
5. the Enlightenment
6. medical model
7. *Wolff v. McDonnell*
8. corrections
9. congregate system
10. penitentiary
11. lease system
12. prison
13. *Hudson v. Palmer*
14. separate confinement
15. *Morrissey v. Brewer*
16. reformatory
17. community corrections
18. *Mempa v. Rhay*
19. mark system
20. rehabilitation model
21. jails
22. *Gagnon v. Scarpelli*

Key People
1. Elizabeth Gurney Fry
2. John Howard
3. Zebulon Brockway
4. Robert Martinson

General Practice Questions
1. Quakers
2. Walnut Street Jail
3. Pennsylvania system
4. separate confinement
5. Zebulon Brockway
6. Elmira Reformatory
7. medical model
8. rehabilitation model
9. jails
10. misdemeanants
11. pretrial detainees

Multiple Choice
13.1.   C
13.2.   C
13.3.   E
13.4.   B
13.5.   A
13.6.   D
13.7.   B
13.8.   A
13.9.   A
13.10. B

13.11. A
13.12. D
13.13. E
13.14. C
13.15. B
13.16. B
13.17. D
13.18. D
13.19. B
13.20. B
13.21. C
13.22. D
13.23. C
13.24. D
13.25. D

True/False
13.1.   T
13.2.   T
13.3.   F
13.4.   T
13.5.   F
13.6.   T
13.7.   F
13.8.   F
13.9.   T
13.10. F
13.11. T
13.12. T
13.13. F
13.14. F
13.15. F
13.16. F
13.17. T
13.18. T
13.19. T
13.20. T

WORKSHEET 13.1: HISTORY OF CORRECTIONS

Imagine that you are the head of a state department of corrections during several eras of American history. Describe each of the following approaches to corrections as you would implement them to make them work as well as they could. Then describe the drawbacks of each approach.

Separate Confinement (Pennsylvania) ______________________________

____

____

Drawbacks: ______________________________

____

____

Congregate System (New York) ______________________________

____

____

Drawbacks: ______________________________

____

____

Rehabilitation Model ______________________________

____

____

Drawbacks: ______________________________

____

____

Community Model ______________________________

____

____

Drawbacks: ______________________________

____

____

WORKSHEET 13.2: CAUSES OF RISING PRISON POPULATIONS

Describe each of the theories used to explain the increase in imprisonment of offenders.

Tougher Sentencing_____

_____

_____

_____

Increased Arrests and More Likely Incarceration_____

_____

_____

_____

State Politics_____

_____

_____

_____

Construction_____

_____

_____

_____

War on Drugs_____

_____

_____

_____

Which theory do you believe provides the best explanation? Explain why.

_____

_____

_____

_____

COMMUNITY CORRECTIONS

Probation and

Intermediate Sanctions

OUTLINE

- Community Corrections: Assumptions
- Probation: Correction without Incarceration
- Intermediate Sanctions in the Community

CHAPTER 14
COMMUNITY CORRECTIONS:
PROBATION AND INTERMEDIATE SANCTIONS

LEARNING OBJECTIVES

After covering the material in this chapter, students should understand:

1.   the assumptions underlying community corrections

2.   the evolution of probation, the nature of probation services, and probation revocation

3.   intermediate sanctions including fines, restitution, forfeiture, home confinement, community service, intensive probation, and boot camps

5.   the difficulties in implementing intermediate sanctions

CHAPTER SUMMARY

Community supervision through probation, intermediate sanctions, and parole are a growing part of the criminal justice system. Probation is imposed on more than half of offenders. Persons with this sentence live in the community according to conditions set by the judge and under the supervision of a probation officer. Intermediate sanctions are designed as punishments that are more restrictive than probation and less restrictive than prison. The range of intermediate sanctions allows judges to design sentences that incorporate one or more of the punishments and hopefully reduce recidivism. Some intermediate sanctions are implemented by courts (fines, restitution, forfeiture), others in the community (home confinement, community service, day reporting centers, intensive supervision probation) and in institutions and the community (boot camps).

CHAPTER OUTLINE

I.   COMMUNITY CORRECTIONS: ASSUMPTIONS

The goal of community corrections is to build ties that can reintegrate the offender into the community. It assumes that the offender must change, but it also recognizes that factors within the community that might encourage criminal behavior (unemployment, for example) must change as well. Central to the community corrections approach is a belief in the "least restrictive alternative," the notion that the criminal sanction should be applied only to the minimum extent necessary to meet the community's need for protection, the gravity of the offense, and society's need for deserved punishment.

II.   PROBATION: CORRECTION WITHOUT INCARCERATION

Probation denotes the conditional release of the offender into the community under supervision. It imposes conditions and retains the authority of the sentencing court to modify the conditions of sentence or to re-sentence the offender. Conditions may include drug tests, curfews, and orders to stay away from certain people or parts of town.

A.   Origins and Evolution of Probation
      John Augustus, a prosperous Bostonian, has become known as the world's first probation officer. By persuading a judge in the Boston Police Court to place a convicted offender in his custody for a brief period, Augustus was able to assist his probationer so that the man appeared to be rehabilitated when he returned for sentencing.

Probation officers began with a casework model to be actively involved in the family, employment, free time, and religion of first-time and minor offenders. With the rising influence of psychology in the 1920s, the probation officer continued as a caseworker, but the emphasis moved to therapeutic counseling in the office rather than on assistance in the field.

During the 1960s, probation officers changed their strategies. Rather than counseling offenders in their offices, probation officers provided them with concrete social services, such as assistance with employment, housing, finances, and education. In the late 1970s the orientation of probation again changed. The goals of rehabilitation and reintegration gave way to an orientation widely referred to as risk control. There is a growing interest in community justice, which emphasizes restorative justice, and how probation can serve to advance restoration.

B. Organization of Probation

Probation may be viewed as a form of corrections, but in many states it is administered by the judiciary, usually with local control. Frequently, the locally elected county judges are really in charge. However, judges usually know little about corrections and probation administration. Perhaps the strongest argument in favor of judicial control is that probation works best when there is a close relationship between the judge and the supervising officer. Some states have combined probation and parole in the same department, even though parolees are quite different than probationers—parolees need greater supervision and have significant adjustment problems when they leave prison.

C. Probation Services

Probation officers have come to be expected to act as both police personnel and social workers. They prepare presentence reports for the courts and they supervise clients in order to keep them out of trouble and to assist them in the community. Most probation officers have backgrounds in social service and are partial to that role. The 50-unit caseload established in the 1930s by the National Probation Association was reduced to 35 by the President's Commission in 1967; yet the national average is currently about 150, and in extreme cases it reaches more than 300.

In dangerous urban neighborhoods, direct supervision can be a dangerous task for the probation officer. In some urban areas, probationers are merely required to telephone or mail reports of their current residence and employment. It such cases, which justification for the criminal sanction--deserved punishment, rehabilitation, deterrence, or incapacitation—is being realized?

D. Revocation and Termination of Probation

Revocation of probation can result from a new arrest or conviction or from failure to comply with a condition of probation. Since probation is usually granted in conjunction with a suspended jail or prison sentence, incarceration may follow revocation. In 1998 a national survey of probationers found that 59 percent of adults released from probation successfully completed their sentences, while only 17 percent had been reincarcerated.

Common reasons for revocation include failing a drug urinalysis test, failure to participate in treatment, failure to report to probation officer (all technical violations) and rearrest for a new crime. The current emphasis is on avoiding incarceration except for flagrant and continual violation of the conditions of probation, thus most revocations occur because of a new arrest or conviction. Some studies show that even serious misconduct will not necessarily lead to revocation.

E. Assessing Probation

Critics argue that, especially in urban areas, probation does nothing. Because of huge caseloads and indifferent officers, offenders can easily avoid supervision and check in only perfunctorily with their probation officers. In such cases, probation has little effect on crime control. Probation does produce less recidivism than incarceration, but researchers now wonder if this effect is a direct result of supervision or an indirect result of people "growing out" of crime.

Due to prison overcrowding, today almost one-half of the nation's probationers have been convicted on felony charges. In addition, upwards of 75 percent of probationers are addicted to drugs or alcohol. Officers can no longer assume that their clients pose little threat to society and that they are capable of living productive lives in the community. The new demands upon probation have given rise to calls for increased electronic monitoring and for risk management systems that will differentiate the levels of supervision required for different offenders.

III. INTERMEDIATE SANCTIONS IN THE COMMUNITY

Intermediate sanctions may be viewed as a continuum--a range of punishments that vary in terms of level of intrusiveness and control. Probation plus a fine or community service may be appropriate for minor offenses, while six weeks of boot camp followed by intensive probation supervision may be the deserved punishment for someone who has been convicted of a more serious crime. Each individual intermediate sanction may be imposed singly or in tandem with others.

A. Intermediate Sanctions Administered Primarily by the Judiciary
   1. **Fines** are routinely imposed today for a wide range of offenses. Recent studies have shown that the fine is used very widely as a criminal sanction and that probably well over $1 billion in fines are collected annually by courts across the country. Fines are rarely used as the *sole* punishment for crimes more serious than motor vehicle violations. In European countries, fines are much more commonly used as the sole punishment.

      Judge may shy away from using fines because they may be concerned that fines would be paid from the proceeds of additional illegal acts. In addition, reliance on fines as an alternative to incarceration might mean that the affluent would be able to "buy" their way out of jail and that the poor would have to serve time.

   2. **Restitution** is repayment to a victim who has suffered some form of financial loss as a result of the offender's crime. It is only since the late 1970s that it has been institutionalized in many areas. It is usually carried out as one of the conditions of probation.

   3. **Forfeiture** is seizure by the government of property derived from or used in criminal activity. Forfeiture proceedings can take both a civil and a criminal form. Using the civil law, property utilized in criminal activity (contraband, equipment to manufacture illegal drugs, automobiles) can be seized without a finding of guilt. Criminal forfeiture is a punishment imposed as a result of conviction at the time of sentencing. It requires that the offender relinquish various assets related to the crime.

      Concerns have been raised about law enforcement self-interest in forfeiture because the forfeited assets are often directed into the budget of the law enforcement agency initiating the action.

B. Intermediate Sanctions Administered in the Community

   1. **Home Confinement** requires convicted offenders to spend all or part of the time in their own residence. Also called "house arrest", offenders may be able to leave their residence for work, school, or treatment. This can be used as a sole sanction or in combination with other penalties and can be imposed at almost any point in the criminal justice process: during the pretrial period, after a short term in jail or prison, or as a condition of probation or parole.

      Electronic devices that monitor offenders can either be passive (in which a probation officer must call in to check that the offender is home) or active (in which a continuous signal is sent by the device, which notifies the probation officer if the offender leaves the home).

   2. **Community Service** is unpaid service to the public to overcome or compensate society for some of the harm caused by the crime; it may take a variety of forms, including work in a social service agency, cleaning parks, or assisting the poor. The sentence specifies the number of hours to be worked and usually requires supervision by a probation officer. Labor unions and workers criticize it, saying that

offenders are taking jobs from crime-free citizens. Some experts believe that if community service is used as the sole sanction, the result will be that certain courts may allow affluent offenders to purchase relatively mild punishments.

3. **Day reporting centers** incorporate a potpourri of common correctional methods. For example, in some centers, offenders are required to be in the facility for eight hours, or to report into the center for urine checks before going to work. In others, the treatment regime is comparable to that of a halfway house—but without the offender living in a residential facility. Drug and alcohol treatment, literacy programs, and job searches may be carried out in the center.

3. **Intensive probation supervision (ISP)** is a way of using probation as an intermediate punishment. It is thought that daily contact between the probationer and officer may decrease rearrests and may permit offenders who might otherwise go to prison to be released into the community. Institutional diversion selects low-risk offenders sentenced to prison and provides supervision for them in the community. Each officer has only twenty clients, and frequent face-to-face contacts are required. Because the intention is to place high-risk offenders who would normally be incarcerated in the community instead, it is expected that resources will be saved.

Judges and prosecutors may like ISP because it gives the appearance of being "tough" on offenders by setting many specific conditions. ISP programs have higher failure rates, in part because officers can detect more violations through close contact. In several states, offenders have expressed a preference for serving a prison term rather than being placed under the demanding conditions of ISP.

C. Sanctions Administered in Institutions and Community
Boot camps now operate in thirty states. They are all based on the belief that young offenders can be "shocked" out of their criminal ways if they undergo a physically rigorous, disciplined, and demanding regimen for a short period, usually three or four months, before being returned to the community for supervision. These programs are sometimes referred to as "shock incarceration."

Other critics note that shock incarceration builds esprit de corps and solidarity, which are characteristics that have the potential for improving the leadership qualities of the young offender and that when taken back to the streets may actually enhance a criminal career. While boot camps have not been effective at decreasing recidivism, many point to the lack of aftercare programs to help transition offenders back into society.

D. Implementing Intermediate Sanctions
In many states there is competition as to which agency will receive additional funding to run the intermediate sanctions programs. Probation organizations argue that they know the field, have the experienced staff, and --given the additional resources--could do an excellent job.

A second issue concerns the type of offender given an intermediate sanction. One school of thought emphasizes the seriousness of the offense, the other concentrates on the problems of the offender. Some agencies want to accept into their intermediate sanctions program only those offenders who *will* succeed. The agencies are concerned about their success ratio, especially as this factor might jeopardize future funding. Critics point out that this strategy leads to "creaming" (i.e., taking the cream of the crop), taking the most promising offenders and leaving those with problems to traditional sanctions.

"Net widening" is the term used to describe a process in which the new sanction increases, rather than reduces the control over offender's lives. This can occur when a judge imposes a *more* intrusive sanction than usual, rather than the *less* intrusive option. For example, rather than merely sentencing an offender to probation, the judge might also require that the offender perform community service.

IV. THE FUTURE OF COMMUNITY CORRECTIONS

There were 3.7 million Americans under community supervision in 1995; by 2003 this figure had grown to almost 5 million. Despite its wide usage, community corrections often lacks public support, in part because it suffers from an image of being "soft on crime." Offenders today require greater supervision based on their crimes, prior records, and drug problems when compared to those placed on probation in previous eras. Probation needs an infusion of resources to fulfill its responsibilities during an era of prison overcrowding. To garner support for community corrections, citizens must believe that these sanctions are meaningful.

REVIEW OF KEY TERMS

Fill in the appropriate term for each statement

recidivism
community justice
technical violation
fines
restitution
home confinement
community service
day reporting centers
intensive probation supervision (ISP)
boot camp
net widening

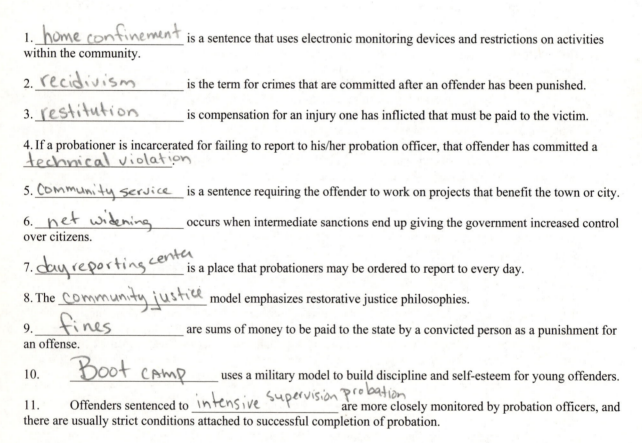

1. _home confinement_ is a sentence that uses electronic monitoring devices and restrictions on activities within the community.

2. _recidivism_ is the term for crimes that are committed after an offender has been punished.

3. _restitution_ is compensation for an injury one has inflicted that must be paid to the victim.

4. If a probationer is incarcerated for failing to report to his/her probation officer, that offender has committed a _technical violation_

5. _community service_ is a sentence requiring the offender to work on projects that benefit the town or city.

6. _net widening_ occurs when intermediate sanctions end up giving the government increased control over citizens.

7. _day reporting center_ is a place that probationers may be ordered to report to every day.

8. The _community justice_ model emphasizes restorative justice philosophies.

9. _fines_ are sums of money to be paid to the state by a convicted person as a punishment for an offense.

10. _Boot camp_ uses a military model to build discipline and self-esteem for young offenders.

11. Offenders sentenced to _intensive supervision probation_ are more closely monitored by probation officers, and there are usually strict conditions attached to successful completion of probation.

GENERAL PRACTICE QUESTIONS

Many intermediate sanctions can be applied in the context of 1. _community corrections_ because offenders who must provide labor under a sentence of 2. _community service_ or are subject to electronic monitoring under a sentence of 3. _home detention_ are not sent away to prison. Although the officers who supervise 4. _probation_ may make some efforts to fulfill the ideal of rehabilitation, many intermediate sanctions actually stem from prison overcrowding rather than from other underlying purposes.

With young offenders, judges may apply either or both 5. _Boot camp_ involving military discipline or 6. _shock incarceration_ to provide a taste of deprivation of freedom. Like other forms of sanctions, these two do not necessarily prevent young offenders from becoming repeat offenders as adults.

SELF-TEST SECTION

MULTIPLE CHOICE QUESTIONS

14.1. What is one reason why criminal justice experts tend to support the use of community corrections?
    a)   It is a harsh punishment
    b)   It is cheaper than incarceration
    c)   It serves to isolate offenders from the community
    d)   It does not assume guilt on the part of the offender
    e)   Offenders have no constitutional rights under a community corrections model

14.2. The public is generally not in favor of increased use of probation because:
    a)   It is too expensive
    b)   It contributes to prison overcrowding
    c)   It appears to be a "slap on the wrist"
    d)   Too many offenders charged with murder receive probation
    e)   The use of probation takes jobs away from non-criminal citizens

14.3. Which of the following concepts are espoused by a community justice philosophy?
    a)   restorative justice
    b)   reparation to the victim and community
    c)   problem-solving strategies
    d)   increased citizen involvement in crime reduction
    e)   all of the above

14.4. Which term describes the approach that seeks to minimize the probability than an offender will commit a new offense by making the punishment fit the crime?
    a)   recidivism
    b)   restorative justice
    c)   intensive supervision probation
    d)   mark system
    e)   risk management

14.5. How many offenders are on probation in the American criminal justice system?
    a)   100,000
    b)   500,000
    c)   2.3 million
    d)   3.8 million
    e)   6.5 million

14.6. Which state developed the first statewide probation system in 1880?
   a)   Delaware
   b)   New Jersey
   c)   Pennsylvania
   d)   Massachusetts
   e)   New York

14.7. According to the Bureau of Justice Statistics, how many adults released from probation successfully completed their sentences?
   a)   17 percent
   b)   28 percent
   c)   59 percent
   d)   76 percent
   e)   96 percent

14.8. According to the Bureau of Justice Statistics, how many adults released from probation had been reincarcerated?
   a)   17 percent
   b)   28 percent
   c)   59 percent
   d)   76 percent
   e)   96 percent

14.9. Which of the following is true about probation?
   a)   Probation can only be revoked for a technical violation
   b)   Probation can only be revoked for committing a new crime
   c)   Probation has a higher rate of recidivism than incarceration
   d)   Probationers are usually the most serious offenders
   e)   Probationers have the right to a hearing before probation is revoked

14.10. How much money is saved by keeping an offender on parole instead of in prison?
   a) $1,000 a year
   b) $5,000 a year
   c) $20,000 a year
   d) $40,000 a year
   e)   there is no savings

14.11. What percentage of probationers are addicted to drugs or alcohol?
   a)   25 percent
   b)   50 percent
   c)   75 percent
   d)   90 percent
   e)   95 percent

14.12. Which of the following can be combined with probation?
   a)   fines
   b)   restitution
   c)   community service
   d)   all of the above
   e)   none of the above

14.13. Which country created the day-fine system in 1921?
    a) Denmark
    b) Sweden
    c) United States
    d) Germany
    e) Finland

14.14. In what case did the U. S. Supreme Court rule that the Eighth Amendment's ban on excessive fines requires that the seriousness of the offense be related to the property that is taken?
    a) *Austin v. United States* (1993)
    b) *Atkins v. Virginia* (2002)
    c) *Ring v. United States* (2002)
    d) *McCleskey v. Kemp* (1985)
    e) *Gregg v. Georgia* (1976)

14.15. Which constitutional right might be violated by electronic monitoring and home confinement?
    a) double jeopardy clause
    b) cruel and unusual punishment clause
    c) quartering of troops clause
    d) unreasonable search and seizure clause
    e) reserved powers clause

14.16. What law passed by the Wisconsin legislature established the model for work and educational release programs?
    a) Walnut Hill Act
    b) Release Program and Probation Act
    c) Labor and Education Act
    d) Intermediate Sanction and Rewards Act
    e) Huber Act

14.17. During the 1960s, what shift occurred in probation?
    a) offenders were given less probation
    b) offenders began to refuse probation and select incarceration
    c) offenders began to abuse probation
    d) offenders were given assistance with employment, housing, finances, and education
    e) offenders were given more counseling

14.18. In the late 1970s, how did the orientation of probation change?
    a) emphasis was placed upon rehabilitation
    b) efforts were made to minimize the probability that an offender would commit a new offense
    c) emphasis was placed upon reintegration into society
    d) efforts were made to eliminate probation
    e) probation did not change during the late 1970s

14.19. Probation seems to work best when the...
    a) judge and the victim of the offender have a close relationship
    b) judge and the offender have a close relationship
    c) judge and the supervising officer have a close relationship
    d) judge and the community are in agreement on probation issues
    e) judge and the defense attorney have a close relationship

14.20. Which of the following is an example of an intermediate sanction administered primarily by the judiciary?
    a) home confinement
    b) day reporting centers
    c) forfeiture
    d) all of the above
    e) none of the above

14.21. Which of the following is an example of an intermediate sanction administered primarily inside institutions and followed by community supervision?
    a) boot camp
    b) day reporting centers
    c) forfeiture
    d) all of the above
    e) none of the above

14.22. Which of the following is an example of an intermediate sanction administered primarily in the community with a supervision component?
    a) home confinement
    b) fines
    c) forfeiture
    d) all of the above
    e) none of the above

14.23. Why don't American judges prefer to impose fines on offenders?
    a) judges do not have time to factor fines into the budget of the court
    b) money and justice should not become intertwined
    c) fines are usually embezzled by court officials
    d) fines are too light of a punishment for even minor offenses
    e) fines are difficult to collect from offenders who are predominately poor

14.24. A passive home confinement system…
    a) Responds only to inquiries from the probation officer
    b) Sends continuous signals and alerts the probation officer when the offender leaves his or her home
    c) Helps decrease net widening
    d) Is used in most prisons to prevent escape
    e) Is generally preferred over an active system

14.25. The inmates in this picture are most likely incarcerated in a:

Work release program
    a) Prison
    b) County jail
    c) Day reporting center
    d) Boot camp

TRUE/FALSE QUESTIONS

14.1. _____The day fine has never been used in the United States.

14.2. _____Before probation can be revoked, the offender is entitled to a preliminary hearing.

14.3. _____The recidivism rate for offenders under community supervision is lower than those who are released from prison.

14.4. _____Fines are used extensively in Europe as punishment.

14.5. _____In regard to forfeiture laws, owners' property cannot be seized if they can demonstrate their innocence by a preponderance of evidence.

14.6. _____Forfeited assets often go into the budget of the law enforcement agency taking the action.

14.7. _____Because incarceration rates and probation caseloads are decreasing, intermediate sanctions probably will not play a major role in corrections during the first decade of the new century.

14.8. _____In most states, laws prevent former prisoners from working in certain types of establishments.

14.9. _____Most work and educational release programs cost relatively little.

14.10. _____Restitution is typically used when it is difficult to calculate damages from crime.

14.11. _____Community service is most often used when offenders cannot pay fines.

14.12. _____In Japan, citizen volunteers are involved in helping newly released offenders adjust to the community.

14.13. _____Conjugal visits have been used in most U.S. correctional systems.

14.14. _____Few released prisoners are subject to conditional community supervision release.

14.15. _____The size of a probation officer's caseload is often less important for preventing recidivism than the quality of supervision and assistance provided to probationers.

14.16. _____Many judges order community service when an offender cannot pay a fine.

14.17. _____There are few technical problems with electronic monitoring devices.

14.18. _____The legislative branch is largely responsible for administering intermediate sanctions.

14.19. _____Probation costs more than keeping an offender behind bars.

14.20. _____A state probationer has a right to counsel at a revocation and sentencing hearing.

ANSWER KEY

Key Terms
1. home confinement
2. recidivism
3. restitution
4. technical violation
5. community service
6. net widening
7. day reporting centers
8. community justice
9. fines
10. boot camp
11. intensive supervision probation (ISP)

General Practice Questions
1. community corrections
2. community service
3. home detention
4. probation
5. boot camp
6. shock incarceration

Multiple Choice
14.1.   B
14.2.   C
14.3.   E
14.4.   E
14.5.   D
14.6.   D
14.7.   C
14.8.   A
14.9.   D
14.10.   E
14.11.   A
14.12.   C
14.13.   C
14.14.   D
14.15.   E
14.16.   A
14.17.   D
14.18.   E
14.19.   D
14.20.   B
14.21.   C
14.22.   C
14.23.   A
14.24.   A
14.25.   E

True/False
14.1.   F
14.2.   T
14.3.   F
14.4.   T
14.5.   T
14.6.   T

14.7.   F
14.8.   T
14.9.   T
14.10. F
14.11. T
14.12. T
14.13. F
14.14. F
14.15. T
14.16. T
14.17. F
14.18. F
14.19. F
14.20. T

WORKSHEET 14.1: PROBATION

If you were a judge, what kinds of offenders would you put on probation? What kinds of offenders would you *not* place on probation?

_____

_____

_____

_____

_____

_____

_____

If you were a probation officer, which aspect of your job would receive your strongest emphasis: surveillance/rule enforcement or social services/counseling to help reintegration? Why?

_____

_____

_____

_____

_____

_____

_____

If you were a judge, what conditions/restrictions would you impose on probationers? Why?

_____

_____

_____

_____

_____

_____

_____

WORKSHEET 14.2: INTERMEDIATE SANCTIONS

Take the following intermediate sanctions and list them in order of the sanctions that you believe are most effective (1 for most effective and 8 for least effective). For each one, describe its strengths and weaknesses with respect to the goals that should be accomplished: fines, restitution, boot camps, intensive probation supervision, forfeiture, day reporting centers, community service, home confinement.

1. _____: _____

_____

_____

2. _____: _____

_____

_____

3. _____: _____

_____

_____

4. _____: _____

_____

_____

5. _____: _____

_____

_____

6. _____: _____

_____

_____

7. _____: _____

_____

_____

8. _____: _____

_____

INCARCERATION AND PRISON SOCIETY

OUTLINE

CHAPTER 15
INCARCERATION AND PRISON SOCIETY

LEARNING OBJECTIVES

After covering the material in this chapter, students should understand:

1.   the goals of incarceration, including the custodial model, rehabilitation model, and reintegration model

2.   prison management and organization

3.   the challenges of managing a "society of captives"

4.   the role of the correctional officer is maintaining order in prisons

5.   the characteristics of inmates

6.   how inmates adapt to incarceration

7.   unique situations of women in prison

8.   the different types of programs available to prisons

9.   violence in prison, including contributing causes, and the role of age, attitudes, race, and gangs

CHAPTER SUMMARY

Since the 1940s, three models of incarceration have been prominent: 1) the custodial model which emphasizes the maintenance of security, 2) the rehabilitation model which views security and housekeeping activities as mainly a framework for treatment efforts, and 3) the reintegration model which recognizes that prisoners must be prepared for their return to society. Popular belief that the warden and officers have total power over the inmates is outdated. Good management through effective leadership can maintain the quality of prison life as measured by levels of order, amenities, and service. Because they are constantly in close contact with the prisoners, correctional officers are the real linchpins in the prison system. The effectiveness of the institution lies heavily on their shoulders. Since the 1960s, the prisoners' rights movement, through lawsuits in the federal courts, has brought many changes to the administration and conditions of American prisons.

In the United States, state and federal prisoners do not serve their time in isolation but are members of a subculture with their own traditions, norms, and leadership structure. Inmates deal with the pain of incarceration by assuming an adaptive role and lifestyle. Today, major problems in prison society consist of AIDS, an increase in elderly and the mentally ill inmates and inmates serving long terms. The state provides housing, food, and clothes for all inmates. To meet the needs of prisoners for goods and services not provided by the state, an underground economy exists in the society of captives. Most prisoners are young men with little education and disproportionately from minority groups. Only a small portion of the inmate population is female. This is cited as the reason for the limited programs and services available to women prisoners. Social relationships among female inmates differ from those of their male counterparts. Women tend to form pseudo-families in prison. Many women experience the added stress of being responsible for their children on the outside. Educational, vocational, industrial, and treatment programs are available in prisons. Educational programs reduce the risk of an inmate committing a crime upon release from prison. Administrators also believe these programs are important for maintaining order. Prison violence is a major problem confronting administrators. The characteristics of the inmates and the rise of gangs contribute to this problem.

CHAPTER OUTLINE

I.   THE MODERN PRISON: LEGACY OF THE PAST

Many people think of prisons in terms of the "big house"—large, maximum security prisons with tough inmates and tough guards. While there are many large prisons that fit this description, our current correctional institutions consist of a number of different types of facilities.

II. GOALS OF INCARCERATION

There are three models that predominate correctional philosophy. The custodial model focuses on security, order and strict discipline in correctional facilities. The rehabilitation model instead focuses on treatment and educational programs in institutions. Finally, the reintegration model attempts to prepare inmates for their eventual return to society.

III. PRISON ORGANIZATION

Prison managers have the difficult task of managing a group of individuals who are being held against their will. Many different kinds of staff members are needed with skills in several different areas (custody, treatment, education, psychology, etc.)

IV. GOVERNING A SOCIETY OF CAPTIVES

Much of the public believes that prisons are operated in an authoritarian manner. Corrections officers presumably possess the power to give orders and have those orders obeyed. John DiIulio has stated that a good prison is one that "provides as much order, amenity, and service as possible given the human and financial resources." Keeping inmates safe, providing their basic needs, and enhancing their lives with training and education are all vital parts of managing prisons.

   A. The Defects of Total Power
       Enforcing commands is an inefficient method of making them carry out complex tasks. Efficiency is further diminished by the realities of the usual high officer-to-inmate ratio and the potential danger of the situation. Thus correctional officers' ability to threaten the use of physical force is limited in practice.

   B. Rewards and Punishments
       Since prisoners receive most privileges at the outset, there is little that can be offered for exceptional behavior. Rewards may be in the form of privileges offered for obedience: *good time* allowances, choice job assignments, and favorable parole reports. However, in many cases inmates are punished for "bad" behavior but are not rewarded for "good" behavior.

   C. Gaining Cooperation: Exchange Relationships
       Correctional officers obtain inmates' cooperation through the types of exchange relationships described in earlier chapters. Officers need the cooperation of the prisoners so that they will look good to their superiors, and the inmates depend on the guards to relax the rules or occasionally look the other way. Thus, guards exchange or "buy" compliance or obedience in some areas by tolerating violation of the rules elsewhere. Secret relationships that turn into manipulation of the guards by the prisoners may result in the smuggling of contraband or other illegal acts.

   D. Inmate Leadership
       Inmate leaders can serve as the essential communications link between the staff and inmates. Inmate leaders distribute benefits to other prisoners and thereby bolster their own influence within the prison. However, today's prison population is divided along racial, ethnic, offense, and hometown lines so that there are multiple centers of power and no single set of leaders.

V. CORRECTIONAL OFFICERS: THE LINCHPIN OF MANAGEMENT

A. The Officer's Role
The officer functions as a member of a complex bureaucratic organization and thus is expected to deal with clients impersonally and to follow formally prescribed procedures, yet must also face and cope with individual prisoners' personal problems. It is difficult to fulfill the varied and contradictory role expectations.

B. Recruitment of Officers
One of the primary incentives for becoming involved in correctional work is the security that civil service status provides. In addition, prisons offer better employment options than most other jobs available in the rural areas where most correctional facilities are located. Because correctional officers are recruited locally, most of them are rural and white, in contrast to the majority of prisoners who come from urban areas and are either black or Hispanic. It is increasingly possible for college graduates to achieve administrative positions without having to advance up through the ranks of the custodial force.

C. Use of Force
Corrections officers can generally use force in the following situations: self-defense, defense of a third party, to uphold prison rules, to prevent a crime, or to prevent escape. Each state department of corrections has detailed policies concerning the above contingencies.

VI. WHO IS IN PRISON?
Prison inmates are primarily repeat offenders convicted of violent crimes. Most prisoners are in their late twenties to early thirties, have less than a high school education, and are disproportionately members of minority groups.

A. Elderly Prisoners
Longer sentences produce increasing numbers of elderly prisoners who have special security and medical needs. The average annual cost to the institution of caring for elderly prisoners is double or triple the cost for the average prisoner. Many elderly prisoners receive better medical care and nutrition than they would in the outside world because, if released, they would return to poor neighborhoods.

B. Prisoners with HIV/AIDS
The rate of HIV/AIDS among prisoners is five times higher than the general U.S. population. Prisoners who test positive create many challenges for preventing transmission of disease, housing infected prisoners, and medical care.

C. Mentally Ill Prisoners
Mass closings of mental hospitals has increased arrests and incarceration of mentally ill people. High percentages of inmates in some facilities are classified as mentally ill. Correctional facilities and workers are often poorly prepared to deal with mentally ill prisoners.

D. Long-Term Prisoners
More prisoners serve long sentences in the U.S. than in any other Western country. The average first-time offender serves about twenty-two months, but an estimated 11% to 15% of all prisoners will serve more than seven years--this amounts to more than 100,000 people. Long-term prisoners are less likely to cause disciplinary infractions, but they present administrators with challenges for maintaining livable conditions.

VII. THE CONVICT WORLD

Inmates in today's prisons do not serve their terms in isolation. They form a society with traditions, norms, and a leadership structure. The *Inmate Code* dictates the values and norms that emerge within the prison social system and help to define the inmate's image of the model prisoner. The code also helps to emphasize the solidarity of all inmates against the staff. A single overriding inmate code really does not exist. In fact, race has become a key variable dividing convict society.

A. Adaptive Roles
Newcomers entering prison must decide how to serve their time: isolate themselves from other inmates or become full participants in the convict social system. Four categories have been used to describe the lifestyles of male inmates as they adapt to prison:

1. **"Doing time"** is the choice of those who try to maintain their links with and the perspective of the free world. They avoid trouble and form friendships with small groups of inmates.

2. **"Gleaning"** is taking advantage of prison programs. Usually inmates not committed to a life of crime.

3. **"Jailing"** is the style used by those who cut themselves off from the outside and try to construct a life within the prison. These are often "state-raised youth" who grew up in foster homes and juvenile detention centers.

4. The **"disorganized criminal"** includes those who are unable to develop role orientations to prison life; often afflicted with low intelligence or psychological problems.

B. The Prison Economy
Prisoners are limited as to what they may have in their cells, restrictions are placed on what gifts may come into the institution, and money may not be in the inmate's possession. Officials have created a formal economic system in the form of a commissary or "store" in which inmates may, on a scheduled basis, purchase a limited number of items--toilet articles, tobacco, snacks, and other food items--in exchange for credits drawn upon their "bank accounts" -- composed of money deposited on the inmate's entrance, gifts sent by relatives, and amounts earned in the low-paying prison industries.

An informal, underground economy serves an important function for inmates in prisons. Many items taken for granted on the outside are inordinately valued on the inside. These underground systems supply items to inmates that are not available at the prison commissary, or they are illegal. The standard medium of exchange in the prison economy is cigarettes. Because possession of coins or currency is prohibited and a barter system is somewhat restrictive, "cigarette money" is a useful substitute. Prison currency may change in the future as more prisons consider banning smoking.

VIII. WOMEN IN PRISON

A. Research on Women in Corrections
Women's prisons are smaller, security is less rigid, the relationships between inmates and staff are less structured, physical aggression seems less common, the underground economy is not well developed, and female prisoners appear to be even less committed to the convict code than men now are. Women serve shorter sentences, and there is perhaps more fluidity in the prison society as new members join and others leave.

Because of the small numbers of women's prisons, these inmates are typically held far from family and other social support groups. Female prisoners are typically young, poorly educated, are members of a minority group, and incarcerated for a serious offense.

B. The Subculture of Women's Prisons
Female inmates tend to form pseudo-families in which they adopt various roles--father, mother, daughter, sister--and interact as a unit. Esther Heffernan views these "play" families as a "direct, conscious substitution for the family relationships broken by imprisonment, or. . . the development of roles that perhaps were not fulfilled in the actual home environment."

C. Male versus Female Subcultures Compared

Male versus Female Subcultures: concepts of adaptive roles, the inmate code, indigenous and imported values, the prison economy, and so on, have explanatory value in both types of institution. A principal difference between male and female prison subcultures is in interpersonal relations.

Male prisoners act as individuals and their behavior is evaluated by the yardstick of the prison culture; autonomy, self-sufficiency, and the ability to cope with one's problems. In prisons for women, close ties seem to exist among small groups of inmates. These extended families may essentially provide emotional support and emphasize the sharing of resources. There are debates among researchers about whether these differences reflect distinctive female qualities (e.g., nurturing, etc.).

D. Issues in the Incarceration of Women

Under pressures for equal opportunity, states seem to believe that they should run women's prisons as they do prisons for men, with the same policies and procedures. Some believe that this comparison is incorrect given the differences in inmate subculture and the specific needs of women prisoners.

1. **Sexual Misconduct**: As the number of women in prison increases, so do accounts of sexual abuse by male guards. Several states have passed laws outlawing sexual relations between inmates and prison staff.

2. **Educational and Vocational Training Programs:** Some have criticized women's prisons for not having the same range of programming available as men's facilities, and for providing programs that are traditionally "feminine" in nature (cosmetology, food service, housekeeping, sewing).

3. **Medical services**: Women often have special or more serious medical problems than men. Pregnancies raise important issues—approximately 25% of incarcerated women were pregnant upon admission to prison or had given birth within the prior year.

4. **Mothers and Children:** The majority of incarcerated women leave children behind to serve their sentence. Many of these children are cared for by relatives or placed into foster care. Most incarcerated women cannot see their children on a regular basis because they are incarcerated long distances from their homes. Some lower-security facilities allow overnight visits with children, but most do not have such programs.

IX. PRISON PROGRAMS

Because the public has called for harsh punishment treatment of criminals, legislators have reduced education and other programs in many states. Administrators must use institutional programs to manage the problem of time. They know that the more programs they are able to offer, the less likely it is that inmates' idleness and boredom will turn to hostility. Activity is the administrator's tool for controlling and stabilizing prison operations. Contemporary programs are educational, vocational, and treatment-based.

A. Classification of Prisoners

Determining the appropriate program for an individual prisoner is usually made through a classification process. Most states now have diagnostic and reception centers that are physically separated from the main prison facility. Unfortunately, classification decisions are often made on the basis of administrative needs rather than inmate needs

B. Educational Programs

Education programs are the most popular programs in prison. In many prisons, inmates who have not completed eighth grade are assigned full-time to a prison school. Many programs permit inmates to earn a high school equivalency diploma (GED). College-level programs are offered in some facilities, but legislation banning federal aid for prisoners has deterred many from taking college courses.

C. Vocational Education

Programs in modern facilities are designed to teach a variety of skills: plumbing, automobile mechanics, printing, computer programming. Unfortunately, some vocational programs are designed to prepare inmates for careers on the outside that are closed to former felons. The restaurant industry, for example, would seem to be a place where former felons might find employment, yet in many states they are prohibited from working where alcohol is sold.

D. Prison Industries

Traditionally, prisoners have been required to work at tasks that are necessary to maintain and run their own and other state facilities: food service, laundry, and building maintenance jobs. Also prison farms produce food for the institution in some states. Industry shops make furniture, repair office equipment, and fabricate items. Prisoners receive a nominal fee (perhaps 50 cents an hour) for such work.

During the nineteenth century, factories were set up inside many prisons and inmates manufactured items that were sold on the open market. With the rise of the labor movement, however, state legislatures and Congress passed laws restricting the sale of prison-made goods so that they would not compete with those made by free workers.

The 1980s saw initiatives promoted by the federal government efforts to encourage private-sector companies to set up "factories within fences" so as to use prison labor effectively. Prison industries are often inefficient due to turnover of prisoners, low education levels, and poor work habits. Also need good security to keep materials from being stolen by prisoners.

E. Rehabilitative Programs

Reports in the mid-1970s cast doubt on the ability of treatment programs to stem recidivism and raised questions about the ethics of requiring inmates to participate in such programs in exchange for the promise of parole. In most correctional systems a range of psychological, behavioral, and social services is available to inmates. Nationally, very little money is spent for treatment services and these programs reach only 5% of the inmate population.

F. Medical Services

Most prisons offer medical services through a full-time staff of nurses, augmented by part-time physicians under contract to the correctional system.

X. VIOLENCE IN PRISON

Prisoners are a natural environment for violence, given the type of people incarcerated there and the many conditions of deprivation.

A. Assaultive Behavior and Inmate Characteristics

1. **Age**: Young people, both inside and outside prison, are more prone to violence than their elders. Not only do young prisoners have greater physical strength, they lack those commitments to career and family that are thought to restrict antisocial behavior. The concept of "machismo"—having a reputation for physically retaliating against those who make slurs on one's honor—can increase violence in prison if embraced inmates.

2. **Attitude**: Some believe there is a subculture of violence among certain economic, racial, and ethnic groups. Arguments are settled and decisions made by the fist rather than by verbal persuasion. These attitudes are brought into the prison as part of an inmate's heritage.

3. **Race**: Racist attitudes seem to be acceptable in most institutions and have become part of the convict code. Prison gangs are often organized along racial lines and this contributes to violence in prison.

B. Prisoner-Prisoner Violence

Most of the violence in prison is inmate-to-inmate. This leads many prisoners to avoid contact with other prisoners or request isolation.

1. **Prison Gangs**: Race and ethnic gangs are now linked to acts of violence in many prison systems. In essence, the gang wars of the streets are often continued in prison. The "blood-in, blood-out" system means that inmates must stab an enemy to be admitted to a gang, and if they want to leave the gang they will risk their own lives. Rival gangs may be placed in different locations to reduce violence, or move members to other facilities.

2. **Protective Custody**: Some inmates are held in protective custody for their own safety. Unfortunately, they remain very isolated and spend most of their time in a cell.

C. Prisoner-Officer Violence
Violence against prison staff does not occur often, and is usually not random. Prisoners sometimes fashion weapons from regular items found in the prison. The threat of attack can contribute to anxiety among guards.

D. Officer-Prisoner Violence
Unauthorized physical violence by staff occurs against inmates in many institutions. Prisoners may have a hard time having their complaints taken seriously. Questions as to what is *excessive* force for the handling of particular situations are usually unclear.

E. Decreasing Prison Violence

1. **The Effect of Architecture and Size**: The massive scale of some institutions provides opportunities for aggressive inmates to hide weapons, carry out private justice, and engage in other illicit activities free from supervision. Modern prisons are designed to increase officer safety and improve living conditions of inmates.

2. **The Role of Management**: Effective management is key for reducing prison violence. Managers must understand the inmate social structure, the role of gangs, and the structure of the facility to keep prisons under control.

REVIEW OF KEY TERMS

Fill in the appropriate term for each statement

custodial model
reintegration model
inmate code
classification

1. The _____ is the model of correctional institutions that emphasizes maintenance of the offender's ties to family and the community as a method of reform.

2. The _____ is the body of norms and beliefs shared by inmates in an institution.

3. The process of determining the correct placement for an inmate is known as _____ .

4. _____ is the model of corrections that emphasizes security, discipline, and order.

GENERAL PRACTICE QUESTIONS

In examining whether 1. ◼◼◼◼◼◼◼◼◼◼◼ in prisons violate the Eighth Amendment prohibition on cruel and unusual punishments, courts previously focused on the 2. ◼◼◼◼◼◼◼◼◼ in those prisons until the Supreme

Although many of its elements remain, the 3. ◼◼◼◼◼◼◼◼ have created and enforced additional rules for their own members which also serve as guidelines for prison life. These additional rules may involve 4. ◼◼◼◼◼◼◼◼ as a form of initiation or as a means of dealing with rivals.

SELF-TEST SECTION

MULTIPLE CHOICE QUESTIONS

15.1. Prison organizations are expected to fulfill goals related to…
a) keeping custody of the inmates
b) using and working the inmates
c) treating inmates
d) all of the above
e) none of the above

15.2. Which prison gang is most likely represented by a swastika tattoo?
a) Black Guerrilla Family
b) Mexican Mafia
c) LaNuestra Familia
d) Texas Syndicate
e) Aryan Brotherhood

15.3. Who is listed at the top of the formal organization of a prison?
a) warden
b) deputy warden
c) counselors
d) physicians
e) accountants

15.4. What is a sub-rosa relationship?
a) a homosexual relationship between prisoners
b) a secret relationship between a correctional officer and a prisoner
c) a violent relationship between a correctional officer and a prisoner
d) a violent relationship between prisoners
e) a friendly and open relationship between correctional officer and prisoner

15.5. Which of the following is TRUE about prisons?
a) prisons have multiple goals and separate lines of command
b) prison goals are characterized by simplicity and consensus
c) individual staff members are equipped to perform all functions
d) all of the above are TRUE
e) all of the above are FALSE

15.6. Which of the following is a situation when a correctional officer CANNOT use force?
  a) self-defense
  b) to defend a third person
  c) when he/she has a right to be angry at an inmate
  d) to prevent a crime
  e) to prevent an escape

15.7. Which of the following is a common criticism of programming for women in prison?
  a) There are too many opportunities for inmates
  b) The programming tends to be conform to sexual stereotypes
  c) The programming is not geared toward women
  d) There are too few programs involving the 'womanly arts'
  e) The programming tends to teach marketable job skills

15.8. What is the concept of male honor and sacredness of one's reputation as a man?
  a) good time
  b) machismo
  c) inmate code
  d) in the life
  e) gleaning

15.9. What is the primary purpose of prisoner classification?
  a) To send the prisoner to the appropriate security level institution
  b) To make sure the prisoner is incarcerated with other gang members
  c) To locate the prisoner close to family and friends for social support
  d) To randomly assign inmates to facilities
  e) To make management accountable for security violations

15.10. Vocational education programs are designed to:
  a) Increase an inmate's level of education
  b) Teach offenders a marketable job skill
  c) Make money for prisons
  d) Control inmates' drug and alcohol addictions
  e) Provide medical treatment for inmates

15.11. Who is most likely to be a victim of rape while incarcerated?
  a) A hard-core old timer
  b) A physically strong, sexual preditor
  c) An older, white, male inmate
  d) An inmate convicted of a white collar crime
  e) A young, physically small "first-timer"

15.12. A program designed to educate members and eventually encourage them to renounce their gang membership
    is called...
  a) deprogramming
  b) deganging
  c) in the life
  d) machismo
  e) gleaning

15.13. Which of the following is TRUE about prison gangs?
    a) they are often large
    b) they are loosely organized
    c) they pursue business interests
    d) they are not a source of inmate-inmate violence
    e) none of the above are TRUE

15.14. Correctional institutions that follow the reintegration model are strongly linked with:
    a) Police officers
    b) Prosecutors
    c) Community corrections
    d) Defense attorneys
    e) Judges

15.15. Which of the following is true regarding prison organization?
    a) All staff perform similar functions
    b) Staff members are not organized by function
    c) The warden is the highest level of administration
    d) The deputy warden is the highest level of administration
    e) The deputy warden for custody is likely in charge of medical services

15.16. What is one reason why prisons have a difficult time recruiting correctional officers?
    a) Correctional officers must have a college degree
    b) Correctional facilities tend to be located in rural areas
    c) Correctional facilities are rather unsecure
    d) Correctional officers are paid too much
    e) There are many opportunities for career advancement for corrections officers

15.17. What is the name given to a new correctional officer?
    a) Fish
    b) Newjack
    c) Teddy bear
    d) Newbie
    e) Rookie

15.18. As opposed to men's subculture in prisons, women's subculture is characterized by:
    a) A black-market economy
    b) Heterosexual relationships
    c) Pseudo-families
    d) Aggression and fighting
    e) Psychpathology

15.19. What is a common method used by prisons for dealing with the mentally ill?
    a) Mandatory sterilization
    b) Counseling and therapy
    c) Electroshock treatment
    d) Torture
    e) Prisons do not provide treatment for mentally ill offenders

15.20. Some researchers have described female prisoners as wanting to avoid "the mix" while incarcerated. This refers to:
   a)   Behavior that can bring trouble with staff & other prisoners
   b)   Working in the kitchens
   c)   Behavior that can earn a prisoner "good time" credit toward release
   d)   Behavior that may earn an inmate a privileged positions in the facility
   e)   The gang lifestyle

15.21. Which of the following is FALSE regarding the difference between men's and women's prison subcultures?
   a)   Women's prisons are generally less violent than men's prisons
   b)   Women tend to respond more effectively to programming than male prisoners
   c)   More women are serving terms for violent offenses than men
   d)   Male inmates are more likely to get to know their guards, while female inmates are not
   e)   Women tend to segregate themselves by race while incarcerated

15.22. Inmates who adapt the role of the "disorganized criminal" while incarcerated tend to:
   a)   cut themselves off from the outside and construct a life in the prison
   b)   take advantage of prison programs
   c)   serve their terms with the least amount of suffering
   d)   become the supplier of illegal goods for fellow inmates
   e)   fail to adapt to any other role

15.23. There has been a significant increase in prisoners over the age of 55. What is likely responsible for this increase?
   a)   The use of alternatives to incarceration
   b)   The increased used of plea bargaining
   c)   Better crime detection methods, such as DNA analysis
   d)   Mandatory minimum sentences
   e)   More older people committing crime

15.24. What do inmates typically use as currency in prisons?
   a)   Cigarettes
   b)   Money
   c)   Drugs
   d)   Food
   e)   Sex

15.25. A prisoner who sees their time incarcerated as a "break" in their criminal career has taken the adaptive role of:
   a)   Doing time
   b)   Gleaning
   c)   Jailing
   d)   Acting as a disorganized criminal
   e)   Fish

TRUE/FALSE QUESTIONS

15.1. _____ The custodial model emphasizes security and order.

15.2. _____ Prison managers can select their own clients.

15.3. _____ Prison managers must rely on clients to do most of the work in the daily operation of the institution.

15.4. _____The most numerous employees in prisons are the custodial workers.

15.5. _____The goals and lines of command often bring about clarity and consensus in the administration of prisons.

15.6. _____The use of force by correctional officers is a controversial issue.

15.7. _____Correctional officers are NOT allowed to rely on rewards and punishment to gain cooperation from prisoners.

15.8. _____Female prisoners are more likely to have HIV/AIDS than male prisoners.

15.9. _____In most of today's institutions, prisoners are divided by race, ethnicity, age, and gang affiliation, so that no single leadership structure exists.

15.10. _____Correctional workers are not responsible for returning inmates to the community no more angry or hostile than when they were committed.

15.11. _____Over the past twenty five years, the correctional officer's role has changed greatly.

15.12. _____Employment as a correctional officer is a glamorous and sought-after occupation.

15.13. _____Correctional officers who are women are NOT allowed to work with female offenders.

15.14. _____Few states have training programs for correctional officers.

15.15. _____A correctional officer may use force to protect an inmate or another officer.

15.16. _____The problem of sexual assault in prison gets too much attention from policy makers and the public.

15.17. _____Violent behavior in prisons is related to the age of the inmates.

15.18. _____Race has become a major divisive factor in today's prisons.

15.19. _____Prisoners have no right against cruel and unusual punishment.

15.20. _____Prisoners have freedom of religion.

ANSWER KEY

Key Terms
1. reintegration model
2. inmate code
3. classification
4. custodial model

General Practice Questions
1. conditions of confinement
2. totality of conditions
3. gangs
4. prison violence

Multiple Choice
15.1. D
15.2. E
15.3. A
15.4. B
15.5. A
15.6. C
15.7. B
15.8. B
15.9. A
15.10. B
15.11. E
15.12. C
15.13. B
15.14. C
15.15. C
15.16. B
15.17. B
15.18. C
15.19. B
15.20. A
15.21. E
15.22. E
15.23. D
15.24. A
15.25. A

True/False
15.1. T
15.2. F
15.3. T
15.4. T
15.5. F
15.6. T
15.7. F
15.8. T
15.9. T
15.10. F
15.11. T
15.12. F
15.13. F

15.14.   F
15.15.   T
15.16.   F
15.17.   T
15.18.   T
15.19.   F
15.20.   T

WORKSHEET 15.1   PRISONS AND THEIR PURPOSES

If you were in charge of a state corrections department, how would you design your prisons? For each question, assume that the prisons have one primary purpose (listed below) and describe the physical design, policies, and programs that you would implement to help the institution advance the overriding goal.

1. CUSTODIAL MODEL_____

_____

_____

_____

_____

_____

_____

2. REHABILITATION MODEL_____

_____

_____

_____

_____

_____

_____

_____

3. REINTEGRATION MODEL_____

_____

_____

_____

_____

_____

_____

_____

WORKSHEET 15.2: PRISONERS' RIGHTS: YOU ARE THE JUDGE

Corrections officers at the main gate receive a report that a fight involving twelve prisoners has broken out in Cellblock C and that the corrections officers in Cellblock C are unable to break up the fight. Seven corrections officers run down the corridor from the main gate toward Cellblock C. As they round a corner, they practically run into inmate Joe Cottrell who is mopping and waxing the corridor floor. One officer grabs Cottrell by the shoulders and throws him aside while saying, "Get out of the way!" Cottrell falls into a wall, dislocates his shoulder, and later files a lawsuit against the officer by claiming that the rough treatment and resulting injury violated his Eighth Amendment right against cruel and unusual punishment. Were his Eighth Amendment rights violated? Explain.

_____

_____

_____

_____

_____

_____

A prison chapel is used every Sunday for Christian services. A small group of prisoners reserve the chapel for each Tuesday evening where they meet to study an ancient religion from Asia that they claim to follow. For two years, they use the chapel every Tuesday to meditate and discuss books about their religion, and they do not cause any trouble. Then, one year Christmas falls on a Wednesday, and the Asian religion group is told that they cannot have their meeting because the chapel is needed for a Christian Christmas eve service. They file a lawsuit claiming that their First Amendment right to free exercise of religion is being violated because they cannot use the chapel on Christmas eve. Are their rights being violated? Explain.

_____

_____

_____

_____

_____

_____

_____

REENTRY INTO THE COMMUNITY

OUTLINE

- Prisoner Reentry
- Release Mechanisms
- Parole Supervision in the Community
- The Future of Prisoner Reentry
- Civil Disabilities of Ex-Felons
- Pardon

CHAPTER 16
PRISON SOCIETY AND RELEASE

LEARNING OBJECTIVES

After covering the material in this chapter, students should understand:

1.   release mechanisms and their impact

2.   problems facing parolees

3.   revocation of parole

4.   pardons and civil disabilities of convicts

5.   community programs following release

6.   the role of the parole officer

7.   problems facing parolees

8.   revocation of parole.

CHAPTER SUMMARY

Parolees are released from prison on the condition that they do not violate the law and they live according to rules designed to help them adjust to society. Parole officers are assigned to assist ex-inmates make the transition to society, and to ensure that they follow the conditions of their release. The problem of reentry has become a major policy issue. Most inmates will receive parole, but they face a multitude of problems such as finding employment and avoiding a return to the criminal life. In addition, parolees who committed felonies cannot vote or hold office. Inmates must abide by certain conditions of release during their paroles. If they fail to abide by these conditions, their parole can be revoked and they can be returned to prison. Parole officers serve many functions, relevant to both law enforcement and social services. The executive branch of government at the state (governors) and federal (President) levels can issue pardons to inmates to remove the stigma of a conviction or remedy a miscarriage of justice.

CHAPTER OUTLINE

I.   PRISONER REENTRY

The issue of "reentry" focuses on offenders returning to their communities after serving their prison terms. Unfortunately, a large percentage of them are expected to reoffend and return to prison. Because many prisons have reduced the number of program options available to prisoners, many do not leave with usable skills.

II. RELEASE AND SUPERVISION

When prisoners are released from incarceration, they are placed on parole. This period of time is used to monitor the offender to assist in their return to the community. The offender is still a responsibility of the government, but they have been given the privilege of release. In return, the offender agrees to abide by certain conditions of release.

A. The Origins of Parole

Tickets of leave were the first form of parole in the United States. Captain Alexander Maconochie was a key figure in developing parole, which began in Ireland. His system allowed inmates to complete their sentences early for good behavior, and they could reduce their level of incapacitation if they behaved well (from incarceration to chain gangs to limited freedom to ticket of leave to full release).

B. The Development of Parole in the United States

Parole developed about the same time as prison reforms took place in the United States—in the middle of the 19th century. Zebulon Brockway was one of the first administrators in the U.S. to begin using parole. In its early stages, members of the community agreed to monitor parolees. Eventually the job was given to professionals.

III. RELEASE MECHANISMS

Several states abolished parole in the 1970's, when the public began to believe the criminal justice system was too "soft on crime". Other states have kept the parole system, but have been reluctant to use it.

A. Discretionary Release

Parole boards can use discretionary release when inmates are sentenced to indeterminate sentences. They can assess whether inmates are prepared to be released and "earn" parole.

B. Mandatory Release

Using this system, inmates must be released when they have served the entirety of their sentence (minus good time).

C. Other Conditional Release

Some states have developed methods to release inmates from prison prior to the end of their sentences by placing them in low-security facilities, such as halfway houses or home supervision.

D. Expiration Release

These offenders have served the maximum court sentence and are not eligible to remain in prison.

E. The Impact of Release Mechanisms

There are several options for correctional administrators who believe inmates are ready to be released, but have not served enough of their sentence according to the state. This discretion allows individualized decisions about when inmates are prepared to leave the prison. There is a great deal of variability in the percentage of the total sentence length served by each inmate. Critics believe discretionary release takes discretion away from the judge, who is the expert on sentencing and legal procedure.

IV. PAROLE SUPERVISION IN THE COMMUNITY

Offenders released from prison must abide by certain conditions of release. These conditions are meant to keep from associating with people who may be a bad influence on them. Most releasees face difficulties finding work, as they usually have little money and/or possessions when they leave prison. Many employers are reluctant to hire parolees given their backgrounds.

A. Community Programs following Release

There are several kinds of community programs available to parolees upon release. Unfortunately, most communities have neither a sufficient number of programs nor space in those programs for all releasees.

1. **Work and Educational Release:** In these programs, inmates are released from the correctional facility during the day to work or attend school. Critics believe it is wrong to provide job opportunities to convicts when there are non-criminal citizens in the public who may want them.

2. **Furloughs:** Fuloughs allow inmates to leave the facility for short periods to visit family. This is thought to assist inmates with reintegration when the return home. This can be a good method to "test the waters" to see how inmates will react to release.

3. **Halfway Houses:** As non-secure facilities, halfway houses allow inmates to work and live in the community while still under supervision. The community can be reluctant to allow halfway houses into their area. These facilities have been decreasing in use since the start of the "punitive era" of corrections.

B. Parole Officer: Cop or Social Worker?

1. **The Parole Officer as Cop:** The parole officer is responsible for keeping track of offenders and making sure they do not violate the conditions of parole. If they find violations, they must report these just as a police officer reports crimes. Parole officers have some law enforcement powers to protect the community.

2. **The Parole Officers as Social Worker:** Parole officers also help parolees by directing them to services they need (finding jobs, restoring family ties). Some believe the roles of police officer and social worker are in conflict, and parole officers should not do both jobs.

C. The Parole Bureacracy
Parole officers have smaller caseloads, but work with more serious offenders. As with probation officers, their caseloads sometimes become much larger than they can reasonably handle and they must prioritize which offenders deserve more of their time.

D. Adjustments to Life outside Prison

1. **General Adjustments:** Inmates returning to the community can have great difficulty adjusting to an unstructured life. When combined with a loss of benefits afford to non-criminal citizens (food stamps, access to public housing, student loans), the adjustment can be even more difficult.

2. **Public Opinion:** Parolees face difficulties adjusting when their community is not receptive to their presence. Thanks to high-profile cases of violent crimes committed by parolees, their communities can fear and even harass inmates post-release. The increased use of sex offender registries can serve to ostracize offenders, who may have been convicted of low-level sex crimes (such as public exposure).

E. Revocation of Parole
A large percentage of parolees are sent back to prison for either violating conditions of parole or committing a new crime. These parolees are entitled to a hearing prior to having their parole revoked.

F. The Reentry Problem
One consequence of the increase in incarceration and "get tough on crime" policies is the corresponding increase in offenders returning to the community. Naturally, this exacerbates the caseload problems faced by parole officers as well as the limits placed on post-release programs.

V. THE FUTURE OF PRISONER REENTRY

Due to the increasing numbers of inmates leaving prison, there is an increased focus on the community for providing valuable reentry services. However, the public is generally not supportive of community programs ("not in my backyard").

VI. CIVIL DISABILITIES OF EX-FELONS

The rights to vote and to hold public office are generally forfeited by offenders when they are convicted. Restrictions on voting and jury service have especially strong impacts on African-Americans and others overrepresented in the criminal justice system, who are not able to participate in and serve their communities even if they have turned their lives around.

VII. PARDON

Pardons are acts of the executive. In the United States, the president or governors of the states may grant clemency in individual cases and release inmates from incarceration. Pardons may be granted to remedy a miscarriage of justice, to remove the stigma of a conviction, or to mitigate a penalty. Pardons are used most often to expunge the criminal records of first-time offenders.

REVIEW OF KEY TERMS

Fill in the appropriate term for each statement

Parole
tickets of leave
discretionary release
mandatory release
other conditional release
expiration release
conditions of release
work and educational release
furlough
halfway house
civil disabilities
pardon

1. The idea of parole began when inmates were issued _____.

2. After leaving a prison, parolees must satisfy several _____ to avoid being reincarcerated.

3. _____ provides for release according to a time frame stipulated by a determinate sentence and/or parole guidelines.

4. _____ is a supervised home for parolees within the community.

5. _____ provides a mechanism for temporary release for a few days in order to visit family and prepare for release on parole.

6. _____ include limitations on ex-convicts' ability to run for public office in many states.

7. _____ is an action under the authority of executive branch officials.

8. _____ provides for release according to a decision by a parole board.

9. _____ is the conditional release of an offender from incarceration but not from the legal custody of the state.

10. _____ is an institution, usually located in an urban area, housing inmates soon to be released and designed to help reintegration into society.

11. Inmates who are released from a correctional facility to go to work or school during the day have received _____.

12. Inmates who are returned to the community through halfway houses, emergency release, and other methods have received _____.

REVIEW OF KEY PEOPLE

Captain Alexander Maconochie
Zebulon Brockway

1. A British penal administrator named _____ was instrumental in developing the idea of parole.

2. _____, the New York prison reformer, assisted in beginning the parole system in the United States.

GENERAL PRACTICE QUESTIONS

Whether a prisoner receives 1. _____, through a determinate sentence and parole guidelines, or a 2. _____, through a decision by the 3. _____, he or she immediately comes under the responsibility of the 4. _____, who tries to watch for improper behavior and also provide social assistance.

SELF-TEST SECTION

MULTIPLE CHOICE QUESTIONS

16.1. What term describes an inmate who repeatedly cycles in and out of prison?
   a) Fish
   b) Newjack
   c) Druggie
   d) Churner
   e) Gang-banger

16.2. Which of the following would most likely cause a revocation of parole?
   a) failing a drug test
   b) credit problems
   c) parking ticket
   d) marital problems
   e) all of the above would cause a revocation of parole

16.3. What is one of the main reentry problems plaguing corrections?
   a) Probation officer caseloads are very low
   b) Parole boards lost discretion to decide when a prisoner was ready to leave prison
   c) Parole officers are not trained to monitor offenders adequately
   d) Programs in prison adequately prepare inmates to re-adjust to life outside prison
   e) Prisoners are often prepared to leave their facilities

16.4. What are the three concepts on which parole is granted?
   a) Honesty, truth, and liberty
   b) Life, liberty, and the pursuit of happiness
   c) Faith, hope, and charity
   d) Grace, contract, and custody
   e) Care, contact, and supervision

16.5. The conditional release of a prisoner from incarceration to the community is called:
   a) Probation
   b) Custody
   c) Detention
   d) Parole
   e) Booking

16.6. Which of the following were means of moving criminals out of prison?
   a) Conditional pardon
   b) Apprenticeship
   c) Transportation
   d) Tickets of leave
   e) All of the above were used

16.7. This is the most commonly used method of returning offenders to the community:
   a) Expirational release
   b) Discretionary release
   c) Other conditional release
   d) Mandatory release
   e) Escape

16.8. Mandatory release occurs when:
   a) An inmate has served their entire sentence
   b) The parole board has decided to release an inmate
   c) An inmate is placed on a work furlough
   d) An inmate is referred to a halfway house
   e) They have 'maxed out' on their time

16.9. What is one criticism of discretionary release?
   a) It shifts responsibility from the parole board to the judge
   b) It shifts responsibility from the police to the parole board
   c) It shifts responsibility from the judge to the police
   d) It shifts responsibility from the judge to the parole board
   e) It shifts responsibility to the inmate

16.10. According to this chart below, which crime has the largest gap between the sentenced as imposed by the court and the sentence actually served?

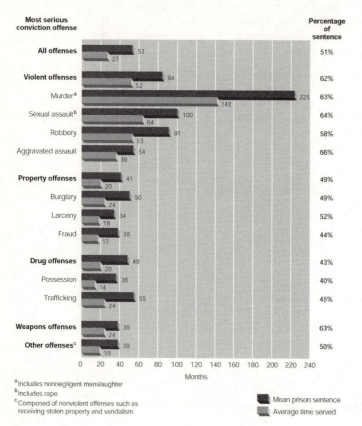

a) Drug offenses
b) Weapons offenses
c) Murder
d) Violent offenses
e) Property offenses

16.11. Which is the only state that does not impose conditions of release on inmates?
a) New Jersey
b) Michigan
c) Texas
d) Maine
e) Maryland

16.12. Why are parolees usually denied work in restaurants?
a) There is too much contact with the public
b) Alcohol is served in restaurants
c) Most inmates do not have food service experience
d) Restaurants are open too late for parolees to work
e) Most parolees don't want work in restaurants

16.13. The largest group of unemployed people in the country is:
a) African-American, male, and under 30
b) African-American, female, and under 30
c) Caucasian, male, and over 55
d) Caucasian, female and over 55
e) Hispanic, male and under 30

16.14. Which branch of government is checked by the pardon power?
   a) executive
   b) judicial
   c) legislative
   d) bureaucracy
   e) executive and legislative

16.15. Which of the following keeps inmates from finding work?
   a) Some jobs require union membership, which can prohibit convicts from joining
   b) Carrying the label of a former convict
   c) Many convicts cannot be licensed for particular careers
   d) Many employers will not hire people who have served prison time
   e) All of the above are reasons why parolees have trouble finding jobs

16.16. Inmates involved in work and educational programs…
   a) Take courses or work during the day at the prison
   b) Leave the prison during the day for work or school
   c) Spend time training other inmates
   d) Generally have a high recidivism rate
   e) Get to stay at home on the weekends

16.17. Inmates can visit family members outside of the prison in:
   a) Furlough programs
   b) Work release programs
   c) Educational programs
   d) Parole programs
   e) Halfway houses

16.18. What does the acronym "NIMBY" stand for?
   a) No, I'm Bored. You?
   b) Not In My Backyard
   c) No one Is Beyond the Law
   d) Nonsense is My Baseline Yardage
   e) No one is my baby, yo!

16.19. Which two roles do parole officers play?
   a) Police officer and teacher
   b) Police officer and social worker
   c) Social worker and judge
   d) Social worker and attorney
   e) Police officers and probation officer

16.20. Why is parole sometimes referred to as "invisible punishment"?
   a) Because parolees have their home phones tapped
   b) Because parolees are generally shunned by society
   c) Because parolees want to return to prison
   d) Because parolees have so many restrictions on their liberties
   e) Because many parolees end up back in prison

16.21. What innovation have some recommended to help inmates return to the community?
   a) Drug courts
   b) Re-entry course
   c) Domestic violence courts
   d) Recidivism courts
   e) Probation courts

16.22. What is the term used to describe the legal restrictions faced by offenders after they have completed their punishments?
  a) Pardons
  b) Clemency
  c) Civil disabilities
  d) Legal remedies
  e) Asphyxiation

16.23. Former inmates who are disenfranchised have lost the right to:
  a) Pray
  b) Speak freely
  c) Work
  d) Drive
  e) Vote

16.24. What purpose does pardon serve?
  a) It remedies a miscarriage of justice
  b) It removes the stigma of a conviction
  c) It mitigates a penalty
  d) It labels officers
  e) Answers A through C are reasons for pardons.

16.25. What was pardon originally called in Europe?
  a) Tickets of leave
  b) Conditional release
  c) Release on own recognizance (ROR)
  d) Royal prerogative of mercy
  e) Expired release

TRUE/FALSE QUESTIONS

16.1. _____Parole release does not impact other parts of the criminal justice system.

16.2. _____Parolees face many problems when released from prison.

16.3. _____In most states, ex-felons do not retain the right to vote.

16.4. _____The pardon power rests with the judicial branch.

16.5. _____Pardons are used to remove the stigma of a conviction.

16.6. _____Parole officers are given little power to restrict the parolee's life.

16.7. _____Parole officers are granted law enforcement powers.

16.8. _____ Before parole is revoked, the offender is NOT entitled to a preliminary hearing.

16.9 _____There are some inmates who "max out" on their time and do not require supervision in the community.

16.10 _____Captain Alexander Maconochie developed a system of graduated release stages, the early forms of parole.

16.11 _____The United States currently uses a nationwide sentencing and release policy.

16.12 _____The Japanese culture does not place a strong emphasis on return to the community.

16.13 _____In an expiration release, a prisoner "maxes out" and cannot serve any more time.

16.14 _____Discretionary release mitigates the harshness of sentencing policies.

16.15 _____Parolees usually have few problems finding jobs after release.

16.16 _____Most inmates have access to reentry programs.

16.17 _____Prison administrators do not like work release programs because they are usually expensive to manage.

16.18 _____Some work release programs allow room and board to be deducted from inmate wages.

16.19 _____Halfway houses are sometimes secure facilities in communities.

16.20 _____Parole used to be focused on transitioning offenders, now it is focused on surveillance and monitoring.

ANSWER KEY

Key Terms
1. tickets of release
2. conditions of release
3. mandatory release
4. halfway house
5. furlough
6. civil disabilities
7. pardon
8. discretionary release
9. parole
10. halfway house
11. work and educational release
12. other conditional release

Key People
1. Captain Alexander Maconochie
2. Zebulon Brockway

General Practice Questions
1. mandatory release
2. discretionary release
3. parole board
4. parole officer

Multiple Choice Answers
16.1.   D
16.2.   A
16.3.   B
16.4.   D
16.5.   D
16.6.   E
16.7.   D
16.8.   A
16.9.   D
16.10. C
16.11. D
16.12. B
16.13. A
16.14. C
16.15. E
16.16. B
16.17. A
16.18. B
16.19. B
16.20. D
16.21. B
16.22. D
16.23. E
16.24. E
16.25. D

True/False
16.1.   F
16.2.   T
16.3.   T
16.4.   F
16.5.   T
16.6.   F
16.7.   T
16.8.   F
16.9.   T
16.10. T
16.11. F
16.12. F
16.13. T
16.14. T
16.15. F
16.16. F
16.17. F
16.18. T
16.19. T
16.20. T

WORKSHEET 16.1　　PRISON PROGRAMS

You are in charge of developing programs at a new prison. For each category of possible programs discuss whether you will recommend such programs for your prison. Why? If so, describe the goals and details of those programs.

EDUCATIONAL PROGRAMS_____

_____

_____

_____

_____

_____

_____

VOCATIONAL PROGRAMS_____

_____

_____

_____

_____

_____

_____

PRISON INDUSTRIES_____

_____

_____

_____

_____

REHABILITATIVE PROGRAMS_____

_____

_____

_____

_____

WORKSHEET 16.2   PRISON PROBLEMS

If you were a prison warden, name three things that you would do to address each of the following issues. How effective do you think your strategies would be?

1. Racial tensions between groups of inmates_____

_____

_____

_____

_____

_____

_____

2. Prison gangs controlling the internal economy_____

_____

_____

_____

_____

_____

3. Mothers of small children serving long sentences in an isolated institution

_____

_____

_____

_____

_____

_____

JUVENILE JUSTICE

OUTLINE

- Youth Crime in the United States
- The Development of Juvenile Justice
- The Juvenile Justice System
- The Juvenile Justice Process

CHAPTER 17
THE JUVENILE JUSTICE SYSTEM

LEARNING OBJECTIVES

After covering the material in this chapter, students should understand:

1. the nature and extent of youth crime

2. the history of juvenile justice, including the four eras: Refuge; Juvenile Court; Juvenile Rights; Crime Control

3. the importance of age and jurisdiction in the juvenile system

4. the role of police, intake, case screening, and preliminary discretionary dispositions

5. adjudication in the juvenile system

6. juvenile corrections, including probation, deinstitutionalization, and community-based treatment settings

CHAPTER SUMMARY

This chapter explores the extent and nature of juvenile crime by listing a variety of statistics regarding juvenile crime. It also traces the history of the juvenile justice system from the colonial era to the modern era using five distinct periods: 1) the Puritan period, 2) the Reform period, 3) the Juvenile Court period, 4) the Juvenile Rights period and 5) the Crime Control period. The chapter examines the development of juvenile courts in the United States, the specific rulings by the U. S. Supreme Court that established constitutional protections for juveniles in the 1960s, and the movement to get tough on juveniles that has developed since the 1980s. A comparative perspective is offered by documenting the juvenile system in Norway and, finally, the problems that are faced today within the juvenile justice system are presented such as whether juveniles should be tried as adults in specific circumstances.

CHAPTER OUTLINE

I. YOUTH CRIME IN THE UNITED STATES

Youth crime peaked from the mid-1980's to early 1990's, possibly due to a large birth cohort or the increased prevalence of crack cocaine. Youth gangs may also be responsible for the increase in youth crime.

II. THE DEVELOPMENT OF JUVENILE JUSTICE

Similar to trends in punishment of adult offenders, juvenile justice trends have swung from rehabilitation to punitiveness. The doctrine of *parens patriae* (the state as parent) has provided the foundation for dealing with juvenile offenders in the United States.

A. Background :The Puritan Period (1646-1824)
Juveniles who committed crime relied on the family to discipline youths. If the family was unable to do, the state stepped in. Puritans viewed delinquent children as "evil".

B. The Refuge Period (1824-1899)

Institutions were created for children who committed crime. These institutions were designed to be both prisons and schools. The state assumed that parents were unable to discipline their children.

C. The Juvenile Court Period (1900-1959)

The "child savers" sough to save children from a life of crime. They believed children could be reformed, and promoted a separate juvenile court system founded on the idea of *parens patriae*. This early juvenile court forms the basis of the modern juvenile courts, in which records are kept sealed and children are protected. In addition, terminology was changed from "criminal" to "delinquent" to imply that children could be rehabilitated more easily than adults.

D. The Juvenile Rights Period (1960-1979)

The early juvenile justice system was very powerful, and juveniles were not always accorded the same rights as adults. Several cases were heard by the United States Supreme Court that were relevant to juvenile offenders:

In *In re Gault* (1967), the Court decided that juveniles were entitled to due process rights. The Court determined procedural rights, including notice of charges, right to counsel, right to confront and cross-examine witnesses, and privilege against compelled self-incrimination.

In the case of *In re Winship* (1970) the Court held that proof must be established "beyond a reasonable doubt" before a juvenile may be classified as a delinquent for committing an act that would be a crime if it were committed by an adult.

The Supreme Court held in *McKeiver v. Pennsylvania* (1971) that juveniles do not have a constitutional right to trial by jury.

In *Breed v. Jones* (1975) the Court extended the protection against double jeopardy to juveniles by requiring that before a case is adjudicated in juvenile court, a hearing must be held to determine if it should be transferred to the adult court.

In 1974, Congress passed the Juvenile Justice and Delinquency Prevention Act, which included provisions for the deinstitutionalization of status offenders (truants, runaways, etc.).

E. The Crime Control Period (1980-Present)

The punitive stance taken recently has spread to the juvenile court. Decisions such as Schall v. Martin (1984) determined that juveniles could be held in detention prior to trial if they threaten the safety of the community. This punitive philosophy has also resulted in more juveniles tried as adults.

III. THE JUVENILE JUSTICE SYSTEM

A. Age of Clients

The upper age limit for a juvenile varies from sixteen to eighteen. In 49 states, judges have the ability to transfer some juveniles to adult court.

B. Categories of Cases Under Juvenile Court Jurisdiction

Four types of cases enter the juvenile justice system: delinquent children, Persons in Need of Supervision (PINS), neglected children, and dependent children. Most cases referred to juvenile court are delinquency cases.

IV. JUVENILE JUSTICE PROCESS
Prevention of delinquency is the system's justification for intervening in the lives of juveniles who are involved in either status or criminal offenses. It is still assumed that the juvenile proceedings are to be conducted in a non-adversarial environment, and that the court should be a place where the judge, social workers, clinicians, and probation officers work together to diagnose the child's problem and select a rehabilitative program to attack this problem.

A. Police Interface
Many police departments have special units to deal with youthful offenders. Most complaints against juveniles are brought by the police, although parents, school officials and others can refer juveniles to the juvenile court. Several Supreme Court decisions relate to police treatment of juveniles:

In *Fare v. Michael C.* (1979), the Court ruled that a child could waive the right to an attorney and the right against self-incrimination. Juvenile courts must be very careful to assure that these waivers were made voluntarily.

According to the Court's findings in *New Jersey v. T.L.O.* (1985), school officials can search student lockers if it is required to maintain order in the school. Random drug testing of students was upheld by the Court in *Vernonia School District v. Acton* (1995).

B. Intake Screening at the Court
Rather than arrest, juveniles are referred to juvenile court through the filing of a petition (intake). About half of all cases are disposed of at this stage through diversion.

C. Pretrial Procedures
For cases in which a formal hearing is warranted, a detention hearing may be held if the court wishes to detail the juvenile prior to trial. Almost 20% of all cases referred to formal hearing involve detention of the accused.

D. Transfer to Adult Court
In serious cases, judges may choose to waive juveniles to adult court. Some juvenile courts are not allowed by law to hear cases involving murder, rape, and armed robbery—these cases must be tried in adult court. One result of the increased used of waiver is that juveniles are being sent to adult prisons more frequently.

E. Adjudication
Adjudication is the trial stage in juvenile court proceedings. The Supreme Court has extended constitutional rights to juveniles at this stage, but the rights of the accused are not always respected in juvenile court. Adjudication is a closed process so as to protect the privacy of the accused.

F. Disposition
If a juvenile is found delinquent, the juvenile receives a disposition (punishment). Most offenders are found delinquent at adjudication, since the less serious cases are typically filtered out early in the process. While the preferred method of sentencing is usually indeterminate sentencing, the trend toward punitiveness in corrections has called for more stringent sentencing practices.

G. Corrections
The different perspective of the juvenile court (parens patriae) results in differences in the correctional models of the adult and juvenile systems. One goal of the juvenile justice system is avoid unnecessary incarceration, as many believe this will harm juveniles more than it will help them. Noninstitutional programs can help with rehabilitation as well as keep them in the family unit.

1. **Probation**: The most common method of handling juvenile offenders is to place them on probation. Juvenile probation has been more satisfactorily funded, and hence caseloads of officers are much lower

in number. Because juvenile offenders seem to be more able to be rehabilitated, a career in juvenile probation can be more enjoyable than on in adult probation.

2. **Intermediate Sanctions**: As with the adult system, intermediate sanctions are sometimes used for juveniles. These programs are meant to keep juveniles from incarceration, which might increase their delinquent behavior.

3. **Custodial Care**: Facilities to hold juvenile offenders can be categorized as secure or nonsecure. Most secure facilities are small, and managing these facilities can be quite challenging. As with the adult system, African American youth are over-represented in secure facilities.

4. **Institutional Programs**: The emphasis on rehabilitation present in the juvenile court has resulted in a number of programs for juveniles, focused on counseling, education, vocational training, and some psychological counseling programs.

5. **Aftercare**: This is similar to adult parole, in which juveniles are monitored and provided assistance with their transition back into non-custodial care.

6. **Community Treatment**: Treatment in community-based facilities has greatly expanded during the past decade. Foster homes developed as a means for implementing a policy of limited intervention into juvenile lives, hoping to keep a child with a family if his or her own family is not available or a negative influence on the child. Group homes are also used to place juvenile offenders.

V. PROBLEMS AND PERSPECTIVES

The juvenile court is an extremely complex organization, with a variety of goals. It must deal with both criminal youth and neglected youth, and strike a balance between treatment and punishment—much more so than in the adult court. The push toward more punitive treatment of adult offenders has also been reflected in the juvenile court, and it is unclear how this will affect juvenile offenders.

REVIEW OF KEY TERMS

Fill in the appropriate term for each statement

parens patriae
In re Gault (1967)
In re Winship (1970)
McKeiver v. Pennsylvania (1971)
Breed v. Jones (1975)
status offense
Schall v. Martin (1984)
delinquent
PINS
neglected child
dependent child
Fare v. Michael C. (1979)
New Jersey v. T.L.O. (1985)
Vernonia School District v. Acton (1995)
diversion
detention hearing
waive
aftercare

1.   In the case of _____, the Supreme Court decided that juveniles have the right to counsel, to confront their accusers and have adequate notice of charges.

2.   _____ is a term used to refer to juveniles who have not committed a crime, but are in need of attention for some reason.

3.   The juvenile equivalent of parole is called _____.

4.   Juveniles can be held in detention prior to trial, according to the findings in the case of _____.

5.   In _____, the Court decided that it was within the rights of a school to search student lockers.

6.   _____ is the concept of the state as the guardian and protector of juveniles and other citizens who cannot protect themselves.

7.   According to _____, juveniles may waive their constitutional rights (such as the right to an attorney)

8.   _____ is a child who has committed a criminal or status offense.

9.   _____ is the process of discretionary decisions that move children away from the system's most punitive consequences.

10. The standard of proof required in juvenile proceedings (beyond a reasonable doubt) was specified in _____.

11. Juveniles cannot be transferred directly to adult court without a hearing, according to _____.

12. _____ is any act committed by a juvenile that would not be a crime if it were committed by an adult but that is considered unacceptable for a juvenile.

13. Prior to being held awaiting trial, juveniles must have a _____.

14. In the case of _____, the Court found that juveniles do not have the right to trial by jury.

15. The Supreme Court determined in _____ that schools can require random drug testing.

16. Judges sometimes choose to _____ juveniles to the adult court system.

17. _____ is a child whose parents are unable to give proper care.

18. _____ is a child who is not receiving proper care because of parental inaction.

GENERAL PRACTICE QUESTIONS

Unlike the 1._____, who sought to develop rehabilitation for juveniles during the Progressive era, contemporary critics of juvenile justice who believe that sentences are not tough enough have ushered in a new era, the 2._____, which represents a change from the preceding era, the 3._____, in which the focus was on judicial decisions, such as the fundamental due process case of 4. ▭, to provide constitutional protections for children.

When a child is declared to be 5. ▭, he or she may be sent to a residential setting with other juveniles, such as a community-based 6. ▭, which is among the treatment settings left after the 7. ▭ movement affected how the government places and treats various troubled populations.

SELF-TEST SECTION

MULTIPLE CHOICE QUESTIONS

17.1. In what case did the Court declare that trial court judges must evaluate the voluntariness of confessions by juveniles by examining the totality of circumstances?
   a) *Fare v. Michael C.*
   b) *McKevier v. Pennsylvania*
   c) *New Jersey v. T.L.O.*
   d) *In re Winship*
   e) *Breed v. Jones*

17.2. According to the following chart, what is the most common offense for which juveniles are arrested in the United States?

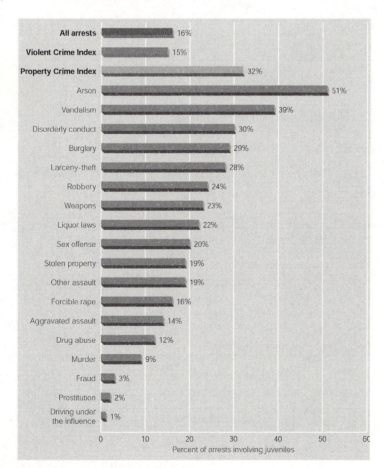

a) vandalism
b) arson
c) burglary
d) sex offenses
e) fraud

17.3. Which of the following is applicable to juveniles but not to adults?
   a) right to counsel
   b) right against unreasonable searches and seizures
   c) privilege against self-incrimination
   d) right to treatment
   e) none of the above are applicable to adults

17.4. What is one possible explanation for the "epidemic" of juvenile crime in the mid-1980's in the United States?
   a) The increased use of marijuana in public schools
   b) Children living in single-parent homes
   c) Increasing numbers of immigrants in the U.S.
   d) The drug trade
   e) Lack of adequate education

17.5. Operation Ceasefire is a program in Boston, Massachusetts designed to:
   a) Reducing drug use among juveniles
   b) Enforcing mandatory curfews
   c) Fighting truancy
   d) Avoid status offenses
   e) Reducing street gang violence

17.6. The juvenile court is guided by the concept of:
   a) *parens patriae*
   b) *mens rea*
   c) *actus rea*
   d) *voir dire*
   e) *persona non grata*

17.7. During the Puritan period, the overriding belief of delinquent children was that:
   a) Children could be reformed
   b) Children should be left to their parents for discipline without interference of the law
   c) Children were evil
   d) Repeat offenders were the biggest problem
   e) Immigration caused delinquency among youth

17.8. In what case did the Court declare that juveniles have the right to counsel, to confront and examine accusers, and to have adequate notice of charges when there is the possibility of confinement as a punishment?
   a) *Fare v. Michael C.* (1979)
   b) *McKeiver v. Pennsylvania* (1971)
   c) *Schall v. Martin* (1984)
   d) *In re Gault* (1967)
   e) *Breed v. Jones* (1975)

17.9. Which of the following is NOT applicable to juveniles in most states?
   a) right to counsel
   b) right to treatment
   c) right to a trial by jury
   d) right against unreasonable searches and seizures
   e) privilege against self-incrimination

17.10. What legislation was the earliest attempt by a colony to deal with problem children?
   a)   Georgia Juvenile Delinquent Act
   b)   Massachusetts Stubborn Child Law
   c)   New York Troubled Child Act
   d)   Illinois Juvenile Court Act
   e)   Virginia Child Protection Act

17.11. Which of the following best describes the House of Refuge?
   a)   One-half prison and one-half nursery home
   b)   One-half school and one-house nursery home
   c)   One-half prison and one-half school
   d)   School
   e)   Prison

17.12. Which of the following acts included provisions for taking status offenders out of corrections institutions?
   a)   Juvenile and Status Act
   b)   Massachusetts Stubborn Child Law
   c)   Delaware Troubled Child Act
   d)   Illinois Juvenile Court Act
   e)   Juvenile Justice and Delinquency Prevention Act

17.13.   The Refuge Period focused its attention on:
   a)   evil chidren
   b)   immigrant children
   c)   reformism
   d)   serious crime by repeat offenders
   e)   juvenile rights

17.14. The "child savers" were influenced by:
   a)   Findings from social scientists that deviance could be treated
   b)   Immigration policy
   c)   The Enlightenment
   d)   World War II
   e)   The Vietnam Era

17.15. Which state created the first juvenile court in America?
   a)   Illinois
   b)   Michigan
   c)   New Jersey
   d)   Ohio
   e)   Massachusetts

17.16.   In most states, the upper age limit for jurisdiction of the juvenile court is:
   a)   15
   b)   16
   c)   17
   d)   18
   e)   19

17.17. What is the difference between a neglected and a dependent child?
  a) A neglected child has committed a crime; a dependent child has no parent or guardian
  b) A neglected child has no parent or guardian; a dependent child is receiving inadequate care from his/her parents
  c) A neglected child is receiving inadequate care from his/her parents; a dependent child is also delinquent
  d) A neglected child is receiving inadequate care from his/her parents; a dependent child has no parent or guardian
  e) A neglected child is a PIN; a dependent child is not.

17.18. What does the acronym PINS stand for?
  a) A person in need of supplies
  b) A person in need of supervision
  c) A prostitute in need of services
  d) A person in suspended animation
  e) A penalty in *nolo suspendere*

17.19. Which of the following is a status offense?
  a) Vandalism
  b) Shoplifting
  c) Running away
  d) Forgery
  e) Assault

17.20. The juvenile court is designed to be:
  a) Nonadversarial
  b) Punitive
  c) Economic
  d) Adversarial
  e) Triangular

17.21. According to the decision in New Jersey v. T.L.O. (1985), under what circumstances can school officials conduct searches of student lockers?
  a) Whenever they feel like it
  b) When the school is in "lockdown" mode
  c) When a student fails a drug test
  d) When there is suspicion of lawbreaking and it is required to maintain order
  e) Officials cannot search student lockers, according to the Fourth Amendment

17.22. Which term in the juvenile court is the adult court equivalent of "trial"?
  a) Diversion
  b) Detention
  c) Waiver
  d) Adjudication
  e) Disposition

17.23. Which sentences is most often used for convicted juvenile offenders?
  a) Probation and release to parent
  b) Intermediate Sanctions
  c) Custodial care
  d) Community Treatment
  e) House of Refuge

17.24. What is the sentencing philosophy most often used in teen courts?
    a)   Punitiveness
    b)   Deterrence
    c)   Restorative justice
    d)   Addiction treatment
    e)   Just deserts

17.25. The juvenile equivalent of parole is:
    a)   Probation
    b)   Discretion
    c)   Diversion
    d)   Referral
    e)   Aftercare

TRUE/FALSE QUESTIONS

17.1. _____Youth gangs are a dangerous presence in most American cities.

17.2. _____Operation Ceasefire was a program developed to prevent date rape.

17.3. _____It is legal in some states to waive juveniles to adult court as young as 10 years old.

17.4. _____England has great influence over the U. S. in the area of juvenile justice.

17.5. _____ A boot camp is a type of secure facility.

17.6. _____ The concept of *parens patriae* refers to the juvenile court acting as parent to delinquent children.

17.7. _____ Even with reforms made during the Refuge Period, juveniles could still be arrested, tried, and imprisoned.

17.8. _____ Juveniles were given the right to an attorney during the Juvenile Court period.

17.9. _____ Juveniles have all the same constitutional rights as adults in court.

17.10._____As of 2005, offenders cannot be executed for crimes they committed as juveniles.

17.11._____The "Child savers" were lower-class reformers who fought to "save" children from the state.

17.12._____Juveniles can be charged and tried for the same crime in both juvenile and adult court.

17.13._____A juvenile under the age of fifteen is harshly punished for a crime in Norway.

17.14._____The terminology used in the juvenile justice system reflected the underlying belief that these children could be "cured" and returned to society as law-abiding citizens.

17.15._____The U. S. Supreme Court began to afford constitutional protections to juveniles in the 1960s.

17.16._____Delinquent children have committed acts that would be considered crimes if committed by adults.

17.17._____Murder is a status offense for a juvenile.

17.18._____While the public currently takes a punitive stance toward adult offenders, this philosophy has not been reflected in the juvenile court.

17.19._____The current juvenile court system mixes together both delinquent and non-delinquent youth.

17.20._____Unlike the United States, there is no separate juvenile court system in Norway.

ANSWER KEY

<u>Key Terms</u>
1. *In re Gault*
2. PINS
3. aftercare
4. *Schall v. Martin*
5. *New Jersey v. T.L.O.*
6. *parens patriae*
7. *Fare v. Michael C.*
8. delinquent
9. diversion
10. *In re Winship*
11. *Breed v. Jones*
12. status offense
13. detention hearing
14. *McKeiver v. Pennsylvania*
15. *Vernonia School District v. Acton*
16. judicial waiver
17. dependent child
18. neglected child

<u>General Practice</u>
1. "child saver"
2. Crime Control Period
3. Juvenile Rights Period
4. In re Gault
5. delinquent
6. group home
7. deinstitutionalization

<u>Multiple Choice Questions</u>
17.1.   A
17.2.   B
17.3.   D
17.4.   D
17.5.   D
17.6.   A
17.7.   C
17.8.   D
17.9.   C
17.10.   B
17.11.   C
17.12.   E
17.13.   B
17.14.   A
17.15.   A
17.16.   D
17.17.   D
17.18.   B
17.19.   C
17.20.   A
17.21.   D
17.22.   D
17.23.   A
17.24.   C

17.25.   E

<u>True/False</u>
17.1.   T
17.2.   F
17.3.   T
17.4.   T
17.5.   T
17.6.   F
17.7.   T
17.8.   F
17.9.   F
17.10.   T
17.11.   F
17.12.   F
17.13.   F
17.14.   T
17.15.   T
17.16.   T
17.17.   F
17.18.   F
17.19.   T
17.20.   T

WORKSHEET 17.1. THE HISTORY OF JUVENILE JUSTICE

For each era listed below, assume the role of the listed official. Describe how much discretionary authority you have to determine which children will be drawn into the system and what will be done with them. Briefly describe what you would decide to do with such children during that era.

THE REFUGE PERIOD (1824-1899). Police officer:

_____

_____

_____

_____

_____

_____

JUVENILE COURT PERIOD (1899-1960). Juvenile Court Judge:

_____

_____

_____

_____

_____

JUVENILE RIGHTS PERIOD (1960-1980). Social Worker:

_____

_____

_____

_____

_____

CRIME CONTROL PERIOD (1980-Present). Prosecutor:

_____

_____

_____

_____

_____

WORKSHEET 17.2. TREATMENT OF DELINQUENTS

Assume each of the following occupational roles. In each role, formulate a recommendation for what should happen to a fourteen-year-old boy whose seventeen-year-old companion killed a man while the two of them attempted to steal a bicycle.

Social Worker:_____

_____

_____

_____

_____

_____

State Legislator:_____

_____

_____

_____

_____

_____

Director of Group Home for Delinquents:_____

_____

_____

_____

_____

_____

Juvenile Court Judge:_____

_____

_____

_____

_____

_____